Testing Freudian Concepts

Irving Sarnoff

TESTING
FREUDIAN CONCEPTS

An Experimental Social Approach

Springer Publishing Company, Inc.,   New York, N.Y.

SPRINGER PUBLISHING COMPANY, INC.
200 Park Avenue South, New York, New York 10003

Library of Congress Catalog Card Number: 70-146658
Standard Book Number: 8261-1191-2, flexible
8261-1192-0, hard

Printed in U.S.A.

This work is dedicated to the memory of the late Arthur R. Cohen. Although his life was tragically short — and blighted in its last years by the constant pain of his fatal illness — it permanently enriched the lives of those who knew him. Despite his extreme personal anguish, he gave unstintingly to the field of psychology. His courageous generosity continues to inspire those who were his students and associates.

Acknowledgments

I am grateful to the following persons, publishers, and journals for granting me permission to quote from their materials: Frances V. Bishop, "Anality, privation, and dissonance." (Doctoral dissertation, New York University, 1965); Philip M. Bromberg, "The effects of fear and two modes of anxiety reduction on social affiliation and phobic ideation." (Doctoral dissertation, New York University, 1967); Edward H. Conrad, "Psychogenic obesity: The effects of social rejection upon hunger, food craving, food consumption, and the drive reduction value of eating, for obese vs. normal individuals." (Doctoral dissertation, New York University, 1968); Harper & Row, Publishers, Inc., for A. Comfort, *The nature of human nature; International Journal of Psychoanalysis* for G. Lindzey, "Psychoanalytic theory: Paths of change"; *Journal of Personality,* for I. Sarnoff, "Reaction formation and cynicism" and I. Sarnoff & S. M. Corwin, "Castration anxiety and the fear of death"; *Public Opinion Quarterly* for I. Sarnoff, "Psychoanalytic theory and social attitudes"; Rand McNally and Company for I. Sarnoff, "Psychoanalytic theory and cognitive dissonance." In R. Abelson *et al.* (Eds.), *Theories of cognitive consistency; Transactions of the New York Academy of Sciences* for I. Sarnoff, "The experimental evaluation of psychoanalytic hypotheses"; and John Wiley & Sons, Inc. for I. Sarnoff, *Personality dynamics and development.*

Preface

This book presents a way of using the experimental method of research as a tool for investigating the scientific utility of Freudian concepts. Although his fascinating ideas grew entirely out of clinical experience, Freud's theory is surely as worthy as other psychological theories for evaluation by methods that most completely satisfy the logical requirements of scientifically adequate evidence. Moreover, in such experimental evaluations the potential explanatory powers of Freudian concepts may be aimed at illuminating the determinants of many phenomena that are of vital and widespread concern to scientists and laymen alike.

My purpose, therefore, is to present guidelines for theoretically appropriate, methodologically rigorous, and ethically acceptable experimental tests of Freudian hypotheses. Because such testing is steeped in personal and societal significance, its advancement depends not only upon an experimenter's technical sophistication but also upon his awareness of the ways in which his own moral values, existential dilemmas, and occupational commitments affect his investigatory decisions.

Accordingly, I begin the book by raising the scientific challenge of Freudian concepts and by articulating a philosophy of deductive research on them. Thereafter, while devoting the bulk of my discourse to a sequential discussion of the logical and operational steps involved in rendering those concepts amenable to experimental study, I make explicit crucial factors of individual and social psychology that influence the planning and the conduct of these experiments. At the same time, developing themes contained in my second book, *Society with tears* (New York: Citadel Press, 1966), I seek to reconcile the goals of scientific epistemology with the ideals of a humane society, indicating how both may be taken into account in devising and implementing the various phases of an experiment.

Having sketched the contents of this work, I must hasten to emphasize the modesty of its scope. Since my chief objective is the presentation of principles of experimentation on Freudian concepts, I do not attempt to explicate the whole of Freudian theory or to submit each of its component concepts to logical examination. Nor do I presume to trace post-Freudian or neo-Freudian developments in psychoanalytic thought and practice, much less to relate Freudian concepts to other theoretical systems within the field of psychology. Instead, assuming that the reader is or may become informed on these pertinent matters through other sources, I confine myself primarily to the question of how one may best proceed with the experimental evaluation of whatever Freudian concept one chooses to study.

Although usually exemplified with respect to Freudian concepts, the central issues discussed in most of my chapters are equally applicable to experimental research dealing with hypotheses derived from other theories of personality. Furthermore, the basic interpersonal factors and implications that I explore are also inherent in social psychological experiments. Consequently, this work may be useful as an auxiliary text in graduate and advanced undergraduate courses dealing with the general principles of research in both personality and social psychology.

While striving to cover essential topics, I have avoided the exposition of a number of elementary matters, such as the fundamentals of statistics, psychological measurement, and research design, which have been extensively treated by other authors and with which readers of this book may be reasonably expected to have become familiar. Thus, I have chosen to highlight investigatory problems and considerations that have impressed me as especially deserving of thoughtful attention and that do not seem to have previously been accorded the emphasis they merit.

My views represent an approach developed from research I have conducted or sponsored. So, for detailed examples, I have drawn almost exclusively from studies in which I have been directly involved as investigator or advisor. Since the total number of such studies is necessarily quite small, I refer extensively and repeatedly to the same set of experiments in illustrating different principles. Happily, this mode of exposition permits the reader to gain a deep understanding of the multitude of interrelated conceptual, procedural, and moral decisions a researcher is required to contemplate and to make in the course of an experiment. Indeed, the fullness and candor with which these problems are discussed constitute, I believe, a special contribution of this book to the furtherance of meaningful and responsible research in this area.

Naturally, I have alluded to alternative strategies of experimentation on Freudian concepts and I have cited findings from other bodies of research, selecting materials especially germane to the points I have sought to make. But I have had no intention of covering the diverse experiments that have aimed to test psychoanalytic hypotheses.

On the other hand, the volume of theoretically pertinent experiments has not grown to fantastic proportions in the quarter of a century since R. R. Sears published the initial review of the relevant empirical literature, *A survey of objective studies of psychoanalytic concepts* (New York: Social Science Research Council, 1943). Indeed, *controlled experimentation* on psychoanalytic concepts is still quite rare, and it is precisely my intention to encourage its growth. But those for whom the monograph by Sears has served as a basic orientation to this subject may find in these pages a fresh and more optimistic appraisal of what can be accomplished by opening the doors of the experimental laboratory to psychoanalytic concepts and by patiently trying to test them in a manner congenial to their particular characteristics.

In my first book, *Personality dynamics and development* (New York: Wiley, 1962), I had occasion to report a variety of findings, which, I felt, argued for the fruitfulness of a marriage between psychoanalytic concepts and experimental research. I should be glad if the present publication were to enhance the felicity and endurance of that relationship.

New York   IRVING SARNOFF
March, 1971

Contents

Figures

Those who have handled sciences have been either men of experiment or men of dogmas. The men of experiment are like the ant; they only collect and use: the reasoners resemble spiders, who make cobwebs of their own substance. But the bee takes the middle course, it gathers its material from the flowers of the garden and of the field, but transforms and digests it by a power of its own. . . . Therefore, from a closer and purer league between these two faculties, the experimental and the rational, (such as has never yet been made) much may be hoped.

Francis Bacon
Novum Organum

The Scientific Challenge of Freudian Theory

In the years that followed his death, Freud's theory became firmly established in the pantheon of great ideas of the Western world. What was once a revolutionary and esoteric doctrine, isolated on the murky fringes of medicine, is now a conventional mode of thought for millions of people in every walk of life. And Freudian concepts, which had once shocked and alarmed genteel members of the middle class, are presently taken for granted in polite society as the most commonplace and self-evident of eternal verities.

From a scientific standpoint, the most remarkable feature of this development is that it occurred in the absence of any logically adequate empirical confirmation of the concepts Freud had set forth. Indeed, it may be fair to say that no other avowedly scientific psychological theory has ever gained even a fraction of such widespread adherence without having been buttressed by data obtained in a manner consonant with minimally acceptable standards of objectivity and precision.

Certainly, it is easy to admire Freud's daring and brilliant conceptualization of universally occurring and emotionally charged human phenomena, which other psychological theorists had not even attempted to address. A scientific psychologist may be moved to say that "it would be possible for Freud to be wrong on all or many of the details of behavior, to be imprecise, to be metaphorical, to be limited in his domain of data, to be biased in his observations, to fail to appreciate the contribution of experimental science, to be swayed by personal problems and situational events, to be unduly influenced by faulty ethnology and transient cultural norms, to follow the lure of an archaic set of neurological formulations, and still have more impact than others simply because of his powerful insights about incest. If the incest taboo has indeed created a basic conflict and

1

consequent developmental frailty that characterizes all mankind, and if only Freud successfully identified this state of affairs, it should come as no surprise that psychoanalytic theory possesses a kind of transcendental vigor that guarantees wide applicability, pertinence, and impact [Lindzey, 1967, p. 1057]." But insights, however transcendent and powerful they may appear to be, are not equivalent to empirical proofs. Indeed, without such evidence, a scientist's purportedly novel insights may be dismissed by skeptical colleagues as ancient follies. Dunlap [1954] for instance, finds "nothing in Freud's system which had not appeared in superstitions which were common several centuries before the beginning of the Christian era [p. 330]."

Consequently, within the framework of science's commonly accepted evidential basis for assessing the merits of its theories, Freud's commentaries on the incest taboo represent an implicit collection of unproven hypotheses. Moreover, while the identification of problems worthy of study is of central importance to the development of science, it is not tantamount to the actual empirical investigation of those problems.

Yet few objective and systematic tests of psychoanalytic hypotheses (Sears, 1943) were launched while Freud was still alive. And although considerably more have been conducted since his demise, the totality of all the available scientific evidence is so flimsy and equivocal that it can scarcely have accounted for the enourmous influence and application of psychoanalytic ideas.

So, to appreciate the tremendous impact of Freudian psychology in Western society, one must turn for enlightenment to non-scientific considerations. Briefly, the following five factors seem to be the most important ones. First, Freud's gift as a writer of exquisite style, erudition, and refinement magnetized attention to his views. Indeed, one of Freud's severest scientific critics has noted, with grudging admiration: "He carried the day with sheer persuasion — with the massing of instances and delineation of surprising parallels and analogies among seemingly diverse materials [Skinner, 1954, p. 300]." Second, Freud was blessed with an unusually talented and articulate band of clinical adherents, who devoted their lives to the exposition, clasification, and furtherance of his ideas. These loyal proponents included his own daughter, Anna Freud (1946), and such early associates as Karl Abraham (1927), Sandor Ferenczi (1955), and Ernest Jones (1936). Third, Freud's writings had a profound effect on many outstanding contemporaries in fields outside of psychiatry and psychology. For example, such eminent authors as James Joyce, Thomas Mann, and Eugene O'Neill infused their literature with psychoanalytic concepts of human motivation and processes of thought, thus subtly and sympathetically communicating Freudian psychology to a vast and undiminished public of readers. Fourth, Freud and his followers stimulated and organized centers of training in psychoanalytic psychotherapy in Western Europe and the Western Hemisphere. Because of Freud's own stature and the lead he took in the field of psychotherapy, therapists trained in or oriented toward the Freudian school were often in a most favorable position to disseminate psychoanalytic views in their roles as educators of physicians, social workers, psychologists, and other members of the helping professions. Fifth, the unhappy condition of modern man, whose problems appeared capable of illumination and amelioration through Freud's concepts of motivation and treatment, disposed many lay persons to turn to Freudian theory and therapy for guidance.

Naturally, professional advocates of the theory were inclined to discover ubiquitous evidence of its truthfulness. And Freudian concepts undoubtedly helped a great many clinicians to cope intellectually with the taxing challenges of their work; to impose cognitive order upon what might otherwise have utterly confounded them as a bewildering assortment of behavioral idiosyncracies. Indeed, Freudian theory at last gave clinicians a comprehensive system of explanation that went beyond the mere phenotypical diagnostic categories that had previously characterized the field of psychiatry. Moreover, while postulating discrete underlying psychological processes for various observable syndromes, Freud simultaneously proposed a theoretically consistent means of uncovering and changing them.

Nevertheless, during his own lifetime, Freud was obliged to face sharp dissent among clinicians who had initially been among his fervent supporters. And even as the ranks of his followers multiplied, others had the temerity to question and to depart from basic tenets of psychoanalytic theory or therapy.

But these rebels were hard put to avoid the stigma of being considered minor artisans in the atelier of Psyche — mere polishers of a few rough edges in Freud's monumental work — and petty, carping, and ungrateful heirs of his priceless legacy. Unquestionably, Freud (1949e) himself so regarded those who, like Jung (1928) and Adler

(1927), had the presumption to compose alternate versions of the phenomena he had sought to illuminate.

Still, the substitution of one scientifically untested set of speculations for another does not represent an increment in reliable knowledge. Of course, it demanded extraordinary courage for any theorist of personality to wrestle with as awesome an intellectual gladiator as Freud. But even the brave may struggle in error, their heroism misspent in a fallacious cause. And how often, in such an impassioned verbal contest, does truth emerge the victor? How edifying is it for observers of these polemical frays to watch a bloody battle of theories — fought by accusation, innuendo, and extravagant pretension — which none of the contestants has the slightest intention of subjecting to the impartial arbitration of scientific assessment?

Fortunately, as hapless as he may be, man has a civilized recourse available for resolving such theoretical disputes: the scientific method. But it is unfortunate that the application of scientific methods of conceptual evaluation to the study of human behavior is a slow and painstaking process. Hence, although they have devised an admirable way of objectively testing the empirical adequacy of their notions, men are frequently loath to use it in examining their own most cherished ideas. This reluctance was plain enough in Freud's case, and it was just as apparent among all the leading theoretical deviants from his position.

On the other hand, among scientific psychologists, one might have expected experimentalists, professionally committed to the creation of knowledge founded on the most logically rigorous of deductive methods, to welcome the opportunity of applying their special skills to the most influential psychological theory of their time. Certainly, there seems to be no clear scientific reason sufficient to account for the fact that experimental psychologists have devoted very little of their research to studies involving Freudian concepts.

Of course, it is entirely possible that some experimenters have shied away from such research simply out of sheer reluctance to face the labor of constructing the methodological foundation that this area of experimentation has been lacking. Also formidable is the intellectual task of teasing out systematic semantic definitions and deducing specific hypotheses from the loose fabric of Freudian prose. And one cannot gainsay the attraction of working on concepts whose operational definitions and techniques of manipulation have already enlisted a fair degree of employment among fellow experimenters.

However, intrinsic interest is precisely the inestimable advantage that psychoanalytic theory has over many other psychological theories, and surely over those that have been the most popular objects of experimental research: In fact, one is led to wonder how any experimentalist could resist the temptation to delve into phenomena that are so inherently fascinating as those with which Freudian concepts are concerned, or reject the opportunity to test the many tantalizing hypotheses that can be derived from Freudian concepts — predictions which, moreover, often seem to be totally unpredictable from other theoretical positions or from the general lore of "common sense."

The ability of a theory to yield testable predictions that do not readily suggest themselves, a priori, from other theories, is certainly as much a scientific virtue as it is an intellectual delight. But when one speaks of a theory's power to stimulate the imagination, one is obviously referring to extra-scientific factors that relate to the motivation of the researchers. Still, insofar as a theory is exceptionally replete with such stimulation, its investigation would ordinarily be expected to be more pleasurable than that of less evocative ones.

So, why have not the majority of experimental psychologists leapt at the chance to animate their studies with the conceptual scintillation afforded by Freud's ideas? Any truly adequate effort to cope with this question would go far beyond the explicit boundaries of this book. However, a good part of the answer would seem to lie in historical influences, particularly in the conceptual models current in the antecedent sciences of physics and biology that shaped the outlook and orientation of experimental psychologists to their own field of inquiry.

Summing up these historical considerations — and asking the reader to make his own allowances for any notable exceptions that come to mind — it may be said that experimental psychology has tended, in general, to develop these three theoretical preferences: a) a preference for the conceptually simple as compared with the conceptually complicated; b) a preference for concepts whose presumed explanatory grasp reaches across species, rather than for concepts that deal with differences between species or among individual members within a particular species; c) a preference for theories that concern overt and directly observable behavior as the phenomena to be investigated, explained, and predicted.

Actually, Freud himself fully embraced every one of these theoretical preferences. Thus, he saw human beings as biological organisms, driven by the same basic instincts as other creatures in the evolutionary family. Moreover, he strove mightily for theoretical parsimony, his most stupendous conceptual accomplishments subsuming an extraordinary variety of observable phenomena under a single imputed variable, such as repression. Nor did he exclude the nuances of overt behavior from his theoretical concern. On the contrary, much of the original and sustaining motivation for the development of his theory arose from his great effort to account for the many unusual, persistent, and troublesome behaviors that had baffled his psychiatric predecessors.

But Freud did not ignore those qualities of the human species that set us off, for better or for worse, from other biological organisms. In fact, it was his incomparably keen interest in and sensitivity to those psychological phenomena — the entire and variegated texture of man's mental experience — that led him not only to his special form of psychotherapy but also to his unique theoretical formulations.

For what is the essential goal of psychoanalytic therapy if not the attempt, by patient and therapist alike, to employ a distinctively human skill — language — to express the particularities of covert human experiences: dreams, fantasies, memories, daydreams, thoughts, affects, and longings? Of course, Freud was interested in every bit of behavior he could see with his own eyes and hear with his own ears. But he was equally concerned with private emotional and ideational states — anxiety, guilt, obsessions, delusions, hallucinations, terrors — which cannot be directly observed, and which can only be inferred from something another individual does or says. No matter what an individual may be observed to do, it is the inner state of his private experience that determines the quality of his life. For ". . . speaking or silent, alone or with others, awake or asleep, a human being can no more escape his stream of thought and feelings, hopes and dreams, moods and fantasies than he can shed his skin and bones. He lives continually within that stream, whether it gladdens or depresses, inspires or rankles, exhilarates or stifles [Sarnoff, 1965, p. 3]."

Of course, these psychological experiences do not occur in a bodiless wraith. And it is entirely logical, in keeping with the naturalistic and deterministic premises of science, to regard them as functions of various material events that impinge upon human beings from their environments, that arise from their own bodies, and that involve interactions between particular environmental and somatic variables. Indeed, to study scientifically and empirically determinants of subjective phenomena one must perforce regard such phenomena as being contingent upon two sets of observable factors: a) the ones assumed to induce given psychological states; and b) the ones assumed to reflect those states.

As an avowed scientific determinist, Freud had no quarrel with these ways of viewing the determinants and effects of man's inner life. His work merely emphasizes, in contrast to that of many experimental psychologists, the desirability of including those subjective conditions as prime objects of inquiry in the scientific study of human psychology. Despite his penchant for biological, chemical, and physical analogies, Freud treated his patients as if they were quite different from other organisms. True, he expressly noted that science might ultimately produce a chemical means of achieving the effects he sought to obtain through his method of psychotherapy (Jones, 1963). Nevertheless, he employed a special type of conversation, rather than drugs or physical manipulations, as the principal medium through which patients might be led to alter enduringly the unpleasant qualities of their inner experiences, including their subjective reactions to their own observed and observable behaviors.

In using words as his primary therapeutic agents, Freud was evoking and responding to symbolic abilities that are unique to our species, and that lie at the root of the meaning we attribute to the concept of "person." By attempting, at the same time, to conceptualize the diverse etiological and therapeutic determinants of his patients' mental experiences, Freud's work has been a great stimulant to many investigators interested in the empirical study of individual differences between persons.

But while Freud was a stalwart intellectual innovator who bravely challenged (Freud, 1950a) the prevailing psychiatric dogmas of his era, he neither initiated nor applauded attempts to place his own concepts in the trying crucible of experimental assessment. Instead, he adamantly insisted that his concepts could only be properly evaluated by psychoanalytic patients or psychoanalytic psychotherapists. "The teachings of psycho-analysis are based on an incalculable number of observations and experiences, and no one who has not repeated those observations upon himself and upon others is in a position to arrive at an independent judgment of it [Freud, 1955, p. ix]."

It is true that, for Freud, the three distinct meanings of the term "psychoanalysis" evolved simultaneously: a technique of psychotherapy, a method of studying behavior, and a general theory of personality. Certainly, his impetus for developing a new form of therapy sprang from his dissatisfaction with the therapeutic techniques available when he began his psychiatric practice (Freud, 1950a). At the same time, his introduction of new psychotherapeutic procedures was usually contingent upon his conceptions of their functional relationships to imputed determinants of behavior and mental phenomena. Thus, he introduced the technique of free association for just such a theoretical purpose, "namely the bringing into consciousness of repressed material which was held back by resistances [Freud, 1950a, p. 72]." Finally, in employing these technical innovations, and in probing into psychological experiences, such as dreams, that especially evoked his curiosity, Freud could infer new concepts and further explore those he had already invented.

But whereas Freud's *modus operandi* obviously exerted a most salutary effect on the emergence of his theoretical formulations, it does *not* logically follow that the conduct of psychoanalytic therapy is an ideal, necessary, or sufficient method for the scientific testing of deductions from his conceptions of personality. Indeed, owing to the multitude of uncontrolled events that occur as patient and analyst interact within any psychoanalytic session, one can safely assert that such sessions cannot even minimally satisfy the scientific principle of control required to test a hypothesis deduced from a Freudian variable of personality.

From time to time, Freud did alter original versions of his concepts, such as his concept of anxiety (Freud, 1949f). However, he always maintained a totally Promethean epistemology, reserving for himself the exclusive right to make and to authorize such revisions.

But never did Freud insist that the presumed explanatory scope of his theoretical creations were restricted to the perimeters of his psychoanalytic consulting room. On the contrary, he set forth his concepts of personality as equally applicable to every human activity and context, seeking to explain such diverse phenomena as obsessions and compulsions (Freud, 1958), religion (Freud, 1949d), and the prehistoric origins of society (Freud, 1938b). Indeed, for all its omissions, extravagances, and ambiguities, his theory is still the most comprehensive and compelling account of the development and dynamics of personality.

Because Freudian concepts were offered as scientifically valid explanations of universally occurring phenomena, they implicitly invite the scientifically committed psychologist to give them as concerned and careful a test as he would accord other concepts. And because the experiment is the most logically convincing means man has devised for testing purportedly scientific concepts, it would seem highly desirable for contemporary experimental psychologists to accept that invitation, however much it may have been spurned by their predecessors.

Psychologists employing the experimental method are now doing research in every substantive area of psychology, including the fields of personality and social psychology. And some of the theoretical orientations, such as the theory of cognitive dissonance (Festinger, 1957), that have recently been commanding a good deal of experimental interest reflect marked departures from the conceptual preferences characteristic of experimenters during Freud's lifetime and for a number of years afterward.

In any event, by bringing the logical powers of the experimental method together with the psychological fecundity of Freudian concepts, researchers are likely to maximize the possibilities of each for contributing to the store of scientific knowledge about distinctively human behavior and experience. The remainder of this book aims at assisting such a rapprochement by discussing precisely how experimental logic and methodology can be brought to bear — with maximal theoretical, social, and ethical relevance — on the task of testing particular psychoanalytic hypotheses.

A Philosophy of Deductive Research on Freudian Concepts

Psychoanalytic theory grew out of the faith of a genius in his own creative thought. In developing and interweaving the many and far-reaching concepts that comprise psychoanalytic theory, Freud performed a colossal feat of inductive reasoning. Nor has his prodigious accomplishment yet been rivaled in psychology.

Nevertheless, the construction of theory is but one half — however indispensable — of the scientific enterprise. The other half, similarly indispensable, involves the work of deductive reasoning, which cannot be satisfactorily fulfilled until specific predictions, derived from particular conceptions encompassed by the theory, are put to empirical tests. The results of these tests, in turn, are applied to an evaluation of the concepts that generated them. From this investigatory yield, old concepts are revised and new ones suggested, thus leading to fresh deductions and their subsequent empirical evaluations.

Of course, the scientific method is not a God-given commandment, which all persons interested in human behavior and experience are pledged to uphold. Instead, like Freudian theory, the scientific method is a human invention, created, oddly enough, as a check on man's self-recognized penchant for basing his beliefs upon his wishes (Russell, 1954). And perhaps man would not have long endured that discipline if it had not so efficiently served his desire to control and to use his environment.

But commitment to the scientific method of acquiring knowledge carries binding responsibilities with it. Insofar as one holds forth a theory as a scientifically valid conceptualization of the phenomena it presumes to explain, one is implicitly obliged to conduct or to encourage the empirical testing of hypotheses derived from that theory.

10

The experiment is merely one scientific mode of hypothesis-testing observation. Nor can it be practically or ethically employed in assessing many derivable psychoanalytic hypotheses. For example, much of the Freudian theory of psychosexual development, (Freud, 1938a) deals with imputed maturational processes, whose predicted effects logically require longitudinal study to permit their observation. And it would be grossly unethical to attempt to control experimentally, over a span of years, the experiences of deprivation or gratification that are assumed by Freud to affect the course of the child's psychosexual development.

On the other hand, insofar as adequately controlled experiments can be done, they are clearly preferable to less conclusive methods of conceptual evaluation. For the whole point of fulfilling the deductive half of the scientific commitment is to put one's ideas to as logically rigorous an empirical test as one can possibly devise. And the fact that Freud gave no encouragement to such testing in no way obviates its scientific desirability.

But to undertake deductive tests with maximal appreciation for their intellectual significance, it is necessary to view them within a broad epistemological context. Thus, the remainder of this chapter will deal with a number of basic assumptions concerning the deductive approach to knowledge about personality in general and about Freudian concepts of personality in particular.

The common linguistic constraints on all approaches to knowledge

In their mindless functioning, human beings, like the rest of nature, are no doubt characterized by an incohate syncretism of matter. But the moment man seeks to conceptualize his own functioning, or that of any other part of nature, he inevitably imposes upon the fluid totality of events the intellectual compartments of his thoughts. Hence, men cannot *think* about themselves or each other without rending the unity of their beings into variables. While we may privately experience intimations of the wholeness and fluidity of our existence, we cannot for an instant speak of it without dividing it into separate and rigid abstractions. Indeed, this peculiar paradox bedevils the existential and Buddhist philosophers, who are obliged to use linguistic compartments in their efforts to convey that which is inherently indivisible; and to name that which is lost in the very process of attempting to name it.

Literary artists and scientific theorists are faced with the same problem of defining and expressing the realities of existence, although they attempt to overcome it in different ways. The literary artist employs an emotionally evocative and mimetic approach, hoping that his stream of verbalized feelings, visions, and thoughts — his cries, snarls, whimpers, and hosannas — will mirror the streaming currents of life; and that his words, in the entirety of their psychological impact, will impart the pristine wholeness of what we see and feel and are.

But the scientific theorist relies upon detachment and intellectual penetration, striving to transcend nature's ineluctability with highly focused mental incursions upon some phenomenon abstracted from its ever-changing totality. Nor does his success accrue from his ability to evoke his reader's capacity to experience the unitary functioning of life. Instead, while verbal facility may help the scientist, as it helped Freud, to get a widespread hearing for his theory, his ultimate effectiveness rests on the extent to which his suggested conceptualizations of temporally and spatially demarcated regions of nature's entire phenomenological domain are sufficiently cogent to withstand empirical tests.

In such tests, the proposed determinants of the specific phenomena remain embedded in the total context of life from which they have been mentally isolated for special study; and those determinants thus remain vulnerable to the unending wash of events of which they are a very small part. Consequently, the deductive scientist can, at best, provide only a relatively limited measure of control over the events deemed relevant to a test of any hypothesis.

From this standpoint, it is noteworthy that so many theoretically derived hypotheses *have* been experimentally supported in human psychology; and all the more so when one considers the sensitivity and reactivity of people — factors that add immeasurably to the contextual fluidity within which a researcher is trying to test a prediction dealing with a tiny segment of what is actually going on within the subjects being studied.

The psychoanalytic psychotherapist appears to stand somewhere between the literary artist and the scientific psychologist in his *modus operandi*. He relies heavily upon empathic communication in fathoming and responding to the wholeness of his patient's inner experiences. At the same time, the therapist attempts to conceptualize the determinants of that experience, as manifested in the patient's behavior, in the language of psychoanalytic theory. And he presumes to respond, at least in large part, to various aspects of the patient's behavior in terms of the determinants that psychoanalytic concepts propose for them.

The therapist's chief source of effectiveness may, in fact, lie in his ability to respond emotionally, empathically, and nonverbally to his patient (Rogers, 1964), while his theoretically based interpretations may have little, if any, effect on them. Hence, insofar as he is effective in his interpretive efforts, a psychoanalytic therapist may wrongly attribute his success to the Freudian concepts on which he based them rather than to his own personal qualities, which were not conceptualized, verbalized, or applied in a theoretically designated manner to particular segments of the patient's behavior.

In any case, the psychoanalytic therapist is continually making theoretical deductions from Freudian concepts; and, in offering interpretations based upon them, he is, in effect if not in intent, conducting a series of uncontrolled experiments, the results of which cannot be confidently applied to a scientific assessment of the concepts involved in them.

By contrast, the experimental scientist can fully devote his critical capacities to the matter of arranging adequately controlled tests of Freudian concepts. He is in a much better position therefore, to assess the ability of each concept to predict the fragment of the total configuration of observable events in respect to which its postulated variable is assumed to exert a more immediately determining influence than any other variables that are simultaneously operative within the individual.

An experimenter need not react with special defensiveness to the charge that his approach to knowledge violates the unitary functioning that actually characterizes the subjects who participate in his research. For anyone who uses language, as we have seen, is open to the same reproach. On the other hand, the experimenter merits approval for his courage to predict the determinants of events that he intellectually abstracts from life's teeming syncretism.

At any rate, given the analytic character of language, men cannot help but conceptualize those determinants as separate dimensions. There is, quite simply, no other way to write about people, discuss their verbal and non-verbal activities in psychotherapy, or construct and test theories about their experience and behavior.

The experimenter confronts this fundamental epistemological dilemma by maximizing the effectiveness of an unabashedly analytic method, seeking knowledge by deliberately limiting his phenomenological focus. Specifically, in any single experiment, he attends only to that number of variables upon which he can impose the greatest possible control over the conditions most immediately relevant to their predicted effects.

As a result of this modest strategy, the experimenter gains in the reliability of the knowledge he acquires. But each of his experiments covers merely a slight portion of the phenomenological wholeness from which he has selected a point of study. Hence, his work helps to reconstruct that wholeness only as it is added to studies that deal with other empirical foci of the same totality.

For the literary artist, the Zen philosopher, and the psychotherapist the situation is often reverse. While beginning a novel or a poem or a discursive essay on a particular feature of life, such authors may freely associate to a wealth of other phenomena that seem variously related to the one with which their work began. This associative tendency is perhaps what Blake meant by the ability "to see a world in a grain of sand." In *Swann's Way*, for example, Proust certainly gives a breath-taking example of what an artist can savor in a tea biscuit. Or, a novelist can delve, as Tolstoy did in *War and Peace*, so sensitively into so many imagined lives within a single book that his readers may finish it with a feeling of having attained a profound understanding of every significant feature of human existence. And yet, on the basis of that reading, a person might be quite unable to formulate any experimentally testable hypothesis concerning the determinants of a specific psychological phenomenon. For Tolstoy did not articulate his insights and impressions with adequate attention to the systematic classification and definition of phenotypes, relating them to similarly classified and defined genotypes.

Perhaps science and art represent two essential cognitive needs of human beings: a need to know as much as is empirically reliable, however restricted in scope, about something; and a need to know as much as possible, however tenuous and illusory that knowledge may be, about everything. Put somewhat differently, science and art may express two different needs regarding man's relationship to nature: a need to bind it to the qualities of human thought and a need to merge with its elusive incoherence.

If such dualities of motivation are indeed inevitable outcroppings of man's condition as both a person and an organism, as both a product of culture and a part of nature, attempts to gratify each are equally desirable. And the fact that different groups of individuals have generally tended to devote themselves either to science or art may reveal nothing more than a passing phase of societal organization, the institutionalized specialization of labor.

Therefore, insofar as the humane use of automation renders such occupational specialization as unnecessary as, from the viewpoint of human realization, it has been undesirable, future generations may be full or artist-scientists, who will move freely and creatively between the two epistemologies; now approaching nature globally and empathically, now directing the full power of analytic thought and scientific test on focal aspects of its totality.

Conceptualization, perception, and deduction in scientific research

Strictly speaking, a scientist never deals with events of nature in their ineffable concreteness. Instead, every datum in science is, in part, a human creation, depending for its very notice upon the human powers of observation, acquiring its particular configuration of perceptible qualities from the characteristics of the human sensorium, and assuming its relevance from the selectivity that is inherent in the way human beings observe the world and attribute meaning to it.

The welter of observable phenomena is amenable to a virtually infinite variety of groupings. A researcher can select any number and kinds of behavior for common classification. Indeed, designating an observable phenomenon as "behavior" is in itself a rudimentary conceptual decision, which is made, however inadvertently, before particular aspects of behavior are singled out as "facts" worthy of special concern. Laing (1968) expresses this selective process with admirable vividness: "The 'data' (given) of research are not so much given as *taken* out of a constantly elusive matrix of happenings. We should speak of *capta* rather than data [p. 62]."

Thus, no observer can classify what he perceives without bringing to it some expectation — however crude, unconscious, and unarticulated — about how its physical attributes may be grouped into communalities. Hence, the mere *perception* of such attributes is a conceptualization of an elementary sort. For every perceived attribute is cognitively wrested, as it were, from its concrete and local phenomenological context and placed into an abstract and universal dimension of thought.

In classifying objects by color, to give a simple illustration, one must conceive an idea — let us say, red — which signifies a visually perceived phenomenon, but which is not that phenomenon *per se*; which distinguishes that phenomenon from others in which it is embedded, such as those we refer to as size and texture; and which embraces a range of variations in the phenomenon's material base — such as when two pieces of chalk from the same box are perceived and classified as equally red, although no two such discrete objects can possibly be absolutely identical in the concrete particulars of their physical composition.

Consequently, abstract thought is always involved in the perception of communalities among objects. However, this fundamental level of abstraction is so closely tied, in time and space, to the objects under observation, that its functioning tends to elude the attention of the observer; and he usually remains unaware of the process of thought intervening between his direct, sensory contact with objects and his classification of their perceptible characteristics (Abercrombie, 1963).

Description, it follows, is merely an application of general classificatory rubrics to specific phenomenological instances, since descriptive language consists of terms referring to abstracted qualities, within which the object of description is given a configuration of concepts, as well as a rough quantitative location on each of the concepts that comprise that configuration. For example, while the description of an individual's physique draws upon a host of concepts, such as height, weight, volume, and fragility, which cover a diversity of traits, the resulting linguistic portrait is no less abstract than it would be if only one of those concepts were utilized. Still, the pattern of quantification imposed on the conceptual dimensions contained in the portrait — as conveyed by such modifying adjectives as "very," "quite," "extremely," and so forth — may well be unique and, hence, communicate a sense of that person's physical individuality.

In contrast to the processes of thought involved in the perception and classification of directly observable physical phenomena, the conceptualization of underlying and not directly observable determinants of those phenomena is much more likely to be experienced by the scientist as an act of imagination. For here the scientist must deliberately attempt to free himself from what confronts his sensorium and conjure the kinds of variables that may have given the objects of his observation their particular appearances.

In the field of personality, the scientist's awareness of the involvement of his imagination in the imputation of determinants of observable behavior is bound to be especially keen, since most concepts of personality are purely hypothetical and do not even pretend to refer to potentially observable phenomena, which may be uncovered, some day, within the body of the individual. Yet the layman may well employ such descriptive concepts without being cognizant of either their abstract or their imputed nature. And the traits he "sees" in others may have, for him, the same perceptual immediacy as the red he unknowingly abstracts from a stick of chalk.

The scientist, however, deliberately uses concepts to bring the boundlessly varied and varying world of nature within the finite grasp of the human intellect. He systematically adapts the pristine complexity of nature to the workings of the mind, reducing the ever shifting mélange of perceptible events to separate, definable, and logically consistent dimensions of thought. With phenotypical concepts, he sorts the overwhelming profusion of observable phenomena into intellectually manageable classes of common appearances. And, striving for explanation, he reduces the large number of phenotypes to a smaller number of imputed genotypes, assuming that each genotypical variable is capable of being manifested, under certain conditions (including interactions with other genotypes), in more than one class of observables. For example, one may postulate from psychoanalytic theory that a single mechanism of ego defense will give rise to extremely divergent social attitudes — depending upon the motive it is functioning to bar from consciousness. Specifically, it can be predicted that the use of reaction formation against aggression will be manifested in altruism, whereas its employment against affection will be reflected in cynicism (Sarnoff, 1960b). And the scientist relies upon deductive research as his means of assessing the empirical adequacy of these kinds of predictions and, hence, of the explanatory concepts from which they are derived.

To be sure, the scientific student of personality does not take refuge in Cartesean dualism. Nor does he regard man's mental life as the emanation of Disembodied Spirit. Instead, while acknowledging man's entire corporeality, he finds it helpful, nonetheless, at this stage in the development of his science, to posit purely imaginary inner determinants of behavior and psychological states, which would otherwise be incomprehensible and unpredictable (Frenkel-Brunswik, 1954). And he presses forward with his research in this inventive fashion, making do until scientific knowledge of man's somatic functioning is so well established that, for example, separately measurable physiological processes can be invoked as discrete determinants of both behavioral and experiential phenomena (Sarnoff, 1962).

Meanwhile, by permitting himself the empirically disciplined and accountable use of his imagination, a scientist of personality may succeed not only in devising a cognitively persuasive account of the determinants of psychological phenomena but also in predicting the specific conditions that will give rise both to those phenomena and to new ones. And while he may personally derive the greatest pleasure in the imaginative aspects of his work, the scientific psychologist always assumes that his conceptualizations reflect and illuminate actual features of human life that are independent of his own being and that can be noted and verified by other observers.

Thus, while the scientific psychologist searches after a world of phenomena he holds to exist outside himself, he realizes that what he finds is not totally independent of how he functions as an observer. And since his observations are inexorably intertwined with his conceptions, he is in constant danger of seeing only what he already believed or wished to be true.

Beset with this epistemological hazard, the scientist turns to the observational safeguards of his method of inquiry as the best means of helping him to minimize his inherently human solipsism and to maximize the veridicality of his perception of the empirical environment and his understanding of how it actually functions. Yet because of the characteristics of his own being, and the fluidity and complexity of what he observes, the scientist can attain only approximate verification of his concepts pertaining to the phenomena he investigates. He must be content with successive and increasingly accurate conceptions of the properties and the determinants of whatever he chooses to study (Needleman, 1968).

But how can a scientist acquire *any* evidential confidence in *any* of his continually modified comprehensions? For the layman, this question may never arise, owing to the implicit faith he may have in the substance of his own thoughts. And it may never even occur to him that his fondly nurtured wishes and his passionately felt beliefs should be doubted, challenged, and put to stringent empirical tests.

The scientist, however, has deliberately and carefully trained himself in skepticism. No matter how strong may be his intuition, he has resolved to take the quite unusual, if not unnatural, attitude of a doubter unto the very concepts that he creates or adopts concerning the phenomena of interest to him.

True, adherence to this resolution is facilitated by the scientist's awareness of the past successes attained by his method of inquiry. "It is the fundamental quality of science that its chief value, the acceptance of truth over wish, is self-policing. If we cultivate illusion or wish at the expense of what is, of the reality principle, our machines will not work nor our crops grow [Comfort, 1968b, p. 196]." Yet even the most conscientious scientist may find himself torn between the clamoring pressures of his immediate needs, such as a desire to be free of excruciating anxiety, and the rational stipulations of conclusive empirical study. Still, it is possible for him to cope with this dilemma satisfactorily by recognizing that what he does in his personal flights from pain and pursuits of pleasure is not necessarily identical to that which should be done to evaluate the scientific efficacy of concepts purporting to be objectively demonstrable explanations of general categories of phenomena.

To take an apt example, the scientist-cum-analysand is a troubled person who is inclined and, indeed, urged to let his capacity for intuition mesh freely with that of his analyst. At the same time, he can preserve his scientific integrity by acknowledging that his own experiences in psychotherapy do not constitute an adequate basis for assessing psychoanalytic concepts of personality. "There is an apparent difference here between interpretations offered in general terms — in Freud's books, for example — as part of an intellectual justification of what is in effect a scientific theory, to be judged as such, and the interpretations offered by an analyst to a conventional scientist in the analytic situation. In the first instance there is no reason to allow psychoanalytic ideas a special rate of exchange — like any other ideas they depend on evidence; . . . the scientist undergoing analysis who required an experimental demonstration of every interpretation offered to him would not, however, get very far, and the analyst who attempted one would not be a very good analyst — in getting insight into raw emotions where these are once exposed, he will need to be guided by theory and training, but his most useful implement is his own intuitive use of the emotional equipment which he shares with his patient, so that in the event the theoretically unsound therapist able to work 'off the top of his head' with a deliberate suspension of self-criticism may get better results than a more rigidly critical thinker [Comfort, 1968b, p. 198]."

But the distinction emphasized by Comfort has not always been fully appreciated by well-intentioned psychoanalysts who have attempted to simulate deductive methods of research within the context of their regular therapeutic sessions. Indeed, this lack of appreciation has generated results whose validational qualities are no more logically compelling than are purely impressionistic clinical reports.

Ezriel (1951, 1963), for example, in purporting to demonstrate experimentally the scientific utility of the psychoanalytic concept of transference (Freud, 1950a), offers as corroborative evidence his observations of the reactions of particular patients to particular interpretations that he presented to them — under conditions that did not provide any empirical controls over the impact of either the theoretically crucial experimental variables — the interpretations — or over the host of other variables, such as the personal characteristics of the therapist, which might very reasonably be hypothesized as alternative determinants of the patients' reactions. So, while Ezriel's interpretations may well have "worked" therapeutically in the manner he describes, his deductive method is too lax in its evidential precautions to yield findings that can be scientifically accepted as experimental support for the general concept, transference, upon which his individualized therapeutic interpretations were presumably based.

True, these kinds of pseudo-experiments can and do help to define the possible behavioral manifestations and evocations of psychoanalytic variables — thereby offering theoretically appropriate leads to their systematic measurement and their controlled manipulation. But the methodological laxity of such studies as Ezriel's undermines the original aim with which, in all sincerity, they were launched. For the basic purpose of deductive research is to objectify the functioning of man's critical intelligence. And there is no quick and easy path to that end; no short-cuts that do not wind back to the very Lotus Land of wish-fulfillment that the researcher had consciously sought to leave.

In inventing their concepts, scientists, like analysands, are best advised to give the freest possible play to their intuitions and to curb excessive critical thought, lest it paralyze their creativity. Indeed, in respect to the formation of original ideas, there is no reason to suppose that the process of creation operates any differently among scientists than it does among artists, writers, or composers (Hutchinson, 1949).

But having dredged a concept from the depths of his own being, or having adopted an idea conceived by someone else, the scientist is professionally trained to shift his mental orientation. Thus, he invokes his arduously acquired skill in ideational self-criticism, bringing it fully to bear on the concept in question. And if he is an experimental scientist, he feels further motivated to ascertain the extent to which the concept is substantiated by observations made under conditions that exclude, as thoroughly as his ingenuity can manage it, the distorting intrusion of his own desires.

Observation and operationalism

To carry out this objective, the scientist relies upon operationalism (Bridgman, 1928), as the means of publicly and precisely identifying the external sources of his perceptual responses to observable phenomena. Although the scientist acknowledges the selective and inventive roles his private conceptual processes play in the abstraction of particular phenomena from the enormous number and kinds of stimuli that activate his sensorium, he strives to objectify his empirical perceptions by systematically fixing their loci outside of himself; that is, by defining them in terms of public and replicable methods of observation. Hence, these operational definitions can be just as readily used by other observers, including scientists whose quirks and biases may differ greatly from one another.

Operationalism is thus the scientist's self-applied protection against his inclination to see only and whatever truths he is personally disposed to attribute to man and nature. Put affirmatively, operationalism is used by scientists to anchor their conceptions of the world in a perceptible reality whose existence transcends their individual subjectivities.

Yet operationalism itself rests upon a cognitive assumption that may be described, without undue irony, as an article of scientific faith; namely, that if an observable phenomenon is demarcated with sufficient precision, all its observers will have a sufficiently similar perception of it to agree upon its objective reality and its appearances. Given the possibility of this kind of empirical consensus, scientists can work meaningfully toward objective proofs for deductive hypotheses. If such agreement could not be attained, the evidential basis of science would never have developed.

Therefore, the effectiveness of operationalism depends upon the occurrence of a social phenomenon — the tendency of most observers to report the same perception when they are confronted by the same operational measurement. It is, paradoxically, this social occurrence that gives scientists their ultimate assurance about the independent existence of a world apart from themselves, and that likewise underwrites their confidence in the particular characteristics of that world.

However, because of wide individual differences in perceptual functioning, not *every* observer to the same operationally defined event can be counted on to agree on what is seen. Nor does it seen possible for scientific psychologists to produce infallibly precise operational measures, particularly since people are susceptible to changes by virtue — and in the process — of being observed (Roethlisberger & Dixon, 1947; Rosenthal, 1966).

So, we must be satisfied with probabilities rather than with absolutes whenever we do experiments on empirically testable hypotheses. Still, we can quite effectively carry out the scientific task involved in such assessments, since adequately reliable operational measures do, in fact, evoke a very high level of agreement among observers concerning the empirical characteristics of the phenomena they are designed to circumscribe.

Investigators may argue heatedly about the theoretical relevance of these measures to the imputed variables they are supposed to define. And these arguments are no small impediments to scientific progress in the psychology of personality. But while operationalism *per se* has not proven to be a panacea for resolving theoretical disputes about the properties of imputed variables of personality, it has provided scientific psychologists with a feasible method for bridging the gap between the perceptible world and their perceptions of it.

Empirically tested concepts: The epistemological
yield of deductive research

Rendering one's perception increasingly objective through the refinement of operational measurement creates the essential preconditions for empirically testing the scientific utility of conceptions of personality. It then remains for the researcher to observe to what extent predictable relationships among the operationally defined variables obtain under conditions specified by, or deducible from, the theory that proposes such variables as scientifically useful. Assuming these conditions are methodologically sound with respect to the preclusion of possibly confounding variables, the scientist can reasonably apply the results of his deductive test to an evaluation of the concept from which he derived his hypothesis.

Within the range of probabilities by which these empirical tests lend support to the concepts that inspired them, the scientific psychologist permits himself a like degree of confidence in the validity of those concepts. Yet he also bears in mind the probabilistic character of the obtained empirical results and, moreover, that concepts of personality, as they are presently formulated, are sufficiently general to permit a great many specific hypotheses to be deduced from them. Hence, he is prepared to let the weight of the empirical evidence from varying tests of such hypotheses accumulate until a logically compelling picture begins to emerge *pro* or *contra* the scientific utility of the concept to which those predictions refer. And he is certainly loath to draw sweeping conceptual generalizations from the results of any particular study.

In this patient, laborious, and cautious manner — tolerating, all the while, the endlessly gnawing disquiet of ambiguity — the scientific psychologist goes about the task of systematically challenging the empirical value of his own concepts. Often, his efforts fail because of the methodological problems that have not yet been mastered by anyone in the field. And even when he succeeds — when his methodology is sound enough to produce a logically satisfying test of a particular hypothesis — he must temper his satisfaction with the awareness that the study is yet to be replicated; that he may have overlooked flaws in his method and his reasoning that others will discover; and that, in any event, the study's results only hold within the boundaries of the statistical levels of confidence obtained, as well as within the characteristics of the subjects and the situations that were actually sampled (Brunswik, 1947). Finally, the scientist is sobered by an awareness that his contribution will in all likelihood be eventually superseded by closer approximations to the truth about the phenomenon he studied, when more accurately predictive concepts than the ones he employed are promulgated and put to deductive test.

Nonetheless, after successfully submitting his ideas to a demanding experimental examination, the scientific psychologist can feel that whatever corroboration he obtains is more reality-based than any he could get by other epistemological methods. And while he may not be able to test his ideas as quickly as he might wish, he has a most legitimate reason for feeling more secure about the validational status of the concepts he has tested than can any purely semantic advocate of those concepts.

Thus, the scientific harvest of deductive research on psychoanalytic theory contains two classes of empirically verified conceptions: a) those that pertain to the properties of variables, including their modes of classification, measurement, and evocation; and b) those that pertain to the relationships among variables, especially relations of cause and effect. Generally speaking, the first type of conception is empirically developed as an instrumentality for attaining conceptions of the second type. For the intellectual objectives of science are ultimately fixed upon explanation; and the work of inferring variables from phenomena and then categorizing and measuring them is, however indispensable, a precursor to the occasion in which theoretically postulated relationships among those variables can be tested.

The conceptual and operational meaning of causation

To bring designated independent and dependent variables together in a predictable fashion, one needs a theoretical account that envisions the effects of the former upon the latter. This account may invoke both visual schemas, such as topological diagrams, and physical analogies, such as forces, energies, and barriers; and it may contain few or many subconcepts in forging a chain of deductive reasoning between the conceptualized independent and dependent variables.

Ideally, too, this chain constains the fewest possible concepts, proposing only those that seem essential to permit one to predict the empirical relationships among operational measures of the relevant variables.

In an actual experiment, these nimble explanatory leaps of a scientist's mind are necessarily translated into operations that are strictly limited to the spatial and temporal requirements of his methods of observation — that is, to the specific measures and manipulations employed. The experimental meaning of causation, as thus empirically delineated, becomes a matter of reporting the observed effects of planfully varied antecedent events, which operationally define the independent variables, on other, consequent events, which are designated, *a priori*, as operationally defining the dependent variable, under conditions that preclude the intrusion of competing antecedents.

It is this deliberate control over the sequence and the locus of observed antecedent and consequent events that gives the experiment its logical force. For the scientist's observation of this spatio-temporal relationship permits him to draw conclusions, with very strong confidence, about the order and place of occurrence of the empirical phenomena under his study. If he predicts that phenomenon B will follow from the institution of operation A_1 — but not of A_2 — the successful outcome of his prediction allows him to maintain, at the very least, that operation A_1 was not preceded by phenomenon B, and that the sequence, $A_1 \rightarrow B$, is empirically different from the sequence, $A_2 \rightarrow$ no B.

Yet the scientist's mentalistic explanation of how manipulation of an independent variable produces effects upon a dependent variable necessarily contains more imagery, dynamism, and syncretism than can be directly transformed into a systematic, discrete, and sequential set of actions and observations. Certainly, the results of any psychological experiment could be reported strictly in the language of the manipulations used to vary the environment of the subject, without any reference to explanatory concepts presuming to describe how imputed characteristics of the subjects mediate their reaction to the given manipulation. Thus, Skinner uses the phrase "schedules of reinforcement" (Skinner & Ferster, 1957) to describe quantitative variations in these environmental contingencies, such as the presentation to subjects of different amounts of food. Yet, despite his militant operational austerity, does not that description *necessarily* imply the existence, within the animals or persons studied, of processes that are capable of being "reinforced" but whose motivational properties Skinner simply chooses not to make any explicit attempt to conceptualize? In any event, when concepts dealing with the intra-organismic functioning of individuals can be translated into experimentally testable hypotheses, they acquire scientific validity to the extent that the predicted sequential relationships between the relevant and operationally defined independent and dependent variables are observed to take place.

Having met the deductive requirements of his epistemological method, the scientist adds an increment of reliable conceptual knowledge to his particular field of interest. That increment is small, tentative, and subject to all the caveats, previously listed, concerning its replication and its range of generalization. Nevertheless, within the limits of all these reservations, the experimenter and everyone who has access to the public report of his deductive study can feel that they now know a bit more than nothing about the objective validity of the concept that was investigated.

Deductive research and the Freudian principle of overdetermination

Implicitly, the principle of "overdetermination" (Freud, 1949b) would appear to oppose the possibility of making systematic and definitive predictive choices among the Freudian concepts that could be invoked to explain the determinants of a particular phenomenon. Of course, it may readily be granted that a given phenotype can be conceived as reflecting the functioning of various kinds of genotypes. Any observable aspect of human behavior can be regarded as the resultant of many simultaneously operative forces. But the ultimate scientific usefulness of any theory depends on its ability to permit one to deduce the specific conditions under which its particular type of determinants will exert specific effects on a phenomenon chosen for study.

The scientific utility of Freudian theory, therefore, depends on its power, first of all, to facilitate differential predictions from its component concepts, such that their particular kinds of imputed determinants can be called into play with respect to the phenomena — and under the conditions — for which they are applicable. Secondly, the theory's lasting scientific value rests on the extent to which such predictions are supported when put to the most objective tests that can be devised for them.

Considered in this light, "overdetermination" must eventually be made to mean a specification of the relative saliency of simultaneously functioning Freudian variables in the determination of a given phenomenon. For if it is not so taken, the term has no scientific implications. Indeed, if it is read as meaning that all possible Freudian determinants of behavior are always operative with equal force and saliency, then the possibility of making differential predictions is completely foiled. And such a possibility is likewise blocked if "overdetermination" is viewed as meaning that any particular bit of behavior or experience can be conceived with equal theoretical aptness as reflecting any number of Freudian concepts.

Clearly, "overdetermination" can simply be a refuge for avoiding commitment to any theoretically derived prediction; and it can also be a ploy used to disavow responsibility for failed predictions. Given the enormous emotional pressures of therapeutic work, one can sympathize with this kind of theoretical hedging with respect to the clinical uses of Freudian concepts. But the validational work of science thrives on the opposite: on firm explication, on the unravelling of conceptual confusions, and on bringing concepts to the point at which their assumptions can be put into the clear articulation of unequivocal hypotheses.

Conceptual validation as the substance of scientific knowledge

In the course of arranging their validational tests, scientists accumulate an ever-increasing supply of techniques and a similarly growing profusion of data for which no *a priori* and theoretically derived predictions had been formulated. Speaking broadly and generically, all this information may be regarded as "knowledge." But from the standpoint of science's explanatory goal, scientific knowledge is not equivalent to technology, however elegant and dazzling, nor to sheer phenomenological data, however abundant and arresting. Rather, scientific knowledge consists of those *conceptions* of the determinants of observable phenomena whose deductive consequences have been subjected to empirical tests that meet objective and logically adequate rules of evidence.

Actually, agreement about this epistemological aim of scientific research is by no means universal among experimenters who are working with psychoanalytic concepts. On the contrary, some of these researchers appear quite ready to grant psychoanalytic ideas an exemption — what Comfort (1968b) in a previously cited quotation has called a "special rate of exchange" — from the standards of evidence that science has developed for the empirical appraisal of concepts purporting, as psychoanalytic concepts do, to be scientifically valid explanations of observable events.

Klein (1967), for example, does not believe that conceptual validation should be a major concern for scientific investigators. Instead, he proposes as the principal goals of scientific research "the accounting of *observed phenomena* and the discovery of hitherto unobserved ones [p. 27]." Thus, he regards psychoanalytic concepts as a set of guiding and expository orientations, suggesting where one might look to find new data and how one might conceptualize, on a *post hoc* basis, data already on hand.

Undoubtedly, such an investigatory prescription can stimulate fresh observations, observational techniques, and conceptual inferences. But it cannot *directly* contribute to scientific knowledge *as herein defined*. For such contributions require controlled predictive tests of the very concepts that one may be employing heuristically either to account for existing data or to generate new observations.

The logical rigor of the deductive phase of scientific research is a stern intellectual constraint. Whether or not one accepts its wearing constrictions is a matter of personal preference. As Freud himself demonstrated, one can be a creative scientist without doing deductive research. Yet insofar as a scientist declines the ardors of such research, he also deprives himself of its unique epistemological powers, which can help him and his fellow men to gain, through the collective and self-disciplined use of human perception, an objective understanding of themselves.

∫ From Concept to Hypothesis

Since Freudian theory contains a multitude of concepts, the first step in any contribution toward its experimental evaluation requires a researcher to choose a particular concept for focal study. Then, the chosen concept must be clarified in linguistic terms that define its particular psychological properties explicitly and precisely. Finally, the semantically defined concept must be theoretically related to a behavioral or experiential phenomenon by stating how and under what conditions the postulated relationship may be observed to obtain.

In formulating Freudian hypotheses, none of these cognitive steps, all of which are essential preliminaries to the final design of an experiment's methodology, can be taken with self-evident assurance. Instead, in taking each of them, the experimenter must actively contend with the logical and semantic hindrances that are rampant in psychoanalytic theory and that must be faced and overcome before a testable hypothesis can be extracted from a psychoanalytic concept. So, it may be useful to examine these difficulties, one by one, with a view toward explicating how they may be resolved.

The selection of a psychoanalytic concept for experimental evaluation

As an inspired author in the classical literary tradition, Freud did not feel obliged to spell out his theory with serious concern for its ultimate experimental assessment, nor to build a careful, cohesive intellectual structure in which his basic assumptions could be systematically presented in an unmistakable hierarchy of logical precedence and accompanied by a thorough exposition of their respective corollaries and deductions. On the contrary, Freud expressed his unfolding concepts — often with their initial bolts of inspiration still glowing in his style — in whatever linguistic form he happened to find convenient: a brief and hurried clinical report; a leisurely, flowing lecture, well spiced with epigrams, parenthetical commentaries, and concrete examples; or a tightly knit and highly abstract essay.

Consequently, Freudian theory is actually a panoramic conglomoration of ideas, some threaded together quite diligently into clusters, which can be classified as sub-theories (Wisdom, 1963), and others left in relative conceptual disjointedness and isolation. For example, in presenting his thoughts about psychosexual development, Freud (1938a) interrelated a wide diversity of concepts dealing with the somatic, behavioral, and experiential effects of both the maturation and the socialization of the sexual instinct. On the other hand, in later postulating aggression as a second and equally significant instinctual motive, Freud (1950b) did not offer a theoretical view of the course and effects of its maturation. Nor did he state how various exigencies of the child's socialization might interact with the maturation of aggression to produce specific alterations in the child's physical and emotional functioning. In short, Freud composed no sub-theory of "psychoaggressive" development to match his psychosexual one. Nor did he attempt a conceptual integration of the somatic and psychological features of the ontogenetic development of both instincts. Furthermore, even within the comparatively well-articulated psychosexual theory, the assumptions made about female sexuality are not nearly as compellingly coordinated as those concerning males — a theoretical shakiness that Freud himself was the first to admit: "If you want to know more about femininity you must interrogate your own experience, or turn to the poets, or else wait until science can give you more profound, more coherent information [Freud, 1949g, p. 174]."

Thus, the experimenter would be well advised to avoid foundering on the question of precisely how his study of a particular concept might fit into an ideally logical program for testing the whole of Freudian theory. Nor is one soon likely to be forthcoming, despite a notable effort by Rapaport (1960) to wrap some tidiness of formal logic about the disarray of Freud's far-flung ideas.

As things now stand, the experimental scientist will find neither in Freud's publications nor in those of his devoted clinical followers a clear logical guide to the order in which Freudian concepts should be selected for study. As Rapaport himself acknowledges: "In the past twenty years attempts at systematic formulation have been made, but no hypothetico-deductive system is in sight [1960, p. 38]."

The task of conceptual selection is additionally complicated by the fact that one cannot be at all certain, since Freud's death, about what concepts can properly be included under the umbrella of psychoanalytic theory. Yet here again the experimenter would do well to by-pass objectively insoluable issues. So little careful deductive research has been done on Freud's personal conceptualizations that no experimenter will have difficulty in finding more than enough concepts to test within the scope of Freud's own writings. Moreover, on the matter of logical precedence, it would certainly seem reasonable to conclude that Freud's original and still quite untested concepts deserve experimental attention prior to those that have been subsequently proposed by psychoanalytic theorists, such as Hartmann (1948), as conceptual improvements. For on what objective grounds can anyone possibly accept the scientific value of such modifications, when neither the earlier nor the later conceptualization has been scientifically validated?

Not having been bequeathed an unambiguous logical model by Freud, the experimenter has no theoretically authoritative frame of reference to guide his choice among psychoanalytic concepts. Yet there does seem, at least, to be an elemental sort of reasonableness in seeking to locate a concept somewhere among Freud's own writings, which are, after all, the foundation of all theorizing that has been done by those who view themselves as having a psychoanalytic orientation toward psychological phenomena. Nor, it may be said, have subsequent psychoanalytic theorists yet added a great many new concepts to those that Freud himself conceived.

Hopefully, in time, the full complement of psychoanalytic concepts that can be experimentally tested will be chosen for such deductive work. It is equally to be hoped that the remaining empirically testable concepts will be evaluated, by other investigators, through the most careful and most appropriate of correlational methods. In this way, we shall gradually acquire a scientifically adequate body of evidence on the validity of the entire spectrum of psychoanalytic concepts: on their separate utility as well as on their combined ability to predict the separately studied components of the subtheories into which they can be categorized. For example, it may be possible to infer from this research not only the adequacy of the concepts of castration anxiety and identification with the aggressor but also the extent to which both concepts predict phenomena that are postulated by their theoretically assigned role in the resolution of the male Oedipal conflict.

Assuming, then, that the experimenter decides to test one of the original Freudian concepts, he must reconcile himself to the fact that Freud did not neatly stack and summarize all of his concepts in a single publication, together with his explicit opinions on their precise rank of significance in the theory's logical architecture. So, anyone desiring to attain familiarity with the Freudian concepts that are available for testing has little choice but to read through the entirety of Freud's writings.

Such a reading will doubtlessly expose the experimenter to a good deal of conceptual redundancy, since Freud was his own best proselytizer and seemed quite capable of repeating himself with undiminished enthusiasm, verve, charm, and wit. However, this voluminous reading cannot safely be diminished, lest the experimenter miss an important new concept that Freud happened to introduce in the context of reiterating previously presented ones. The redundancies will also help to deepen the reader's understanding of the concepts involved and their postulated inter-relationships. For Freud tended, with each repetition, to make fresh observations about the meaning of the concepts and the ways in which they presumably act and interact in the determination of various categories of behavior and experience.

But even as the researcher is engrossed in his Freudian readings, he remains a live human being, impelled by his particular tastes, dispositions, and problems. It is likely that his personal motivations, however unconsciously operative, will play a very large part in determining which concepts he eventually selects for empirical study. Yet this individual choice is all to the good from the standpoint of sparking and sustaining the experimenter's investigatory interests and efforts. And, assuming he properly applies the observational safeguards of the scientific method — inadvertent deviations from which the scientific colleagues who ultimately read and replicate his published experiment stand ready, in due course, to discover, publicize, and correct — the experimenter need not hesitate to follow his subjective feelings of affinity for the concept he has chosen to study.

Of course, the experimenter may initially be motivated by curiosity about a particular phenomenon rather than by concern with a particular concept. Thus, he may arrive at the selection of a concept only after concluding a search for theoretical comprehension about the phenomenon that originally aroused his interest. It is likely that most existing research on psychoanalytic concepts derived its initial investigatory thrust from such a phenomenological source, after which the investigator dug into psychoanalytic theory as a repository of ideas that promised to shed explanatory light on the determinants of the phenomenon that had gripped his attention. Hence, although he may launch a predictive experiment primarily out of an interest in empirically uncovering the determinants of a phenomenon, the experimenter's resulting data are also applicable to an evaluation of the concept that permitted him to envision those determinants and to predict their effects.

On the other hand, an experimenter's conceptual choice may be less influenced by personal considerations than by extrinsic ones, such as the requirements of an ancillary role he may be playing as an assistant to a researcher who is eager to work on a particular concept or who is developing a program of studies encompassing several psychoanalytic concepts or, alternatively, phenomena whose determinants can be appropriately conceptualized in psychoanalytic terms.

Finally, both intrinsic motivational and fortuitous situational factors may combine to determine what psychoanalytic concepts an experimenter chooses to study. Surely, while familiarizing himself with Freud's theoretical writings, the researcher ought, with good reason, to become acquainted with the experiments that others have already conducted on psychoanalytic concepts. His very awareness of that experimental literature may, in consort with his temperament, shape the outcome of his decision. Thus, if he tends to be cautious, the experimenter may suppress his spontaneous interest in an empirically neglected concept and gravitate toward one for which there exists some base of feasible measures and manipulations. However, if he is a very adventurous person, he may persist in his initial leanings, in spite of the fact that they lead him toward an almost totally unexplored concept and require him to create the methods for any adequate deductive study of it.

Actually, this differentiation between cautious and adventurous experimenters is a highly relative one, made among people who are necessarily quite definitely on the adventurous side of that temperamental continuum. For given the pioneering state of experimental research on psychoanalytic concepts, anyone who opts for such research possesses, by definition, more than an average amount of scientific daring. And not the least of what he must dare, once he has selected a concept, is to forge a clear and consistent meaning for it.

The semantic clarification of the Freudian concept selected for experimental study

Unfortunately, as even his most ardent scientific admirers are willing to concede, Freud did not spell out his concepts with vigilant care for the precision and consistency of their semantic definition. No matter how deeply he respects and honors Freud's words, an experimenter will have to make use of his own in welding his chosen concept into a semantic form that is a suitable guide to the systematic deduction of hypotheses. "Thus," as Rapaport (1960) says of Freud's theory, "the experimental psychologist who approaches it must assume the responsibility of clarifying and specifying theoretically the propositions which he undertakes to test [p. 120]."

Keeping this responsibility fully in mind, the conscientious experimenter will nevertheless wish to make every effort to fathom the essence of Freud's meaning of the concept selected for empirical study. For it was Freud who provided the fountain of intellectual stimulation that produced the concept. Besides, it would be foolish and self-defeating to undertake the considerable labors involved in the experimental study of a psychoanalytic concept without first becoming as knowledgeable as possible about what the concept's author had to say about it.

But actually finding out Freud's views on his own concepts is not as straightforward a task as it might appear — unless one is able to read him in the original German publications of his work. For those not sufficiently proficient in Freud's native tongue, there is no alternative but recourse to a translation in their own language. Yet, as is true of all linguistic translations, a certain amount of meaning is likely to have been lost or distorted in the process of putting Freud's German writings into another language.

Some Freudian theorists, who are proficient both in German and in the language into which Freud's writings are to be translated, have approved the authenticity of particular translations, such as the English version by Strachey (1953-1966). And the experimenter can consult this translation, which was approved by Anna Freud, if he is in doubt about the accuracy of any other translations available to him. But most of the existing experimentation on psychoanalytic hypotheses was done before the completion of Strachey's "Standard Edition." Accordingly, the references to Freud in this book cite a variety of other translations. It should also be kept in mind that translation from German to English is not a simple procedure whose outcome can be expected to evoke complete agreement among experts in both languages. Thus, the mere existence of an "authorized" translation of Freud is far from a perfect assurance that its readers will thereby be granted perfect access to all the conceptual nuances that are contained in Freud's original texts.

Having become as familiar as he can possibly get with Freud's writings, the researcher may feel the need for further semantic clarification about the concept he has singled out for experimental investigation. In particular, he may wish to obtain a more concise statement of that concept than he can piece together from the allusions to it that are scattered among the diverse forms of Freud's publications. For this kind of elucidation, the experimenter can turn to the writings of psychoanalytic theorists, some of whom were trained by Freud and worked closely with him. However, every secondary source also involves acute hazards of translation, since it necessarily conveys not Freud's ideas, *per se*, but its author's understanding of those ideas. For example, in reading Fenichel (1945), it is often impossible to tell how much of his own independent thinking is intermingled with his conceptual explications of Freud. Moreover, a goodly number of these secondary sources were themselves written in a language other than the one into which it was translated for the benefit of particular populations of readers, thus multiplying the possibility of conceptual distortion inherent in linguistic translation.

Despite these problems of written communication, the experimenter may find his readings in these secondary expositions of Freudian theory helpful insofar as he can glean from them a measure of consistency in the usage of the concept whose meaning he is seeking to define in a stable fashion. And he may attain further clarification in the course of discussions with colleagues or mentors who have a similar interest in defining Freudian concepts.

Yet for all of Freud's liberties in expounding his concepts, their ambiguity cannot be entirely attributed to his lack of proper respect for semantic precision. Nor will their diligent explication by his interpreters completely eliminate that ambiguity. For the present language of *all* theories of personality is essentially generic; that is, the vocabulary of daily life is used to formulate the linguistic terms that comprise the concepts of personality. Hence, those concepts are rife with the semantic problems that becloud communication in ordinary discourse.

Ideally, each concept of personality should be phrased in exact technical terms that impart its special and specific properties as a distinct psychological variable. But generic language is fraught with a multitude of connotations, both abstract and phenomenological, and with a plethora of emotional evocations and moral attitudes (Sarnoff, 1962). Consequently, the language of personality raises profound difficulties for the experimenter, who hopes to define his concepts in such an unambiguous manner that people of varying backgrounds and dispositions will be able to comprehend it in precisely the same way as he does himself.

So, no matter how thoroughly he reads and digests Freudian concepts, the experimenter must face the fact that, after he actually writes down his most well-considered semantic definition of his chosen concept, the terms of his definition will still be so laden with connotative ambiguity, as well as emotive and moral evocation, that his readers may disagree about what he means to say. They may also take harsh issue with him about whether or not — or to what extent — he has faithfully articulated Freud's own original meaning of the concept.

Properly forewarned about these semantic swamps, the experimenter will not permit himself to become bogged down in them. For given the intrinsic semantic shortcomings of the generic terms that must also serve as the technical vocabulary of his scientific concepts of personality, the experimenter cannot hope to achieve perfect lucidity in his semantic definitions. Nor can he expect those definitions to compel agreement among fellow scientists. Instead, the experimenter should do the best semantic job he can with his concept in the light of all his acquaintanceship with its use in the Freudian literature.

Then, having at least satisfied his own critical judgment, the researcher can only rely on the results of actual experimentation to accumulate an objective empirical verdict on the scientific utility of the Freudian concept — as he has ultimately defined it for the purposes of deductive research.

Thus, operationalism is the empirical language, as it were, upon whose observational terms it is possible to go beyond sheer subjective debate about the adequacy of a concept's semantic definition. And unless and until one moves from the semantic to the operational levels of definition, one has no satisfactorily objective way of resolving questions about the linguistic definition of a concept.

Some day, psychologists may have on hand a technical language of personality whose terms have such precise, limited, and specialized connotations as to permit virtual unanimity among scientists working with them. But the arrival of that day is too far off and uncertain to warrant the suspension of experimentation on the promising and interesting Freudian concepts, however abundant they may be in surplus meaning. How else will scientists build such a technical language if not out of careful honings of the present conceptual terms, sharpening each of them against the hard stones of operational definition and empirical test, so that they become increasingly free of connotative implications and increasingly shaped to proven observables? Unless experimenters try to go from the conceptual to the operational planes of meaning, they shall not be able to see which of the Freudian concepts lend themselves with relative ease to semantic definition, the necessary prelude to operational definition, and which are so linguistically elusive that they virtually defy coherent articulation.

Since Freud did not do the preparatory work necessary to render his concepts scientifically testable, the experimenter must either do it himself or rely upon such relevant efforts as may already have been made by other deductive researchers. Insofar as the eventual results of experimental tests of the concept tend to support its validity, credit accrues to Freud's genius, which the systematic and experimentally oriented explications of his ideas only helped to become scientifically confirmed. And, insofar as such tests yield negative results, the scientific utility of the concept involved is cast into doubt — and, with it, Freud's ability to explain the aspects of human functioning to which the concept refers.

In either event, the persons who help to put Freudian concepts into semantic terms congenial to their subsequent scientific investigation can scarcely avoid adding something, however small, of their own cognitive facility to that of Freud's. This awareness is burdensome, for the experimenter is not presuming to articulate his own concept but is, rather, merely aiming to prepare the Freudian one for testing. However, motivated and sustained by his enthusiasm for the explanatory potentials of Freudian concepts, the experimenter takes upon himself both the risks and the responsibilities involved in attempting to clarify what Freud was content to leave unclear, and then to evaluate empirically what Freud was satisfied to accept untested.

It is only from such research that a scientifically based psychoanalytic theory can eventually emerge. What is scientifically useful in this conceptual and empirical reworking of Freudian theory will be retained; the rest will fall away. It is fruitless for anyone to speculate on the extent to which the concepts tested are worded precisely as Freud would have wanted them to be for he had no desire to see such work done, much less to assist it actively.

In any case, those concepts which are of scientific utility in Freudian theory can only be established by removing them from their rambling discursiveness and placing them into focused definitions; and, then, by going from these semantic foci to operational ones. And if the theory that cumulates from the transformation of clinical musings into deductive research is not Biblical Freud but is, instead, somewhat secularized in the process of preparing and submitting psychoanalytic concepts to objective evaluation, so much the worse for non-empirical acolytes of Freud and so much better for those who dare to search for reliable knowledge of human psychology.

The formulation of a specific, experimentally testable Freudian hypothesis

In accordance with the analytic structure of verbal language, the semantic clarification of a Freudian concept results in its definition as a genotypical variable of personality whose psychological properties are explicitly stated. As a purely linguistic statement, any such definition may be praised or condemned with the greatest impunity. Some of its readers may denounce it as deficient in theoretical scope or in connotative meaning, while others may regard it as a model of aptness and lucidity.

Left in its semantic form, the concept would be impervious to empirical judgment. And the fund of scientific knowledge would not be any richer than it was before the concept was linguistically refined. There would still be no objective basis for deciding who was more correct: those who defended its validity or those who attacked it.

So, to bring the concept into the court of scientific evidence, the experimenter must draw out the empirical implications of its hypothetical properties, predicting the conditions under which the antecedent presence of the genotype can be expected to exert specific and observable consequences on other variables, both phenotypical and genotypical.

In regard to a psychoanalytic genotype, however, assumptions concerning its effects are not contained entirely within the statement of its special properties. Instead, some of those assumptions are contained in the defining properties of other Freudian concepts, which are presumed to mediate its effects. Therefore, to formulate theoretically appropriate hypotheses from any single Freudian concept, the experimenter must be aware not only of its own properties but also of the relevant properties of the other concepts likely to be immediately involved in its functioning.

Perhaps a concrete example may help to illustrate this conceptual complication. Projection (Freud, 1949h), a mechanism of ego defense, can be differentiated from all other such defenses in that it prevents an individual from perceiving a consciously unacceptable motive by permitting him to attribute it to others rather than to himself. However, to make a specific prediction about the behavioral or experiential consequences of projection a researcher should know, first of all, the Freudian assumption about the behavioral properties of motives; namely, that for every motive there is an overt response that is maximally reductive of its tension (Sarnoff, 1962). Hence, the activation of the motive tends to provoke that response. For instance, the arousal of aggression is maximally reduced through the expression of hostility.

Second, the experimenter ought to be cognizant of the Freudian assumption that motives are capable of being repressed, if consciousness of them has become associated with catastrophic threats to the individual; and that a motive, while unconscious, continues nevertheless to press for discharge and, hence, for intrusion into the individual's awareness.

Third, the experimenter should be familiar with the Freudian premise that a motive is capable of being contained in an enduring condition of unconsciousness by a variety of mechanisms of ego defense, some of which, like projection, also allow the individual to discharge some of its tension without having to acknowledge its existence in himself.

Fourth, the experimenter should assume, with Freud, that ego defenses are relatively permanent and automatically functioning variables, which were gradually shaped out of the individual's long experience of struggle to resolve motivational conflicts.

Fifth, the researcher can postulate, from the Freudian definition of motives, that the motive being kept unconscious by a mechanism of ego defense is capable of transient environmental stimulation, thus calling into play a like increase in its pressure for overt discharge and representation in consciousness. Under such circumstances, the defense habitually used to obscure the motive from awareness will become saliently operative, exacerbating the usual effects of its functioning.

Finally, the researcher must have a conceptual grasp of the properties of the dependent variables likely to be affected by the action of a particular ego defense against a particular motive. These dependent variables may be other psychoanalytic genotypes, such as anxiety (Freud, 1949d). However, they may be genotypes, such as attitudes (Sarnoff, 1960a), or phenotypes, such as eating behavior (Conrad, 1968), which are widely employed in research on other psychological theories. In any case, the experimenter has to be equipped with definitions of the properties of these dependent variables if he is to predict how they are likely to reflect the influence of the independent one.

Keeping all these definitional assumptions in mind about both the variable of projection and the variables directly concerned with and affected by its employment, the experimenter is in a position to deduce a specific hypothesis about projection. For example, he can hypothesize that the ascription of hostile intent to others will be greater among individuals who are high in the use of projection against aggression than among individuals who are low in this respect; and, that, moreover, this difference will be greater under conditions of intense arousal of aggression than when aggression is only slightly aroused.

Thus, despite his care in semantically defining the psychologically distinctive properties of projection, the experimenter cannot formulate a testable derivation from that definition without, at the same time, drawing upon assumptions about other variables, which, owing to the conceptual focus of the hypothesis, are not themselves the immediate subject of empirical evaluation. Put somewhat differently, while projection is placed in the center of the empirical stage, it cannot step forward into the limelight of experimental test without the assistance of other concepts. And although those concepts, for the particular study, occupy supporting places in the shadows of the stage, they are indispensable to the sheer playing, by projection, of the leading role.

It would be logically more elegant and satisfactory if a psychoanalytic concept contained, by itself, all the psychological implications necessary to link it deductively to dependent variables whose properties would be the only other conceptual information an experimenter would be required to have on hand. But Freudian theory, especially as a result of its postulation of unconscious processes, cannot be experimentally studied unless one is willing and able to sort through assumptions, as indicated above, about variables directly impinging — in hypothetical time and space — upon the functioning of the independent variable whose conceptualization one wishes to test.

Yet Freudian concepts are not unique in this respect. For every theory is, by definition, a network of logically interrelated concepts. And the experimental study of any concept in such a network necessarily impinges upon other concepts with which it is functionally linked in the theory. On the other hand, in comparison with most other psychological concepts, Freudian concepts are embedded in a much larger theoretical network; and their constituent assumptions tend to be both more numerous and less semantically clarified.

Still, a theoretically knowledgeable experimenter will not be dissuaded by the difficulty in sorting out the assumptions most germane to the test of an hypothesis that focuses upon an empirical implication of a particular Freudian concept. For he realizes that the very number of inter-related concepts available in Freudian theory makes it possible to make deductions whose potential predictive capacity far exceeds that inherent in any other theory of personality. And, to the extent that he becomes versed in the multitudinous theoretical properties of Freudian variables, the experimenter can formulate hypotheses that promise to illuminate the determinants of previously unexplored subtleties of human behavior and that cannot be derived from other psychological theories.

Thus, to extend the illustration already used, the Freudian mechanisms of ego defense cover a variety of ways in which the same motive can be excluded from an individual's awareness as belonging to himself. Hence, while the projection of aggression should lead to its attribution to others, reaction formation against that motive should be manifested in idealizing others as essentially nonaggressive, and the rationalization of aggression permits one to vent his aggression freely upon others while perceiving his behavior as animated by interest in the salvation of their souls or some other beneficent intention. Accordingly, by assessing in advance which of these three defenses is preferred by individuals in coping with their unconscious aggression, it is possible to make very specific predictions about how they should differ in responding to the experimental evocation of aggression.

Certainly, the predictive potentials of a Freudian concept are not exhausted by a single hypothesis, for, clearly, many hypotheses can be derived from each concept, taking into account the mediation of other concepts on its empirical effects. Thus, hypotheses concerning projection can be formulated not only in regard to its action against consciously unacceptable aggression, but also against other consciously unacceptable motives. Moreover, the effects of the use of projection against these diverse motives can be formulated in predictions dealing with different kinds of dependent variables, ranging from the genotypes of anxiety and attitude, to the phenotypes of speech disturbance, ocular focus, and social withdrawal.

Of course, Freud did not compile an exhaustive inventory of experimental hypotheses that could be theoretically deduced from each of his concepts. Nor is it possible for the most ardent systematizer of Freudian theory to be so omniscient as to anticipate how every potential experimenter may succeed in making logical deductions from every concept to particular categories of empirical phenomena.

Thus, the validation of a Freudian concept, like that of other psychological concepts, is a quite open-ended process, resting on gradual accumulation of tested hypotheses. Certainly, no Freudian concept — nor any other psychological concept — can reasonably be regarded as having been confirmed or disconfirmed, at whatever degree of statistical confidence, on the basis of a single test of one hypothesis derived from it. Quite apart from the considerable issue of replication, a single hypothesis is simply too small a sample of the predictive range intrinsic in the concept's definitional assumptions.

So, as Cronbach and Meehl (1955) have similarly remarked in respect to the general issue of conceptual validation, many psychoanalytic hypotheses must be tested and replicated before the concepts from which they are deduced can be held scientifically useful or deficient. Just how many of these empirical studies will be needed for scientists to render such well-supported judgments cannot, once again, be determined on a firm *a priori* basis. Understandably, a scientist may feel more incentive to pursue a concept whose initial predictive test yields positive rather than negative findings. But all predictions are statistically articulated in terms of the null hypothesis. Hence, from a purely scientific standpoint, negative results are as important as positive ones. Indeed, negative findings are more logically compelling than positive ones. For it is literally impossible to prove that an empirically supported explanation will continue to receive such support in all future tests of its predictability; or that it is the best of all conceivable explanations for the obtained results, since no person is sufficiently godly to conceive all alternative possibilities. In contrast, however, the implication may be much more plausibly rejected by an explanation's predictive failure.

Perhaps, if the relevant methodology were sufficiently developed to eliminate it as a source of likely *post hoc* explanations for failed hypotheses, experimenters would be as sanguine about obtaining negative results as supporting ones. Nor would their motivation to follow up initial predictive failure with tests of other hypotheses deduced from the same concept be decreased by the opportunity to publish experiments that yield negative results — and by the receipt, moreover, of as much professional reward and research funds for such studies as for ones reporting positive findings.

Clearly, social values and scientific research interact strongly in this matter. And it is equally apparent that scientists, at any rate, are in a good position to call this problem to the attention of their fellow citizens, the quicker to obtain help in remedying it.

Regardless of the investigatory choices an experimenter may make, the fact remains that many empirical studies, conducted in the face of negative results and probing the limits of positive ones, will have to be done before anything like a scientifically mature verdict can be delivered on any Freudian concept.

Meanwhile, interested experimenters will wish, at least, to do theoretical justice to the assumptions contained in the concepts that capture their imagination, and they will be inclined to reflect those assumptions as faithfully as possible within the hypotheses they formulate. Yet, as has been amply illustrated, the derivation of such hypotheses is not a simple and automatic procedure, with each conceptual assumption transforming itself, at the merest glance, into a testable prediction. On the contrary, in a much more extensive manner than is involved in the semantic clarification of the concept, the experimenter must tap into his own creativity and individuality for the logical cement and bricks needed to build a deductive passageway from the concept to hypotheses appropriate to its empirical evaluation.

About creativity, little more can be added to what has been said — or, more precisely, to what science has been unable to say — about its workings. In respect to the sheer mechanics of hypothesis-formation, familiarity with the ground rules of deductive logic may not be amiss. But training in logic *per se* cannot confidently be recommended as an appreciable aid to the psychological reasoning inherent in Freudian concepts — some of whose intricate assumptions have evoked the censure of professional logicians (Hook, 1959). Certainly, general conversance with other kinds of psychological theory may be obliquely helpful insofar as it gives the experimenter conceptual access to dependent variables which can be employed in predicting the effects of the Freudian variables. Similarly, a wide reading in literature and a varied experience of life may suggest categories of phenomena that could usefully be introduced as dependent variables. And, to be sure, actual work in a clinical setting would bring the experimenter into contact with the very phenomena from which Freudian concepts were derived, and hence the phenomena, when systematically conceived as dependent variables, to which experimentally testable psychoanalytic hypotheses might well be addressed. Finally, the experimenter may receive some creative stimulation toward the formation of hypotheses through surveys of the relevant empirical literature, both experimental and correlational.

Choosing the dependent variables in formulating Freudian hypotheses

In discussing the selection of a Freudian concept for focal study, allusion has been made to the role that the experimenter's own existential dilemmas may play in determining his choice. The same sort of conflicts may also be at work in guiding the experimenter's decisions about the content of the dependent variable he chooses in formulating an hypothesis from the selected concept. For example, if an experimenter is concerned about his problems in dealing with aggression, he may decide to test an hypothesis about projection dealing with the attitudinal effects of the projection of aggression. Similarly, if the sexual motive is of greater concern to him, he may wish to test an hypothesis about the attitudinal consequences of projected sexuality.

In carrying out the tests of Freudian hypotheses, therefore, experimenters may be seeking not only to inform an anonymous world, but also to enlighten and unburden their private darkness. In this area of science, an experimenter, like an artist, may well be striving to master his own erupting conflicts in the very process of objectifying them through a special form of expression; and insofar as he succeeds in thus articulating them, the scientist, no less than the artist, may free himself of their formerly uncontrolled tensions. So, rather than feel self-consciously chagrined about the prospect of revealing his personal problems in the Freudian hypothesis he chooses to study, the experimenter can welcome the chance to resolve these problems in the course of formulating and testing his hypotheses. Indeed, if he is overly guarded about self-revelation, he may not be able to do any research on Freudian concepts. For no matter which one he chooses to investigate, and no matter what specific hypothesis he deduces from it, his work is always open to interpretation as reflecting a personal conflict whose content is manifest in his investigatory choices. Therefore, the experimenter would do well to follow his own conceptual inclinations and acknowledge, in advance of any such interpretations, that what he voluntarily selects for study is indubitably an affirmation of himself, and that, moreover, he is glad to assume complete responsibility for his affirmation, albeit that he himself may be far from sure about how much of it is determined by buried tensions within himself.

But intraindividual conflicts comprise only one part of the existential forces that motivate the experimenter for formulating particular

Freudian hypotheses. The other part is, broadly speaking, interpersonal; and it pertains to the tensions experienced between the experimenter and the society in which he lives. More particularly, these tensions concern the discrepancies between an experimenter's own ideals about how people ought to relate to each other in society and the ways in which they are, in fact, treating each other.

An experimenter's awareness of such discrepancies may motivate him strongly enough to take them into explicit consideration in formulating Freudian hypotheses. Thus, he may feel initially impelled to conduct an experiment largely because he wishes to contribute toward the alleviation or prevention of a social phenomenon that affronts his conception of human decency or that, indeed, represents a direct and palpable menace not only to his personal existence but also to millions of people who occupy a place in social reality that is similar to his own. For example, a Jewish researcher may choose to study anti-Semitism because that prejudice has been a central precipitating factor in the massive slaughter of Jews. And having first decided to investigate that social phenomenon, he may select a Freudian concept whose attributes appear to permit the formulation of an hypothesis concerning the psychological determinants of anti-Semitism.

But a researcher need not feel so imminently threatened by a social phenomenon to decide to study it. Nor need he select it for study prior to selecting a potentially fruitful explanatory concept through which to investigate its psychological determinants. And it may be that the fusion between concept and phenomenon most often occurs in a single act of creative reasoning, whereby the experimenter's interest in a specific Freudian concept and his concern for a particular social phenomenon come together in a solution to: a) the intellectual problem of formulating an hypothesis that is an appropriate deduction from the concept; and b) the emotional problem of finding a promising way of conceptualizing, and hence of systematically studying, the determinants of the social phenomenon.

Using social attitudes as dependent variables in Freudian hypotheses

Thus, the experimenter can meet the logical requirements of his scientific commitments while simultaneously actualizing his social values. In testing hypotheses that are conceived with these two ends in view, the researcher can, in every experiment, produce empirical data that are equally applicable to the scientific evaluation of Freudian concepts and to the scientific comprehension of social problems. And insofar as people possess reliable knowledge about the determinants of their societal difficulties, they can use it for their social betterment.

Just how an experimenter effects such happy mental rapprochements between his interest in a Freudian concept and concern for a social problem is no clearer today than is the inventive process of problem-solving, wherein elements of a solution are sudenly brought together in a flash of insight (Wertheimer, 1945). But recognition of the possibility and the desirability of such solutions, vis-a-vis the formulation of Freudian hypotheses, may help the experimenter to create them.

In this respect, the phenomena of social attitudes would appear to lend themselves particularly well as vehicles through which the validity of Freudian concepts can be tested and the explanatory potentials of psychoanalytic concepts can have societal impact. For, conceived as relatively enduring dispositions to react positively or negatively to a class of objects (Sarnoff, 1960a), social attitudes are genotypes that affect a wide range of the individual's thoughts, feelings, and actions toward other people. Indeed, every type of interpersonal reaction can be conceptualized as being mediated by an attitude relevant to some social attribute of the persons involved: their class, caste, color, ethnic membership, religious affiliation, age, sex, occupation, and so forth.

But social attitudes can be conceived, in turn, as dependent variables; that is, as having been determined by the functioning of other variables. Viewed in this perspective, knowledge of the determinants of attitudes can permit the scientifically based introduction of social changes designed to produce widespread attitudinal changes. And, insofar as attitudes mediate behavior, the resulting changes in attitude should be manifested in consonant alterations in social behavior.

Insofar as social attitudes are conceived of as dependent variables, they can be most appropiately used in hypotheses that seek to test the validity of Freudian concepts. For such hypotheses deal with the Freudian concepts as independent variables which are theoretically expected to exert specific attitudinal effects. And such a linkage can be made with perfectly logical appropriateness, since virtually all Freudian concepts have decidedly social implications embedded in their psychological properties.

Actually, apart from Freud's inherently biological concepts, libido and the death instinct, the whole of Freudian theory refers, directly or indirectly, to psychological variables that are shaped in the course of the individual's interaction with his social environment. But even the behavioral fate of the postulated innate instincts is explicitly regarded as a function of the individual's social history. Thus, for example, Freud's theory of psychosexual development might be more accurately described as "psycho-socio-sexual" in character, for its component concepts are replete with assumptions concerning the enduring psychological effects of social vicissitudes experienced by the child at various stages of his sexual maturation. Such concepts as *frustration* or *gratification* clearly refer to ways in which the child's caretakers habitually respond to the expression of his libidinal motivation. Similarly, the concepts of trauma and fixation refer to psychological consequences of those social responses.

Over time, therefore, the child's personality is formed not only from the maturational unfolding of his sexuality but also from the interaction between his efforts to reduce the tension of his sexual motives and the manner by which those efforts are socially confronted. In this respect, Freud's Oedipal theory, which is a crucial part of his account of psychosexual development, is largely an attempt to conjecture universal characteristics of that social confrontation at a particular point in the child's sexual maturation. And just as the Oedipal theory assumes the presence of a mother toward whom the male child can direct his sexual tensions — and about whom those tensions can be represented, epiphenomenologically, in his fantasies — so does it assume the presence of a father who forbids the child to covet the mother sexually.

Certainly, the adult actors in this social drama need not be the child's biological parents, as Malinowski (1927, 1929) long ago emphasized in describing the disciplinary role of the boy's maternal uncle among the Trobriand Islanders. But the important point to be noted here is that the Oedipal conflict is conceived as being both precipitated and resolved by the child's social relationships. And every one of the concepts involved in Freud's explanation of the resolution of the Oedipal conflict reflects, as it were, lasting psychological residues of societal forces — transmitted within the familial microcosm through the person of the father — opposed to the practice of incest. Thus, the concepts of *castration anxiety, identification with the aggressor, repression*, and *displacement* refer to the various inner transformations whereby the child, threatened with extreme punishment, adopts his father's prohibitions, permanently pushes his incestuous desire out of consciousness while renouncing his mother as a sexual object, and turns his heterosexual inclinations toward other, non-taboo females.

Presumably, these psychological transformations can be subsequently modified, at least to some extent, through the kind of insightful uncovering of their interpersonal origins as occurs in psychoanalytic theory. Ordinarily, however, the accretions to personality that occur during the Oedipal and other periods of psychosexual development are conceived as relatively fixed psychological dimensions that remain with the individual throughout his life. But since each of these enduring variables of personality was originally established in a context of social interaction, it may be readily applied as an explanatory concept to relevant aspects of the individual's subsequent social behavior. Hence, insofar as they mediate such behavior, social attitudes can also serve as most appropriate dependent variables for the testing of hypotheses derived from Freudian concepts.

However, to make such use of social attitudes, the experimenter will need to think creatively about the kind of impact that a particular Freudian variable may have on a specific attitude. Certainly, the attitude *per se* is no reliable guide to its potential psychoanalytic determinant. For any attitude may be conceived as arising from a variety of motivational sources, including the entirely conscious desire to use it as means of reducing the tensions of a motive of which the individual is completely aware. For example, "Individual A may *deliberately* behave in a manner that leads his prejudiced neighbors to infer that he shares their anti-Negro attitudes: he may, for instance, grin at anti-Negro jokes, nod his head at bigoted remarks made in his presence and offer his own negative pronouncements about Negroes. Approving of the anti-Negro sentiments that they see in his behavior, Individual A's neighbors patronize his store and help to reduce, thereby, the tensions of his motives to make money [Sarnoff, 1960a, p. 169]."

But Freud did not invent his theory to conceptualize the calculated expressions of consciously acceptable attitudes. On the contrary, Freudian concepts exclusively refer to consciously unacceptable motives and to the unconsciously operative processes whereby those motives are excluded from awareness. And it is only from this frame of reference that attitudes can be approached, with theoretical appropriateness, as effects of psychoanalytic variables. "From the standpoint of his consciously unacceptable motives, the individual's attitudes toward objects are determined by their function in facilitating: (1) covert ego-defensive responses aimed at precluding the perception of consciously unacceptable motives and (2) overt symptomatic responses which permit the individual to reduce the tension produced by his consciously unacceptable motives [Sarnoff, 1960a, p. 266]."

But since an attitude can also be adopted and maintained for other motivational reasons, as previously noted, an experimenter must carefully consider "which *combination* of consciously unacceptable motive and ego-defense might plausibly account for the *particular* overt response from which the attitude is inferred [Sarnoff, 1962, p. 169]." Following such consideration, an experimenter can formulate a specific hypothesis in which an attitude is used as a dependent variable in a test of a Freudian concept. But since an experiment involves the planned manipulation of independent variables, with consequent observation of their effects on dependent variables, the hypothesis would involve the prediction of a change in the relevant attitude. And since the independent variables involved are of two kinds, unconscious motives and ego defenses, the attitudinal change would have to be predicted as a result of either:

1. The manipulation of the ego defenses that presumably function to obliterate the perception of the consciously unacceptable motive whose functional relationship to the attitude had been postulated; or
2. The arousal of a motive against whose conscious perception the individual is supposed to be defending himself by the use of a particular mechanism of ego defense [Sarnoff, 1962, p. 170].

An example of the first type of hypothesis can be found in the experimental work of Katz, Sarnoff, and McClintock (1956), wherein the reduction of anti-Negro attitudes was predicted as a consequence of the provision of insight into the possible ego-defensive basis of those prejudices. The second type of hypothesis is exemplified in the prediction (Sarnoff, 1960b) that the arousal of affection would produce more cynicism among subjects high in the use of reaction formation than among those who were low in the use of that ego defense against affection.

Sometimes, however, an experimenter may be interested in the attitudinal effects of failure of the ego defenses to work effectively. In such instances, Freudian theory would expect the afflicted individual to experience anxiety (Freud, 1949f), which presumably signals the incipient emergence into awareness of a consciously unacceptable motive. But since anxiety is also conceived as a motive in its own right (Sarnoff, 1962), it is possible to predict its effects on attitudes likely to function as channels for the reduction of its tensions. Moreover, by specifying its distinctive psychological properties and by differentiating them from those connected with other but seemingly similar motives, such as fear, one can derive subtle and striking hypotheses concerning the impact of anxiety on interpersonal orientations. Thus, Sarnoff and Zimbardo (1961) were able to predict that the experimental arousal of anxiety would lead people to prefer social affiliation.

Similarly, by an assiduous shifting of assumptions contained in the several Freudian concepts involved, it is possible to categorize anxiety by type. These premises concern the psychological properties of the unconscious motive, the interpersonal history that fostered its chronic rejection from consciousness, the symbolic representation of that history in consciousness, and the interpersonal stimuli likely to arouse it. Thus, one might assume that castration anxiety among males, induced by paternal prohibition against incest, can be aroused by heterosexual stimuli; and that while the original castration threat *per se* might be too traumatic to admit to consciousness, its occurrence would be lastingly experienced in the symbolic form of concern over the possibility of incurring physical injury, including the ultimate injury, death.

Insofar as such fears can be grouped together as a common class of phenomena, they may serve as the cognitive basis of an attitude. Hence, one can utilize such attitudes as dependent variables in predicting a positive relationship between castration anxiety and the fear of death (Sarnoff & Corwin, 1959). Moreover, Bromberg (1967) related castration anxiety to two different kinds of fear, showing that, as predicted, its relationship with the fear of physical injury was more pronounced than its relationship with the fear of being separated from other people.

4 Interactive Designs for Freudian Experiments

In the interests of coherent exposition, this volume presents the various phases of deductive experimentation in separate and sequential chapters. But as will become increasingly evident through the issues raised within each of those chapters, the proper planning of an experiment necessarily involves highly intertwined processes of thought, reflecting the interrelated theoretical and operational implications of all the procedures employed. For no methodological step toward the testing of an hypothesis can be sensibly taken without simultaneously considering how it may best implement preceding and succeeding ones.

Thus, after evolving a specific hypothesis, a researcher must envision the general conditions required to generate the observational data that can provide the most logical basis of inference regarding the relative empirical truthfulness of his prediction. The experimental design constitutes this logical framework, laying down broad procedural guidelines within which the experimenter subsequently makes his decisions concerning the specific operational measurement and manipulation of the relevant variables.

Ideally, an experiment's design should be determined by the substantive nature of the theoretical question contained in its hypothesis. But because the potential range of such questions cannot be anticipated, any commentary on the abstract principals of experimental design is destined to be deficient in its theoretical aptness and applicability. Still, as a fundamental orientation to this topic, the reader may find it very helpful to become familiar with the excellent monograph by Campbell and Stanley (1963).

Regarding the substance of Freudian concepts, however, a particular kind of interactive design recommends itself as most theoretically appropiate for their experimental study. This interactive design, which juxtaposes relevant variables of persons and situations, will be the model on which this chapter will focus and to which most of the illustrative experiments in this book will refer.

An interactive model for the design of experiments on Freudian hypotheses

It seems eminently reasonable, as Lewin (1954) has noted, to view behavior as a function of the individual *and* his environment. Brunswik (1947), accepting the same premise, has stressed the importance of adequately and systematically sampling both individuals and the stimuli presented to them as a prerequisite to valid generalization in psychology. Similarly, Cronbach (1954) has argued for the integration of the "two disciplines of scientific psychology" — the correlational and experimental — into a single investigatory approach, which would permit the simultaneous study of the separate and combined effects of individual and situational variables.

In conceptual terms, such a unified strategy of research would regard any dependent variable as a function of two sets of independent variables: those that are intrinsic to the individual and those that characterize the situation in which the individual is studied. Clearly, by combining both types of independent variables in the same studies, researchers can acquire more information about the determinants of the dependent variable than they could by including only one type of independent variable. A combination permits a researcher to sort out how much of a particular facet of behavior or experience (the dependent variable) is separately determined by each type of independent variable and how much is determined by the interactions of those independent variables.

Regarding tests of Freudian hypotheses, the relevant independent variables that deal with differences in personality are conceptually defined, we have seen, as relatively enduring traits — the mechanisms of ego defense and motives or motivational conflicts that have been chronically repressed. Operationally, therefore, such traits require definition through procedures of measurement. For it is assumed that they cannot be induced, *de novo*, within the spatial and temporal confines of a controlled experiment. However, these traits are conceived as amenable to differential evocation and engagement by relatively transient states of motivation or cognition, which fluctuate in accordance with ongoing environmental stimuli. Accordingly, these transient states can best be operationally defined for systematic study through procedures of experimental manipulation.

Thus, to utilize maximally the logical advantages of studying individual and situational determinants of behavior within a single investigation, it is desirable, even while formulating Freudian hypotheses, to consider how those two types of independent variables may contribute, both separately and in consort, to whatever effects a researcher is seeking to predict. Put operationally in its simplest form, this consideration would lead a researcher to conceive how quantitative variations in a nonmanipulated (measured) trait of personality and like variations in a situationally manipulated state of motivation or cognition separately and jointly affect measurable quantitative variations in a given aspect of behavior or experience (dependent variable).

Figure 1 summarizes the operational essentials of an interactive design applicable to tests of Freudian hypotheses:

In Figure 1, it will be noted that only two levels of quantitative variation are depicted for the independent variables. However, as the ensuing discussion makes plain, it is often possible and desirable to study the effects of finer quantitative gradations in the independent variables. Similarly, the effects of more than one nonmanipulated independent variable and one manipulated variable may be studied within the same interactive experiment; and, of course, more than a single effect (a single dependent variable) may be predicted and measured. Finally, various numbers of different individuals (N individuals) may be included in each of the combinations of independent variables juxtaposed in an experimental design. Naturally, however, an experimenter would want to include enough individuals to obtain a statistically adequate test of his hypotheses (Cohen, 1965); and their assignment to the groups should be done in such a way as to preclude the intrusion of an experimenter's inadvertent biases. Thus, subjects possessing different degrees of the measured independent variable of personality should be randomly assigned to the different experimental conditions, and the experimenter dealing with them in those conditions should not know how much of the variable of personality is possessed by particular individuals assigned to a given condition.

Although such interactive designs, however complex, contain only

FIGURE 1

The Prototype of an Interactive Design for Experimentation on Freudian Concepts

		Quantitative Variation in a Situationally Manipulated Independent Variable of Motivation or Cognition	
		HIGH	LOW
Quantitative Variation in the Nonmanipulated (Measured) Independent Variable of Personality	H I G H	Measured Effects on the Dependent Variable (N individuals)	Measured Effects on the Dependent Variable (N individuals)
	L O W	Measured Effects on the Dependent Variable (N individuals)	Measured Effects on the Dependent Variable (N individuals)

two types of independent variables, it is possible to advance three sets of *a priori* hypotheses concerning the impact of those variables on the dependent ones: (1) hypotheses dealing solely with the effects of the nonmanipulated independent variables of personality; (2) hypotheses dealing solely with the effects of the manipulated independent variables of motivation or cognition; and (3) hypotheses dealing solely with the interactions between the nonmanipulated and manipulated independent variables.

Of course, insofar as good theoretical grounds exist within Freudian theory for formulating these three possible sets of predictions in a given experiment, it is scientifically desirable for an experimenter to do so. For the more widely, definitely, and stringently a concept can be tested within a single experiment, the more information will that experiment yield concerning the concept's scientific utility.

However, Freudian concepts were originally conceived as habitual individual differences in personality that determine individual differences in behavior and experience (dependent variables). Moreover, it is often readily possible to deduce how those enduring differences in personality may be systematically engaged by (interact with) transiently induced variables of motivation or cognition to produce various behavioral and experiential effects. But Freudian theory does not often permit one to predict how those transiently induced variables *per se* will affect specific dependent variables.

Thus, in most cases, an experimenter may be able only to advance confident *a priori* hypotheses regarding either the interaction between the two sets of independent variables or that interaction and the main effects of the nonmanipulated variable of personality. But testing the effects of a nonmanipulated independent variable would merely require a correlational study, whereby the designated measure of that variable could be correlated with a measure of the designated dependent variable. Consequently, it is the hypotheses dealing with the interactions between enduring variables of personality and the transient ones of motivation or cognition that ordinarily require an experimental rather than a correlational method of investigation to be designed.

If an experimenter has a firm theoretical basis for predicting interactions between the types of independent variables *and* the main effects of the nonmanipulated one, he has the advantage of being able simultaneously to conduct an experimental and a correlational study, thus fulfilling both the letter and the spirit of Cronbach's investigatory prescription. However, this very opportunity also brings with it certain methodological problems, which will presently be discussed.

*Problems to be overcome in the systematic
use of interactive design for
Freudian experiments*

A. *Theoretical problems of interactive designs.* Despite its impeccable logic as a strategy for extracting the greatest possible amount of explanatory information from any single experiment, the interactive model of experimental research cannot be meaningfully applied unless an experimenter is equipped with a theoretical basis for making *a priori* decisions about which of all possible individual and contextual variables should be operationally brought together as the most likely determinants of particular psychological phenomena. But most psychological theories have tended to treat only one or the other set of potential determinants with explicit and systematic concern.

For example, social psychologists, who might have been expected, following Lewin's formula, to give equal conceptual attention to both sets of variables, have generally omitted *systematic* concern for individual differences in personality in their theoretical formulations. And this omission is characteristic even of such theories as Festinger's (1957) theory of cognitive dissonance, which centers upon, and makes various assumptions about, intraindividual states of conflict and their manner of resolution.

Of course, Festinger and other social psychologists (cf. Brehm & Cohen, 1962; Insko, 1967) recognize that individual differences in personality may affect the dependent variables in their experiments, But they have typically attempted to control for such effects by randomly assigning subjects to the various experimental manipulations without first attempting to measure any differences among the subjects on independent variables of personality that may mediate the impact of those manipulations. However, despite this randomization, these experiments are usually left with a considerable amount of variance unaccounted for by the main effects of the manipulated independent variable of motivation or cognition. And this "error" variance is just as usually presented as if it ought not to require any further explanation.

Naturally, errors of measurement in respect to the dependent variables can be expected to contribute a fair amount to the unaccounted variance in these experiments. Actually, however, as Campbell and Stanley (1963) note, sampling procedures involved in the assignment of subjects to groups are often not nearly as random as the statistical ideal would require. Hence, some experimental groups are likely to differ, in unknown ways, on personality variables that may crucially affect their reactions to the manipulations. Moreover, even if the sampling were perfectly random, one might still reasonably expect part of the variance obtained to reflect the operation of those variables in advance, one would be in a position to predict for effects randomly distributed groups, to interaction with the particular manipulated variable. If one could measure such habitual, intraindividual variables in advance, one would be in a position to predict for effects that cannot be otherwise explained. The resulting gain for scientific knowledge would be increased accordingly.

The basic theoretical problem, of course, is to conceive precisely which nonmanipulated independent variables of personality may predictably interact with the manipulated ones of motivation or cognition. Lacking the appropriate conceptions, a researcher cannot make such specific predictions, and he may well choose to measure variables of personality that provide little elucidation of the variance not accounted for by the main effects of the manipulations. Fortunately, Freudian theory is abundant in its conceptualization of variables of personality that can facilitate these predictions. But it is manifestly deficient in the degree of explicitness with which it conceives the situational factors involved in the formation and elicitation of the individual's presumably internalized and enduring traits of personality. Certainly, the interpersonal connotations of Freudian concepts are overshadowed by Freud's stress on their imputed intraindividual dynamics.

Largely as a result of this conceptual emphasis, a good deal of past research on Freudian concepts has implicitly tended to view the individual as a quite self-contained, if not hermetically sealed, psychological unit, whose mode of functioning is so impervious to on-going environmental influence that he can be studied without systematic concern for the social context in which his personality is measured. Thus, for example, in his manual for the Thematic Apperception Test, Murray (1943), although by no means entirely Freudian in orientation, likens his test to an X-ray, which can reveal by itself the inner workings of the personalities of the individuals responding to it.

Nevertheless, the sympathetic and interested researcher can tease out many of the social implications of Freudian concepts, as already illustrated in discussing how Freudian theory can be utilized in studies on the motivational determinants of social attitudes. Similarly, it is possible to conceive the kinds of situational stimuli — including social ones — that are most likely to evoke particular Freudian variables of personality. Thus, insofar as an experimenter succeeds in making clear the theoretical connection between Freudian variables of personality and the situational variables that ought to mediate their effects in specific ways, he can (as will soon be concretely illustrated) make optimal use of interactive designs as guidelines for testing Freudian concepts.

B. *Methodological problems of interactive designs.* The systematic incorporation of a variable of personality in an interactive experiment undoubtedly creates methodological problems, even if one has resolved the first theoretical difficulty of deciding which variable to include. "Secondly, one must find or develop a reliable measure of that personality variable, often no mean task in itself. Thirdly, one must develop a rationale which covers, with ostensible reasonableness, the administration of the premeasured variable of personality and the induction of the manipulated variable. Fourthly, one may be obliged to contend with knotty 'ceiling' effects, when, for example a correlation exists between the personality variable and the dependent variable in before-after experiments that predict particular changes in attitude as a function of the interaction between level of the personality variable and level of the manipulated variable [Sarnoff, 1965a, pp. 284-285]."

These difficulties can be dealt with by recourse to a variety of techniques of measurement, experimental staging, and statistical analysis. For example, the construction of theoretically apt, easily administered, and reliable measures of personality can be aided by the use of item analysis and factor analysis. Imaginative presentation of an experiment can handle problems of credibility and emotional involvement, encompassing the administration of pre-experimental measures and the experimental inductions. 'Ceiling' effects may largely be mitigated in advance by measures of the dependent variable that permit ample room for registration of changes in one's initial position on the measures at issue. The methods of multiple regression and analysis of covariance can be used as statistical controls in instances where the measure of personality is shown to correlate with the "before" measure of the dependent variable.

We shall dwell upon these methodological devices in detail as their consideration arises in respect to the implementation of the various sequential stages of an experiment. But it is now important to concretize the logic of interactive design, showing how it may be applied in its two basic versions: the "after-only" and the "before-after" experimental procedures.

"After-only" and "before-after" versions of the interactive design

As Campell and Stanley (1963) point out, the after-only experimental design is as logically sound as the before-after one. It also has the advantage of being generally quicker to conduct, of being less vulnerable to the confounding effects of experiences — including exposure to the measure of the dependent variable — intervening in the lives of subjects in before-after experiments, and of being less susceptible to the loss of subjects who initially agree to participate in it. Certainly, hypotheses that involve *only* interactive effects can be logically and satisfactorily tested through after-only versions of the prototypic interactive design in which the dependent variable is measured only once — after the manipulations of the independent variables of motivation or cognition.

However, hypotheses involving interactive effects and the main effects of the variable of personality may best be tested through "before-after" versions in which the dependent variable is measured twice — before and after the manipulations of the independent variables of motivation or cognition. Any hypothesis dealing with a *habitual* relationship between an independent variable of personality and a designated dependent variable can be most logically observed before the dependent variable has been affected by any experimental manipulation. Still, by taking measures of the dependent variable both before and after the manipulations, an experimenter can use the resulting before-after change in the dependent variable as a criterion for assessing his hypotheses concerning the way in which those manipulations would interact with the nonmanipulated variable of personality.

Before-after variations in the interactive design are also useful in experiments investigating the endurance of effects produced by the interaction between particular nonmanipulated and manipulated independent variables. For example, Katz, Sarnoff, and McClintock (1956) took two "after" measures of the attitude whose change represented their dependent variable: one measure immediately after subjects were exposed to the experimental manipulations, and the second five weeks later. Thus, the changes in attitude induced by the manipulations could be traced over time by comparing the "after" measures both to each other and to the "before" measure.

Finally, an experimenter may wish to study unequivocal, empirically observed change within the *same* individual, and not simply *assume* that he had changed thus and so with respect to a group matched in personality but exposed to a different experimental condition – the basic assumption behind the after-only procedure. There is a good deal of empirical reassurance in the attainment of such actual, as opposed to presumed, changes.

On the other hand, exposure to a "before" measure or an experimental manipulation could conceivably so disclose what is being studied and why as to greatly influence the responses of subjects to an "after" measure. And these uncontrolled influences could, in turn, undermine the test of the hypothesis an experimenter had hoped to study. In due course, such confounding influences, together with suggestions for coping with them, will be discussed in detail. But it can be said in advance of those considerations that an experimenter would be wise to use an after-only approach if he had good empirical reasons – from his own pilot work or other studies – to believe that a before-after procedure might involve adverse methodological consequences.

The following examples are intended to illustrate the application of "after-only" and "before-after" types of interactive designs to tests of Freudian hypotheses. It should be noted that each illustration involves the use of an attitude as a dependent variable.

An after-only interactive design: Anality,
privation and dissonance (Bishop, 1965)

In devising her design, Bishop sought, in part, to replicate the
study of Festinger and Carlsmith (1959). However, her experiment
modified theirs to include a Freudian variable of personality.

Working strictly within the confines of dissonance theory, those
experimenters had first exposed their subjects to a very boring task
for considerable periods of time. They then asked subjects to
volunteer to tell other purported subjects, who were awaiting participation in the experiment, that the task was interesting rather
than boring. In one experimental condition, subjects were promised $20.00 for relating this information, which was so contrary to
their actual cognitions about the task. In the other condition,
subjects were offered only $1.00 for agreeing to carry out the
experimenter's wishes. A subsequent check on their own attitudes
toward the task showed, as predicted from dissonance theory, that
subjects in the low reward conditions were more favorable in their
attitude toward the task than subjects in the high reward condition.

Bishop argued, however, that this kind of relationship between
incentive and attitude change would not be found among all
possible subjects. Indeed, she reasoned, drawing upon Freud's theory
of the anal character . . . that subjects high in anality would
react quite differently from subjects low in anality under identical
conditions of privation. Specifically, she predicted that, under
conditions of low privation, high anal subjects would be more
favorable than low anals toward a boring task they had volunteered to describe as interesting to potential subjects. Conversely,
under conditions of high privation, she predicted that high anals
would be more negative to the task than low anals. In her case,
degree of privation was varied by leading subjects to anticipate
the winning of a $20.00 reward for their participation in the
experiment, and then having a 'drawing' from a punch board
which limited the high privation group to $1.00, while the an-
ticipated winnings of the low privation group were only reduced
to $19.00. And the interaction between the personality measure
of anality and the manipulated variable of privation yielded the

predicted differential patterns of attitude change [Sarnoff, 1965a, p. 285].

Bishop was primarily concerned with predicting the interaction between the nonmanipulated independent variable of anality, as measured by the Ah (anal hoarding) scale of the Dynamic Personality Inventory (Grygier, 1961), and the manipulated independent variable of privation, as induced by differentials in the amount by which an individual perceived his originally anticipated winnings to be reduced. This predicted interaction, whose effects on the dependent variable of favorableness to the boring task are indicated by plus (+) signs for more and minus (−) signs for less. is graphically presented in the interactive design given in Figure 2 (see page 64).

A before-after interactive design: Castration anxiety and the fear of death (Sarnoff & Corwin, 1959)

On the theoretical bases explicated in Chapter III, this experiment sought to test: 1) A correlational hypothesis concerning the relationship between habitual castration anxiety (CA) as a nonmanipulated independent variable, and the fear of death (FD) as a designated dependent variable, and 2) An hypothesis concerning the effects on the fear of death of the interaction between habitual castration anxiety and the manipulated independent variable of heterosexual motivation. Specifically, it was predicted that a positive correlation would obtain between habitual castration anxiety and the fear of death and that this relationship would so increase with heterosexual arousal (SA) that individuals high in habitual castration anxiety would become more fearful of death than those low in castration anxiety.

To test these hypotheses, it was first necessary to measure both the independent variable of habitual castration anxiety and the dependent variable of fear of death. Then it was necessary to place individuals who were high and low in habitual castration anxiety in experimental conditions that quantitatively varied the manipulated variable of heterosexual arousal. Specifically, this placement yielded four different groups of subjects (High CA-High SA, Low CA-Low SA, High CA-Low SA, Low CA-High SA), permitting each level of both independent variables to have a quantitative control. Finally,

FIGURE 2

*The After-Only Interactive Design Used
in Bishop's Experiment*

		Quantitative Variation in the Situationally Manipulated Independent Variable of Privation	
		HIGH	LOW
Quantitative Variation in the Nonmanipulated (Measured) Independent Variable of Anal Hoarding	H I G H H	Measured Effects on the Dependent Variable Of Attitude Toward the Boring Task (−)	Measured Effects on the Dependent Variable Of Attitude Toward the Boring Task (+)
	L O W	Measured Effects on the Dependent Variable Of Attitude Toward the Boring Task (+)	Measured Effects on the Dependent Variable Of Attitude Toward the Boring Task (−)

after exposure to their particular experimental condition, the subjects were given the "after" measure of the dependent variable, FD.

Various and additional aspects of the methodology of this experiment will be discussed subsequently. But for the moment it suffices merely to note that the obtained results gave statistically significant support to both hypotheses listed above. That is, the measure of CA correlated positively with the "before" measure of FD, and, following the high SA manipulation but not the low SA one, individuals high in CA showed a greater before-after increase in FD than did individuals who were low in CA. The predicted interaction is graphically represented in Figure 3 (see page 66). The + and − signs in the body of the diagram indicate the direction and the relative amount of before-after change in the dependent variable.

The theoretical meaning of quantitative "controls" for the independent variables in interactive designs

By definition, a psychological variable is a continuum whose quality is quantitatively distributed among individuals to whom it is imputed. Thus, psychologists interested in the operational measurement of Freudian variables of personality have developed their measures with a view toward reflecting quantitative variations in those variables. And while such measures, as we shall see, may contain various defects, they are at least constructed with the aim of permitting inferences about the degree to which the individuals measured by them may be imputed to possess the variables concerned.

However, the same principle of quantitative variation has not been as systematically applied in the operational *manipulation* of independent variables involved in experimental tests of Freudian concepts. Indeed, one of the first such experiments in which I participated (Katz, Sarnoff, & McClintock, 1956) failed to provide for quantitative variation in our manipulated variables of cognition.

True, we had built such variation into our premeasured variable of personality, having sorted out three levels of ego-defensiveness: high, medium, and low. But our experimental manipulations simply consisted of three unvaried conditions: Interpretation, Information,

FIGURE 3

*The Before-After Interactive Design Used
in the Experiment by Sarnoff and Corwin*

		Quantitative Variation in the Situationally Manipulated Independent Variable of Heterosexual Motivation	
		HIGH	LOW
Quantitative Variation in the Nonmanipulated (Measured) Independent Variable of Habitual Castration Anxiety	H I G H	Measured Effects on the Dependent Variable of Fear of Death (+ +)	Measured Effects on the Dependent Variable of Fear of Death (−)
	L O W	Measured Effects on the Dependent Variable of Fear of Death (+)	Measured Effects on the Dependent Variable of Fear of Death (−)

and Control, a group which received no intervening communication prior to being retested on the attitude scale in the "After" condition. . . .

Thus, we had no way of knowing whether the subjects received a little or a lot of interpretation and information; whether more or less of those manipulated variables would have made a difference in terms of changes in the dependent variable; or, finally, whether or not various levels of the manipulated variable would have interacted simultaneously with the levels of the personality variable.

But making provision for the quantitative variation of the manipulated variable has a significance above and beyond those just stated. Indeed, it is virtually the only way to satisfy oneself that one has some genuine comprehension of the crucial properties of the variables one is presuming to manipulate. For if one can demonstrate that, as an independent variable rises or lowers in intensity, it has systematic and predicted effects on a dependent variable, one can feel more confident about having isolated the independent variable in accordance with the theoretical conceptions of the manner in which it is presumed to function.

In the absence of such a demonstration, however, it is impossible to assert with any assurance that one has grasped the theoretically defining aspect of an independent variable, regardless of how strong an impact its manipulation of unknown strength has on a dependent variable. Certainly, for example, in our experimental manipulation of insight aimed at reducing ego-defensiveness, we had no way of knowing what aspect of our 11-page interpretive communication conveyed the theoretically pertinent variable of insight. Yet, to gain this important knowledge, one would have to show that, by varying the intensity of the theoretically pertinent property of that communication, one could induce like variations in both insight and attitude change.

The provisions just discussed cannot be adequately made by the substitution of a nonmanipulated control group for a group exposed to a quantitative variation in the experimentally manipulated, independent variable. That is, it is not a logically satisfactory solution to the problem of understanding cause-effect relationships in psychology simply to compare a group receiving an induction of unknown intensity with one which did not receive that induction. For human beings are sentient organisms who are continually reacting to their environment and continually trying to fathom its meaning. So, putting people into a control group requires giving them *some* rationale for the enlistment of their cooperation and telling them something about why they are being called upon to respond to whatever measures of the dependent variable one wishes to impose upon them.

Accordingly, the term 'control group' generally represents a wistful and quite inaccurate euphemism. Clearly, every so-called control condition is a manipulation of some psychological variable or variables, albeit that experimenters have typically made no attempt to determine what, in fact, was stirred up among subjects placed in it. Indeed, it would be more apt to label such conditions 'uncontrolled,' insofar as they affect subjects in ways unknown to the experimenter.

Thus, from a theoretical standpoint, it makes more sense to have at least two degrees of variation in a manipulated variable than it does to have a single manipulation of indeterminant strength versus a control group. On the other hand, there are some experimental designs, notably those involving interactions between premeasured and manipulated independent variables, in which the addition of a nonmanipulated control group may contribute appreciably to the understanding of results. However, in those designs it is advisable for the experimenter to keep in mind that the group is being exposed to some eliciting stimuli, if only those that urge him again to fill out a questionnaire he had filled out some time in the past [Sarnoff, 1965a, pp. 281-282].

> *The possible utility of a nonmanipulated control group for the manipulated independent variable in interactive designs*

A. *The use of a nonmanipulated control group in "after-only" interactive designs.* As previously indicated, the "after-only" design ordinarily cannot be used to study a predicted habitual relationship between the independent variable of personality and the dependent variable. For such a relationship would have been contaminated by the intervening effects of the manipulated variable of motivation or cognition.

However, the experimenter interested in including the uncontaminated study of such a relationship may be able to do so by adding an extra, nonmanipulated control group to an "after-only" version of the interactive paradigm. Specifically, he could sample a group of individuals who are not exposed to any degree of quantitative variation in the experiment's manipulated independent variables.

A researcher could thus obtain a sufficient sample in which no manipulation intervened between the measure of the personality variable and that of the dependent variable. And the data from such a control group could be used for the purpose of a correlational study, which would have been grafted on to the experimental one. For example, if Bishop (1965) had included such a nonmanipulated control group to her previously described experiment, she would have been able to assess the habitual relationship between anal hoarding and attitudes towards the kind of repetitive task employed in her experiment. Accordingly, she might have been able to see whether and to what extent individuals high on the measure of anal hoarding are *generally* inclined to perceive such a task as less boring than individuals who are low on that measure.

B. The potential uses of a nonmanipulated control group in "before-after" interactive designs. The following accounts give a detailed explication of two experiments. In the first, the findings, which were somewhat equivocal, could not be further clarified owing to the absence in the original design of a nonmanipulated control group. In the second example, it will be shown how such a problem of equivocality was remedied by obtaining an additional, nonmanipulated control group that was not originally included in the experimental design.

1. Separation fear and the fear of death: Ross 1966). Dealing with the theoretically presumed effects of separation fear on the fear of death, Ross predicted that: "children who possess high, habitual levels of separation fear would be more fearful of death than children whose habitual level of separation fear is less intense; and experimentally induced separation fear would interact additively with ha-

bitual separation fear, thus causing subjects high in habitual separation fear to become even more fearful of death than subjects low in
habitual separation fear.

Actually, she found the predicted correlation between separation
fear and the fear of death. Under the experimental condition of
low arousal of separation fear, the children high in habitual
separation fear became more fearful of death than those low in
habitual separation fear. However, under the experimental condition of high arousal of separation fear, even the magnitude of
the differences obtained under low arousal did not appear, thus
clearly contradicting the expectation that the high arousal condition would induce greater differences than the low arousal condition.

Thus, far from yielding the predicted interaction, the high arousal
condition appeared to have obliterated the effect on fear of death
of habitual individual differences in separation fear. Indeed, the
experimenter argued, *post hoc,* that the high arousal condition
may have had just that massive an impact. Certainly, it is logical
to assume that, when environmental conditions are sufficiently
extreme, they may obscure individual differences in response that
would show up under less overwhelming circumstances. To be
sure, the children in the high arousal condition were exposed to
nothing more extreme than listening to the story of a lost child.
(Subjects in the low arousal condition heard a less poignant version of the same story, in which the child was only briefly separated from his parents.) Still, for young children the high arousal
may have been sufficiently moving to wipe out the individual
differences in habitual levels of separation fear that show up as
decisive determinants of the fear of death under less threatening
conditions.

At any rate, this line of reasoning would be more compelling if
the experiment had included a nonmanipulated control condition,
in which no degree of separation fear was deliberately elicited.
It would have then been possible to make an empirical comparison
between the before-after patterns of change in that nonmanipulated
group and the two manipulated groups. If one found that the non-

manipulated group demonstrated no differences in change in fear of death between subjects high and low in habitual separation fear, one could begin to speculate with firmer justification on the possibility that the interaction between habitual and manipulated separation fear operates in a curvilinear rather than in a linear fashion. Here, certainly, is the sort of instance, previously referred to in connection with the quantitative variation of independent variables, where a nonmanipulated control group might have been most usefully incorporated into the experimental design [Sarnoff, 1965a, pp. 285-286].

2. Reaction formation and cynicism: (Sarnoff, 1960b).   Regarding the last point, a related problem arose in connection with an interactive, before-after experiment conducted on the relationship between reaction formation against affectionate feelings and cynicism. It had been predicted a positive correlation would be found between the independent variable of personality, reaction formation against affectionate feelings, and the dependent variable, cynicism toward people. This prediction was empirically supported by the findings. However, it had also been hypothesized that this relationship would be intensified under conditions of high arousal of affection, such that subjects high in the use of reaction formation would become more cynical than those low in its use, as compared with the differences between the two sets of subjects under the low arousal of affection.

But the results showed, instead, that the mean cynicism scores of subjects both high and low in reaction formation declined under each condition of arousal. Still, the difference between the two kinds of subjects was significantly greater under high than under low arousal, the subjects high in reaction formation showing very little drop in their cynicism scores as compared with the sizeable reduction in cynicism for subjects low in reaction formation under the same condition of high arousal. Under the low arousal condition, by contrast, no statistically reliable differences in the decline of cynicism was found between subjects high and low on the personality measure.

Thus, although the experimental predictions about a differential rise in cynicism were not confirmed, the results suggested that the subjects high in reaction formation were more resistant to a decline in cynicism than were the subjects low in reaction formation under conditions that strongly aroused affectionate feelings. Yet the fact that the subjects high in reaction formation did drop in cynicism under both experimental conditions might merely have reflected the operation of statistical regression, since, owing to the positive correlation between the independent variable of personality and the dependent variable, subjects high in reaction formation tended to come into the experimental conditions with higher scores in cynicism than did subjects low in reaction formation. The resulting drop in cynicism among the subjects high in reaction formation may have been consonant with the frequently observed statistical tendency of scores on a test to regress toward the mean upon the second administration of that test to the same group of subjects. At the same time, it was found that subjects low in reaction formation did not go up in cynicism, even in the low arousal condition, which is what might have been expected of them if they were merely showing the effects of statistical regression.

Since the results were equivocal with regard to the subjects high in reaction formation, a control group was subsequently run, consisting of subjects among whom no attempt was made to arouse any level of affectionate feelings. Using this nonmanipulated group as a baseline of comparison, the before-after changes in cynicism of the high and low reaction formation subjects were plotted and their slopes tested against each other in all three conditions: high arousal, low arousal, and control. These results did, in fact, give statistical support to the inference that, when both groups of subjects had their affectionate feelings highly aroused, the subjects high in reaction formation were more resistant to change in cynicism than subjects low in reaction formation.

Interactive designs as precautions against "experimenter effects"

Interactive designs contain built-in controls for the unwitting influences experimenters may exert on subjects. This is a very solid bonus, itself virtually justifying the employment of interactive designs and more than compensating whatever pains one must take to cope with their methodological intricacies. For, as Rosenthal (1966) amply emphasizes with reference to many different kinds of experiments, the experimenter is often able, somehow, to communicate his private expectations to subjects even if he makes no conscious attempt to do so and even if his mode of communication cannot be detected by observers. Indeed, it appears that such expectations can even be inadvertently imparted through recorded instructions which are played to subjects in the physical absence of any experimenter.

True, in their methodological and statistical critique of Rosenthal's studies, Barber and Silver (1968) raise doubts about the extent to which experimenters should be guided by his findings and conclusions in the design of their experiments. Nevertheless, as Rosenthal (1968) indicates in his rebuttal to that criticism, his cumulative results supporting the presumption of "experimenter effects" seem to be so extensive that it would appear consistent with scientific prudence for investigators to take whatever precautions they can to preclude their possible and unwanted intrusiveness.

Accordingly, an experimenter may derive considerable assistance from interactive designs, whose hypotheses involve particular combinations of both personality and situational variables. Even if the experimenter is quite aware of the hypotheses and is privately keen to see them fulfilled, his influence on subjects cannot systematically implement his unuttered expectations. For, assuming he does not deviate overtly from his experimental instructions — and that he tries to present them as compellingly as possible — his private expectations confront subjects of different personality groups within an experimental condition he is conducting. And assuming, further, that he has arranged in advance to take the precaution of having subjects assigned to experimental conditions in a manner that prevents his knowing their personality designation, the experimenter, even in manipulations conducted with one subject at a time, is literally unable, however covertly and unconsciously, systematically to adjust his unspoken expectations about the interaction between person and condition from subject to subject. Hence, his expectations cannot reasonably be advanced as a plausible alternative explanation of the interactive results that are predicted on *a priori* theoretical grounds.

This control on the experimenter's expectancies is effective to the extent that he cannot accurately guess the personality designation of the subjects. Certainly, an experimenter can check on this possibility by having himself — or those who run the experiment — rate each subject on the relevant personality dimension after conducting him through the experimental condition. For it may be that the nature of a given experimental task will induce a subject to display his personality grouping in the very process of responding to it. Insofar as that revelation occurs prior to the administration of the measure of the dependent variable, the experimenter has a chance to adapt, as it were, his private expectations to the particular interaction at hand, and is thus in a position to influence the subjects' responses to the dependent variable in a systematic manner.

To guard against this possibility, a researcher can arrange to conduct his subjects through his experimental conditions on a group basis, having samples of subjects representing every level of the relevant personality variable participate simultaneously in the same experimental condition. Bromberg (1967) followed such a procedure in having small groups of subjects, both high and low in habitual castration conflict, present during the induction of both his heterosexually-arousing and pain-anticipating conditions. Moreover, each subject was seated in his own booth, shielded from the sight of the others by partitions, and all subjects received their common instructions from a pre-recorded tape. Thus, while Bromberg was physically on hand in the experimental room, he did not know which subjects were high and which were low in castration conflict. But even if he had known, the simultaneous presence of both kinds of subjects, and his lack of focal interaction with them, would have precluded his effectively transmitting his private expectations to each of them.

A further safeguard against the possible confounding influences of experimenters' private expectations would involve the simultaneous induction of different experimental manipulations to subjects of varying positions on the theoretically relevant premeasured variable of personality. Such an administration was involved in the previously mentioned experiment of Katz, Sarnoff, and McClintock (1956), in which the crucial experimental induction — insight versus information — were distributed in written communications that were silently read by subjects of varying degrees of ego defensiveness assembled in the same classroom. However, it is exceedingly difficult to apply such a procedure with the optimal amount of impact and smoothness required for the intellectually and emotionally compelling manipulation of the kinds of independent variables with which Freudian theory is concerned. For the evocation of such variables typically appears to require, as shall be seen, engaging more media of manipulation than the mere distribution of printed material.

Anticipating alternative explanations for the
predicted results of Freudian experiments

In the preceding discussion of "experimenter effects," the concluding point of this chapter has actually been introduced; namely, that the results of *any* experiment may be determined by independent variables other than those under test. So it behooves an experimenter to do his utmost to anticipate alternative explanations for the results he predicts from the conceptual perspective guiding his hypothesis, and to incorporate those anticipations into the structure of his experimental design.

Naturally, there are practical limits to the number of such controlled alternatives that can be provided for in any study. And there are likewise limitations on the range of possibly relevant conceptions that a researcher can have grasped prior to designing a study. Still, the atmosphere of social accountability that flows from the existence of contending theories tends to make researchers more conscientious than they might otherwise be about trying to establish empirically the most convincing explanation of all that are offered for the same phenomenon. Thus, theoretical controversy can be resolved by recourse to a common set of evidential rules and the weight of empirical data can utimately squeeze out all erroneous concepts, permitting all contending scientists to agree upon the superiority of the view that endures the rigors of empirical evaluation.

Certainly, the aim of determining the comparative scientific value of opposing theories would be facilitated by pitting them against each other simultaneously and seeing which one correctly predicts the consequences of the same set of antecedents. However, in psychology at the present time, most theories are not truly competitive in the sense used here, since they were inferred from different sets of data — indeed, often from species as different as man and mouse — and presume to explain quite different categories of phenomena (Sarnoff, 1962).

But even when two concepts appear to be referring to identical phenomena, crucial tests of their comparative predictive superiority are virtually precluded, owing to the practical difficulty of attaining consensus among the theorists concerning the most appropriate operational articulation of deductions from their concepts. Thus, contending parties in the field of personality, for example, cannot be expected to agree on a single and a common set of measures, procedures, and manipulations that would satisfactorily define and evoke the independent variables stipulated by their divergent hypotheses.

Nevertheless, for any given hypothesis, the effects predicted may conceivably be deduced from other concepts of their determinants. But these other conceptions are potentially so diverse that provisions for their adequate control cannot be encompassed in any general explication of them. However, later chapters will illustrate how various kinds of anticipated alternatives may be operationally handled through theoretically appropriate procedures of measurement and manipulation. So let us end this chapter by indicating the range and nature of the alternative concepts that may have to be taken into systematic consideration in a Freudian experiment.

The plausible alternatives may often be much more theoretically parsimonious than the Freudian concepts being evaluated. Thus, they may challenge the very necessity of invoking Freudian concepts, which are admittedly replete with explanatory complexity. Indeed, these alternatives may be exceedingly straightforward and generic concepts, which, like the concept of an experimenter's inadvertent communication of his expectancies, are not necessarily connected to any formally articulated theoretical network. Specifically, they may refer to demographic independent variables, such as socioeconomic status, sex, religious affiliation, ethnic membership, and educational attainment. Or, they may pertain to more conceptually complex psychological variables, such as intelligence or non-Freudian variables of personality. In any case, these characteristics of the individual cannot, by definition, be created through experimental manipulations. Hence, they can only be controlled statistically, through measures, sampling procedures, and analyses of data that logically eliminate them as competing bases for explaining the results predicted by a particular Freudian hypothesis.

On the other hand, some conceptions of likely alternative explanations for results predicted from Freudian concepts may be quite complicated; and they may pertain, moreover, to an independent variable of motivation or cognition, which requires experimental manipulation for its proper control. Finally, alternative explanations for a deduction from a Freudian concept may be suggested by another Freudian concept, given the many interconnected relationships among those concepts within Freudian theory as a whole.

Of course, it may not be as easy to ascribe ranks of immediately applicable explanatory relevance among Freudian concepts as it is to non-Freudian ones. Still, as noted previously in criticizing Freud's principle of "overdetermination," it is scientifically desirable to make explicit and to test points of predictive contention that are implicit among whatever Freudian independent variables may be viewed as the most salient alternative determinants of particular dependent variables. It may thus become increasingly possible to accumulate an empirical frame of reference on the basis of which the explanatory abilities of Freudian concepts can be compared among themselves, just as provision for the control of non-Freudian variables may construct a similar empirical foundation for making comparisons between Freudian and non-Freudian conceptualizations of the same behavioral and experiental phenomena.

5 The Experiment as Social Contrivance and Drama

From an interpersonal viewpoint, every psychological experiment is a theatre of observation — a scientific stage in which subjects are constrained to act and react within the specific situational confines established by the experimenter for the measurement and evocation of the particular variables relevant to his hypothesis. For the experimental laboratory is explicitly sought after by a researcher to impose such confinement, without which it would be impossible to exercise the theoretically and logically required degree of control over the spatio-temporal relationships pertinent to observing the impact of particular antecedent events on consequent ones. Indeed, it is the very limitation of its observational scope — its highly controlled empirical narrowness — that gives the laboratory experiment its potential evidential strength.

The contrived character of human society

Regarding psychological experimentation with human beings, the scientific experiment should not be invidiously contrasted with the conditions of daily life, as if the latter were utterly free of social containment and contrivance. For human life is always contained within the context of a culture, and all cultures are products of human contrivance, their fundamental ingredients consisting of man-made values and institutions (Sarnoff, 1962). Thus, whatever man does is conditioned by an interaction between learned values and the situational constraints upon their expression.

A person may become so thoroughly conditioned in this respect that his behavior in a given situation may appear virtually reflexive, as when drivers slow down and stop their cars at a traffic signal whose light has turned red — a reaction shown by empirical social research (Allport, 1934) to be quite universal indeed. Similarly, individuals may become so mentally locked in the embrace of their culture that they lose an appreciation of its contrived character and regard its mores and rituals as sacrosanct manifestations of nature (Redfield, 1947).

Alternatively, the essentially arbitrary quality of the social norms and structures that encompass human existence everywhere may be so painfully apparent to some men as to drive them to despair. And they may, like the fictive, anti-hero of Sartre's *Nausea*, spend much of their time in anxious, numb, and heartsick rumination — at a loss to find some values or vocations or relationships more inherently meaningful than any others.

Some conditions of life, like that of the independently wealthy artist, are, to be sure, relatively unstructured and free, providing a fairly wide and spontaneous latitude of responses. Others, like that of the worker on an assembly line, are extremely structured and limiting, demanding a single stereotyped response to a repetitive stimulus. Yet, even the artist is constrained by the very concept he has acquired of his vocation, and by the social expectations imposed upon him by others who also have — albeit, perhaps, different — concepts of his role. And, outside the factory, the worker's behavior is also constrained by his concept of his occupational role, as well as by the expectations that role evokes in other people.

Thus, as a result of their histories of socialization, individuals in all societies are imbued not only with general conceptions of the goals of life to which they should strive, but also with the particular conceptions of their roles as occupants of various social statuses: vocational, familial, sexual, and so forth. They are obliged to express these conceptions within the confines of the social structures available for such expression; for example, within the bureaucratic office, the nuclear family, and the laws governing sexual relationships. Nor can anyone escape either the internalization of these conceptions or the contexts of their evocation and prohibition, since every society, however preliterate, is characterized both by conditioning to roles and by the social organization of those roles.

In effect, therefore, "everyday" life in society is an uncontrolled experiment, with people acting various roles — playing out their learned aspirations — under various conditions of evocation and constraint. And when many people are induced simultaneously to enact the same role under very similar conditions, the result is remarkably similar behavior — a consequence that approaches the uniformity of response predicted, yet all too rarely obtained, in a particular condition of experimental arousal.

Daily life and the psychological experiment as social inventions

It would be incorrect, then, to characterize experimentation as "artificial" and daily lise as "real," implying that they represent polar opposites of human inventiveness. Rather, both situational contexts are inherently inventional in character, their only essential difference arising from the fact that the social contrivances of everyday life generally impinge upon people in a fairly loose and unsystematic fashion, whereas those of the scientific experiment are systematically imposed.

Moreover, experiments are designed to test theoretically derived hypotheses, each of which necessarily deals with but a few selected aspects of the individual's potential repertoire of behavior and experience. Because of its special and restricted purpose, scientific experimentation cannot be appropriately condemned for its failure to satisfy the hunger for immediate and practical relevance that people may bring to psychology in their desperate search for ways to deal with the various cultural contrivances that destructively afflict them in their societies. Nor, on the other hand, is it fair for an experimental scientist to expect that the social contrivances of daily life, however varied and multitudinous, will suggest all the theoretical concepts needed to visualize the significant determinants of psychological phenomena. Some of these suggestions, surely, may be reasonably expected to flow from experimentation itself.

Accordingly, it behooves an experimenter always to be open to every source of conceptual and methodological inspiration. In refining and testing his concepts, it may be helpful for him to remember that his ultimate scientific question potentially applies to many different circumstances in which human beings may function. Thus, he should ask himself: Given these or those behavioral or experiential phenomena, abstracted in space and time from all other such phenomena, what are their most likely determinants?

Insofar as the theoretical answer to this question results in concepts whose component variables lend themselves to manipulation within the spatial and temporal grasp of an experiment, subsequent deductive research on the validity of those concepts can be experimentally pursued. If, however, that answer produces concepts whose investigation cannot be carried out via controlled experimentation, their empirical validity can only be assessed through less logically rigorous methods of observation. In such an instance, the interested researcher is obliged to go outside the laboratory and into everyday life, albeit the pursuit of his scientific queries perforce limits him to a very highly selected observation of that generic totality — to those aspects that are theoretically presumed to reflect and to contain the particular variables involved in his focal concept.

Hence, even in the most methodologically flexible of studies, conducted by "participant-observers" who actually reside, as do anthropologists, among the communities whose people they investigate, a scientist who wishes to gather data regarding the validity of a particular concept must focus his observations on particular behaviors presumed to reflect the assumptions inherent in that concept. And he can only communicate his inferences about theoretically postulated variables by describing aspects of the culture, both those putatively internalized and those explicitly externalized, to which the variables refer.

Of course, a researcher can attempt to design his experiment in such a way as to facilitate the application of his results to a specific situation in the current social reality of daily life. Insofar as he conceives them as theoretically congenial to the conditions needed for the testing of specific hypotheses, he can include some of the defining features of those social situations in the establishment of his experimental manipulations — just as he can try to select as dependent variables phenomena intimately related to particular social problems, such as ethnic prejudice. Yet, given the growing social influence of science, it may not be too facetious to imagine a time when nonscientists may look to the experimental setting as the locus of genuine "reality," regarding their more familiar contexts of daily life as "artificial" and "superficial" by comparison.

The terms "real" and "artificial," as used in the previous passage, do not denote existential differences that are crucial to the aims of deductive research in psychology; instead, those words connote invidious cultural distinctions in situational prestige, and, far from being universal and eternal, those distinctions are parochial and transient.

For example, in American society, the context of business was once considered supremely "real" in comparison with the "unworldliness" of the campus — a distinction that has been disappearing insofar as academic staffs have received more pay, have become the "gate-keepers" to youth's upward occupational mobility via higher education, and have secured important consultantships with government and, indeed, with leading business corporations.

Within American universities, the shift in the material fortunes of scientific departments after World War II imbued them with a glamor and significance that overshadowed the importance traditionally accorded, by educators and students alike, to the liberal arts. In more recent times, however, the association of many scientists with the production of deadly weapons for the military forces has repelled a fair number of students from scientific study, leading them back to the humanities in the hope of finding life-preserving intangibles to pit against the "realities" represented by Dr. Strangelove.

Having acknowledged the scientific value of his planful contriv-ances — and their societal value, as well, insofar as he attempts directly to illuminate the determinants of phenomena linked to social problems — a researcher is ready to devote himself to the staging of his experiment with all the calculating ingenuity he can find in his imagination. For the success of experimentation on psychoanalytic hypotheses depends very heavily upon the extent to which subjects give themselves over to it, responding to the manipulations with the kind of involvement and credibility needed for an adequate test of the hypotheses under study. Since these manipulations are theoretically aimed at either unconscious motives or ego defenses, their successful impact requires that subjects will take the experiment seriously enough to permit themselves, albeit unknowingly, to be affected in those presumably critical areas of their functioning. Moreover, the experimental conditions have to extend for a sufficiently long period of time to allow for the measurement of their predicted effects. And those conditions have to be preceded by introductory steps, which not only can expedite the administration of whatever measures of nonmanipulated variables the hypothesis contains but also can give the subjects an emotionally involving rationale for participating in the study.

Thus, although human beings are no less real and human in a laboratory than they are in everyday life, they must be so moved, emotionally and intellectually, by the experiment as to permit a test of its particular hypothesis. Accordingly, an experimenter is confronted from the outset with an essentially theatrical challenge. For he must create a setting and a performance in which subjects can be stimulated to manifest the theoretically required variables. Yet, while thoroughly and appropriately involving the subjects in the experiment, he must succeed in preventing them from correctly guessing his hypotheses — and the relationship to those hypotheses of their specific modes of participation.

Societal power and the capacity to control the conditions of a scientific experiment

Naturally, the power to direct an experimental drama exactly to the theoretical requirements of one's hypothesis is contingent upon the amount of control one can exercise over the participants in it. If a person is granted virtually dictatorial authority over people below him in a hierarchy of invidious distinction, his power to stage the conditions for experiments in which they participate can be extremely great. And he may be able to keep them entirely unaware of the very fact that they are participating in an experiment.

Indeed, in an authoritarian organization, it may be possible for oligarchs to exercise such complete control over every relevant aspect of the social environment of those in the hierarchical pyramid as to leave the experimental subjects quite in the dark about their having been systematically manipulated and observed. But since such oligarchs may often be more concerned about the preservation and extension of their social, economic, political, or military power than with the furtherance of scientific knowledge, they may not be interested in publishing the results of such experiments. Nor may they be interested in conducting them for any other reason but to attain more effective means of using fellow human beings as mere instruments of their self-aggrandizing motives (Sarnoff, 1966).

Military organizations certainly represent a likely place for such secretive experimentation, for soldiers can be expressly ordered about by their superior officers, and everyone in the military hierarchy is expected to give unquestioning obedience to everyone above him in rank. Thus, subjects could simply be commanded to report here or there and to do this or that in accordance with the requirements of an unrevealed experimental design. And an entire experiment, operationally articulated within the context of the ordinary military routine, could be perceived by subjects not as a psychological experiment but as the fulfillment of their regular military duties.

Given sufficiently totalitarian powers, governmental officials are also easily capable of this type of experimentation. And the essentially totalitarian organization of the economy in every modern nation makes it possible for economic oligarchs to do the same kind of research.

Thus, it is apparent that the capacity to manipulate independent variables in an experiment is largely a function of an experimenter's power to control the lives of other people. Yet questions concerning the legitimacy and proper use of that power are not matters that can be resolved by scientific investigation. Rather, they are moral questions, which are answerable only in terms of the values people hold and the qualities of life they wish to nurture.

Experimental control and the values of realization

Since totalitarian control and hierarchical organization are clearly incompatible with the equalitarian ideals that form a part of the values of realization (Sarnoff, 1966), no person deeply devoted to equalitarian values can uphold societal arrangements which not only permit, but which glorify, the pursuit of power. Thus, whoever really cherishes participatory democracy must abominate the socioeconomic hierarchies of invidious distinction that characterize the overall structure of all modern societies, whatever their official and self-designated ideologies, and that are especially blatant in our organizations of work. Hence, insofar as the conduct of scientific research implements the pursuit of power for its own sake and helps to perpetuate the hierarchical structures within which it is carried out, it is open to the identical moral condemnation.

It is for this reason that a democratically oriented researcher would find it inconsistent with his values to experiment on subjects without their freely given consent. Obviously, to obtain such consent, the subjects must at least be presented with the possibility of willingly participating in a study, thus explicitly having the option of declining to be studied.

It would also be in keeping with democratic values for a researcher to undertake his experiments solely for the sake of contributing toward human liberation from ignorance and oppression. Thus, he would refuse to engage in secret research, or to let others decide whether or not his results should be submitted for publication. He would refuse the sponsorship of industrial, governmental, military, or other oligarchs who might wish to reserve the right to withhold from publication any findings that might call adverse social attention to (and hence impede) their thrust for exploitative aggrandizement.

By applying these humane considerations to his scientific efforts, a researcher necessarily and severely restricts the amount of social control he can employ in the conduct of his experiments. *In fact, he is limited precisely to the degree of control that subjects in his experiments are willing to give him.* For in the democratic contract involved in his solicitation of them, the essential feature is their freedom to accept or to refuse participation in his experiment. Certainly, under present social conditions, subjects openly invited to participate in a study may not always feel as free to decline the invitation as would be ideal from the standpoint of equalitarian values. Some subjects may be in a financial bind and may accept the invitation largely because of the money being offered for their participation. In other cases, where money is neither offered nor sought, a subject may feel inwardly coerced by the perception of his occupational vulnerability with respect to the person who solicits his participation. For example, a student may not feel as secure in refusing to participate in a professor's experiment as he might in reacting to one being conducted by a fellow student. Nor, for similar social psychological reasons, may students decide to leave an experimental condition that they discover to be repugnant after volunteering to participate in it, if they think they may thus displease the professor who is conducting the experiment.

But these inwardly felt constraints upon their freedom of action represent, for the participants involved, the demoralizing and dehumanizing effects of having been reared in and surrounded by a society of aggrandizement. Thus, money can only be a great incentive for people who have strongly internalized the value of material wealth, or for those permitted by an unjust society to suffer material privation. And a willingness to obey unjust authority reflects the extent to which a person has adopted the value of power and the legitimacy of its hierarchical distribution. Indeed, with regard to the matter of authoritarianism, Asch (1948) and, more recently, Milgrim (1964) have commented on the appalling readiness with which students have been willing to comply with the most outlandish, arbitrary, humiliating, and horrendous requests made of them by experimenters in whose research they had agreed to participate.

It is very understandable that much of the scientific experimentation in psychology currently takes place in a university milieu, a societal setting for many people keenly interested in intellectual values and in other values of realization. Given the traditionally authoritarian structure of academic organizations, it follows that those who conduct experiments, professors and graduate students, have relatively greater power and status than those who generally participate in them — the undergraduate students (Sarnoff, 1969). Indeed, in many universities, the faculty members of departments of psychology have succeeded in insuring the supply of subjects for their research by making a given amount of participation in such studies mandatory for all undergraduate students enrolled in the introductory course, which is often, in addition, an educational prerequisite to all the more advanced courses. Of course, a student could refuse to study psychology altogether rather than to submit to such arbitrariness. Or he could try, from the brief description usually given of the studies involved, to devote his requisite hours of participation entirely to those researches that sound most interesting to him. Or, alternatively, he could organize protests with other, similarly affected students, aimed at forcing the department to drop its mandatory requirement.

Undoubtedly, it would be best for all concerned if participation in psychological experiments were a truly voluntary activity within an actually democratic educational organization, uncrimped by any sort of intimidation, however subtly conveyed. Under such wholesome circumstances, experimenters and subjects would be working together as social equals, each relating to the other as respected and valued partners in the resolution of their common existential problems.

Presently, throughout the world, some students and professors are working explicitly and whole-heartedly to bring about the organizational changes that could transform our basically authoritarian universities into unequivocally democratic ones. And the humane academic psychologist has good reason to assist in this transformation. For if it were to succeed, it would produce an environment more congenial than the present one to both his personal values and his scientific activities. Indeed, in an atmosphere where people are spared the degradations of aggrandizement and encouraged to fulfill their unique capacities as human beings, the scientific and all other approaches to knowledge could flourish as they have never flourished in the past.

If universities — and the societies that maintain them — were to become fully devoted to human realization, the scientific study of human psychology would probably become an almost universal avocation. For people would wish to know as much as could be reliably learned about the factors determining their functioning, the better to enhance the quality of their lives. Under such circumstances, people would be very willing to cooperate with researchers, and there would be no shortage of volunteers for psychological experiments.

Aware of all these contingencies, subjects in experiments might even be glad to extend their participation to considerably more time than the few hours which at present generally represent the maximum that can be expected of even paid subjects. Nor would they object to the manipulative element that is, by definition, inherent in any experimentation. For assuming they were in no danger of either acute or permanent injury as a result of their participation — a proviso guaranteed by the humane values of the experimenter — they would accept the manipulations as an indispensable feature of the experiment's epistemological method.

Regarding contemporary experimental reseach in psychology, no agreement prevails among researchers concerning the extent to which they are prepared to expose subjects to stressful or painful manipulations, some of which may perhaps be enduringly injurious — at least in a psychological sense. The ethical problems attendant upon these possibly damaging effects shall be explored in the chapter dealing with the manipulation of independent variables.

Deception as a methodological necessity in the scientific study of human psychology

The most harmless of psychological experiments necessarily involves an element of deception, even if it is merely the withholding from subjects of the hypotheses under study. Usually, however, the degree of deception practiced must be quite appreciable in order to evoke adequately the independent variables requiring manipulation. And while psychologically sophisticated subjects — both now and in the hopefully more humane future — may gladly submit to it as a price worth paying, and necessary to pay, for the knowledge it facilitates, humane experimenters will perhaps always be tormented by the moral dilemma that the systematic use of deception raises for them.

Indeed, the most troubling irony of scientific research in human psychology is that the empirical approach to truth must be protected by a lie. For human beings, as has been repeatedly noted, are extremely susceptible to change in the very process of being studied. Hence, whatever people know or guess about the objectives of the research in which they participate as subjects is likely to influence their behavior in the investigatory situation. And, as has also been thoroughly discussed, such influences are likely to confound the results obtained, introducing unwanted and uncontrolled variables, which, rather than the ones selected on a theoretical basis for special study, may account for the observed effects on the dependent variables.

Although the use of deception *per se* cannot be defended on ethical grounds, the most morally upright of researchers cannot avoid lies of omission, lest he undermine the whole purpose of his inquiry. Nor can he do without lies of commission, if he wishes to create the experimental conditions that depend upon them. Thus, an experimenter has to console himself with the awareness that the scientific knowledge he acquires for mankind could not have been obtained without the conscious use of deception. And if he cannot so exonerate himself, he may have to stop doing research with human beings.

Yet it is possible to take a stand that permits an experimenter to continue to do his research and, at the same time, appropriately and constructively relieve the feelings of guilt engendered by his scientific use of deception. Thus, while using a transient deception, he can resolve to undo its falsity as quickly as possible, giving the deceived subjects a truthful explanation of why the deception was necessary in the light of what was being studied.

In the process of disabusing the subjects, a topic to be discussed in a later chapter, an experimenter can also invite them to express all of their reactions to his confession and to pose questions about various aspects of the study. Thus, by establishing an entirely honest relationship with the subjects following the completion of the experiment proper, a researcher can affirm his solidarity with them as human equals, freely exposing his own psychological functioning — just as they had voluntarily agreed to be accessible to him. Indeed, the very act of his confession eliminates any implicit or explicit social advantage he may have had over them during the experiment.

Obviously, the impact of a researcher's post-experimental revelations depends greatly upon the actual degree of sincerity that he feels and expresses. Yet reparation for the ethical violation involved in the scientific application of deceit is not entirely in the hands of the experimenter who perpetrates the deception and who seeks expiation for his guilt. It rests also upon the dispositions of the subjects, whose forgiveness and compassion is sought. And, insofar as there are vastly more subjects than experimenters, the problem becomes one of societal dimensions: that is, will the general public countenance the inevitable deceit on which scientific research in psychology must rely? Or will there be growing and adamant opposition to it, the vanguard of which, in fact, now includes psychologists themselves (Kelman, 1967)?

Within our present societies of aggrandizement, humane individuals may well associate the scientific use of deception with the deceits practiced by oligarchs who sponsor and use psychological research to promote their own egoistic and inhumane ambitions. And the academic rule of "publish or perish'" has given rise to a widespread, and perhaps not groundless, suspicion that many researchers are similarly motivated, conducting a seemingly endless stream of trivial and scientifically worthless experiments — and working countless deceptions on subjects — merely to advance their personal status and income.

But while it is possible to envision — and to work toward — a society whose basic values and institutions do not motivate people to exploit and deceive each other, it is impossible, for the reasons previously examined, to conduct scientifically meaningful and conclusive research in psychology without making use of deception. No matter how honestly and decently societies of the future may encourage people to relate to each other, people will always have to tolerate the unavoidable deceits of psychological research if they wish to obtain, through its auspices, scientific knowlege of themselves.

As has been suggested, people in a humane society might gladly extend such tolerance to scientific psychology, since its findings could give them increasingly accurate conceptions of pathways to

their common and fondest social goal: the realization of human capacities. And in knowingly agreeing to the transient deceptions of
scientific psychology, they would be accepting an intransigent absurdity
of human existence: the requirement that they be deceived in order
to contribute to the uncovering of more and more reliable truths about
themselves.

Having completely and consciously accepted moral culpability
for his part in this existential absurdity, an experimenter can un-
ashamedly employ deception for the only humane purpose that depends
absolutely upon its use: the attainment of scientific knowledge of
human behavior and experience. He can then construct his experimental
methods with a view toward introducing whatever fabrications are
necessary to provide a theoretically appropriate test of his hypotheses
— albeit his scientific lies are petty, transient, and revealed to the
subjects after the conclusion of his experiments.

Since a humane experimenter would wish neither to conduct
research secretly nor to exert any control over the subjects outside
the spatial and temporaly boundaries of the experiment *per se*, he
would want to solicit the participation of people in his research.
It is for these reasons that experiments are typically quite limited
in their temporal span, while involving a similarly restricted locus
of occurrence which, for expository reasons, has merely been called
a "laboratory," although the situational context in which an experiment
is actually conducted may be a room or an open space whose fur-
nishings and atmosphere scarcely conjure the images of test tubes
and sinks generally associated with that term.

The psychological experiment as an
unfolding drama

An experimenter must realize that, from their very first contact
with his solicitation, subjects are psychologically "in" his research —
that is, developing their emotional and cognitive reactions to it. Consequently, the staging of an experiment must begin with the initial
procedures adopted for the recruitment of subjects. Nor does that
staging end until the subjects are disabused of their deception by
the experimenter, following the collection of all the data contingent
upon the maintenance of the deception.

In selecting his procedures, an experimenter must dwell upon each and every measure and manipulation that will be required of his subjects, striving to embrace the experiment's entire sequence of events in an overall plan for presenting and rationalizing the research to potential subjects. To be sure, as we shall see, all measures and manipulations require introductions with instructions and rationalizations specifically constructed to produce the theoretically stipulated motivations and cognitions of the subjects. Still, insofar as a series of separately perceptible methodological steps have to be taken by the subjects, it is vitally important for the subjects to have a compelling sense of meaningfulness — however planfully erroneous the experimenter contrives to be — concerning the investigatory purpose under which those steps are subsumed.

An experimenter has a chance to implant an impression of that purpose at the time subjects are recruited, after which he can reinforce it at various junctures in the experiment. As with every other aspect of methodology, an experimenter's decisions about how to make and to rationalize the first contact between his research and his subjects are necessarily guided by a blend of considerations, usually reflecting compromises between what is ideally desirable and what is practically feasible. Yet insofar as an experimenter is the systematic user of scientific deception, he may greatly increase the realm of feasibility. Like the dramatist, he can find in his imagination devices for transcending the limitations of his own persona, giving himself — or those who may assist his work — whatever roles are temporarily needed to evoke theoretically demanded orientations and reactions; and writing whatever scripts, setting whatever props, and using whatever audiovisual aids may help to insure the full impact of the drama.

But whereas an audience in a theater is aware of having chosen to attend a drama in which the actors are known to have been explicitly cast to play particular roles, subjects in experiments on psychoanalytic hypotheses must be deliberately deceived about the dramatic intent of those who act upon them. These subjects are caught up in a drama within a drama, the ostensible rationale given for what they see being only a pretext for affecting them in ways — and toward ends — of which they must be kept unaware until the end of the experimental performance. Unlike an ordinary theatrical audience, experimental subjects are invited to the drama in order to be involved in it as active participants — thus displaying or failing to display the behavioral propensities predicted for the particular evocations by the hypotheses being tested. Yet the subjects' mode of invitation and involvement must be deviously arranged, lest their participation be determined by variables other than those of immediate theoretical relevance to the *a priori* hypotheses.

The media available for producing such evocations are as abundant and varied as those utilized in the explicitly artistic realms of drama. In addition to mime and the spoken articulation of rehearsed parts in live performances reminiscent of traditional theater, an experimenter may wish to use films, slides, television, stereophonic sounds, and stroboscopic lights. He may also readily adapt to experimentation in scientific psychology the new techniques of conveying information and sensory impressions that are continuously being developed in the fields of mass communication and entertainment, as well as in visual art, poetry, and the diverse forms of creative writing.

Because all these methodological aids are easily accessible to him, an experimenter can enormously extend the scope of his own personal capacity to devise the conditions needed for appropriate tests of psychoanalytic concepts of interest to him. By letting his imagination freely range over those technical possibilities, he may well discover viable means of testing hypotheses that he might otherwise have considered untestable, or that, indeed, might not even have entered his consciousness in the first place had he restricted his thinking to the kinds of conditions that have ordinarily been associated with experimentation in such a "classical" area of scientific psychology as that of learning.

Much of the early experimental work on psychoanalytic hypotheses (Sears, 1943, 1946) suffered from this unfortunate constriction of methodological imagination. And the rather dismal view presented by Sears of the prospects for scientific progress in this area of research may have stemmed, in large part, from his failure to see how fully and appropriately its experimental methods could be enlarged beyond the procedures that had been conventionally employed in laboratory experiments suggested by the theories of learning prominent at the time he offered his comments. Nor could the nimbleness of his vision have been increased by the fact that so much of that experimentation on learning had used rats and other animals as its subjects.

Historically, perhaps the greatest single impetus behind the imaginative use of experimental methods in the systematic study of human psychology was provided by Kurt Lewin, whose search for such methods was entirely in keeping with his theoretical stress on the importance of contextual factors in the determination of human behavior. Moreover, Lewin's strong desire to contribute to the alleviation of pressing social problems (Lewin, 1948) probably added urgency to his interest in developing methods peculiarly suitable for engaging human intellectual and emotional involvement.

Following Lewin, his students, notably Festinger (1953), continued that methodological development, explicitly emphasizing the scientific uses of deception in social psychological experiments. And while such experiments tended to avoid the study of differences in personality, their methods paid a great deal of attention to the ways in which, from the standpoint of the intraindividual perception of the subjects, every step of the experimental procedure could contribute toward the induction and the maintenance of the psychological conditions required by the hypotheses under investigation. Thus, especially since the end of World War II, experimental social psychologists have taken the lead, among all their scientific colleagues, in showing how much it is possible to contrive systematic variations in very subtle psychological states, while both adequately motivating and deceiving the subject. (See, for example, the many studies of this type reported in Jones and Gerard, 1967).

The details of the staging for any particular experiment depend upon the specifics of its hypothesis. But the very concept of staging alerts an experimenter to the desirability of contriving everything the subject sees and does with the utmost care to insure that it will, at once, put him in the theoretically required frame of mind and deceive him about the specific hypothesis under test. And since the first thing the subject sees is some form of request for his participation, an experimenter's concern to provide his research with such insurance must necessarily include that initial contact. This contact must be diligently maintained thereafter, always bearing in mind the expectations likely to be carried forward by subjects from one methodological point to the next — expectations based, of course, upon what the experimenter had led them to believe at earlier points in the experimental procedure.

Such experiments may be construed as evolving dramas, with each scene built upon previous ones. Taking nothing for granted, therefore, about any subject's prior expectations, an experimenter ought not to overlook the slightest aspects of wording, manner, dress, and setting that may conceivably affect the reactions of subjects to what they are asked to do, how they are introduced to measures and manipulations, and the contents of everything presented to them.

The experimental application of theatrical skills and devices

As in the case of a successful drama, a well-conducted experiment requires a good deal of rehearsal in advance of its final staging. In due course, various aspects of this rehearsal, germane to different procedures in the overall methodology, will be discussed and illustrated. But certainly, an experimenter should be prepared to try out and to discard any number of preliminary ideas that occur to him regarding those procedures. In addition to pilot studies with subjects similar to those planned for inclusion in the formal staging of the experimental test, an experimenter may wish to ask groups of colleagues, or others presumed to be experts in one or another phase of his methodology, to respond to his exploratory attempts to devise experimental rationales, instructions, measures, and manipulations.

Such preliminary scouting and checking is virtually inescapable insofar as there is available no solid body of empirical literature from which to extract methods of demonstrated feasibility. And, given the general paucity of such methods with respect to deductive research on Freudian concepts, it is difficult to imagine how any experiment on a previously untested psychoanalytic hypothesis could be sensibly and confidently mounted without first devoting a considerable amount of exploratory work to its proper staging.

Depending on the theoretical requirements of his hypotheses, an experimenter may well wish to present himself to subjects in a variety of guises: sometimes as his actual occupational self, relying entirely on the wording of the experiment's rationale and instructions to dissimulate his specific experimental purposes; sometimes assuming a different persona for the occasion, transforming himself temporarily from graduate student to member of a visiting scientific organization or whatever other status is necessary to gain the serious participation and credibility of his subjects. Indeed, within the same experiment, he may even play two different occupational roles, in one condition a professional psychologist, and, in another, an undergraduate student — while, in both instances, actually being a graduate student (Bonchek, 1966).

On the other hand, an experimenter may deem it best not to conduct a particular study himself, lest his age or sex or ethnic membership militate against an adequate test of his hypothesis. In such instances, an experimenter may employ others to conduct the study, being himself publicly unconnected with it while the data is collected by others. In other cases, the experimental procedure may be so intricate as to oblige a researcher to seek the assistance of confederates, to whom he may delegate responsibility for the recruitment of subjects, the administration of measures, or the manipulation of the independent variables.

Regarding the presentation to the subjects of written or spoken rationales for their participation in these experiments, a similarly large variety of possibilities for the theoretically indicated deception is open to an experimenter. At one extreme, he can present the experiment as the flimsiest of exploratory studies, launched by someone who really is quite uncertain about what he is looking for, and why. At the other extreme, an experiment can be presented as the well-developed, reliable, and nationally replicated work of an organization of specialists widely recognized for the excellence of their work, the results of which are regularly applied by highly practical and prestigeous universities or governmental bureaus. These differing rationales can be communicated by persons dressed — and acting — to convey the indicated differences in experience and prestige; and, insofar as those rationales are put into written documents, the neatness and slickness of the format and the verbal smoothness of the text can reinforce the disparity of perception of recognized competence with which subjects are supposed to be differentially imbued.

Since the conduct of an experiment does not occur in a social psychological vacuum, an experimenter is often required to take local considerations into account, in addition to the purely theoretical ones inherent in his hypotheses, from the earliest phase of his experimental staging. For example, whether or not an experimenter can risk "passing himself off" as one fictitious identity or another may rest on the extent to which he is already known to the subjects whose participation he is obliged to solicit. Similarly, in conducting an interactive, after-only experiment, an experimenter known to a group of potential subjects may wish to be dissociated, in their perception, from the experimental inductions. Thus, he may himself administer the relevant personality measures in a separate pre-experimental session with the subjects, while letting a confederate solicit their participation in the subsequent experimental sessions and conduct the subjects through them. Until the experiment is over, the subjects will remain unaware of the fact that their participation in two presumably different studies is, in fact, participation in two different phases of the same experiment.

Naturally, too, effectiveness in communicating false perceptions and expectations to subjects is partly contingent upon the skill with which those communications are formulated and expressed. A flair for writing can be useful in this regard, as can facility in acting. Still, for any particular experiment, a researcher may wish to supplement his own abilities in both those skills by enlisting the services of other writers and actors (cf. Ross, 1966, Sarnoff, 1960b).

Thus, a researcher, by mobilizing his own expressive talents as well as those of others, can put on a dramatic performance of quite compelling proportions. Although it is true that the esthetic features of the staging are merely ancillary to the experiment's purposes, they must be handled with sufficient sensibility and expertness to accomplish the scientific objectives, keeping the subjects deceptively engrossed until the experimenter feels it safe to disclose the denouement.

As with theatrical training, the acquisition of the skills requisite to the writing and enactment of a moving experimental drama is a gradual process of trial and experience. And the same may be said of the development of the judgment by means of which an experimenter can decide what written or acted efforts of others are likely to be useful to diverse phases of his experiments.

On developing the attitude of a humane experimental dramatist

Essential to the nurturance of all such abilities is an eager willingness to acquire them. Researchers with formal training in other branches of experimental psychology may be most highly motivated in this regard, having already found the logic of systematically contrived manipulation congenial to their scientific outlook. Others, however — and these seem to by especially numerous among those with an interest in doing clinical work — may feel inclined to reject the planful, scientific use of deceit as too jarring a contradiction to the ethical intentions that consciously impel them to offer interpersonal help to troubled persons. One could point out to such demurrers that mere good intentions do not, unfortunately, vouchsafe positive results. For, as Bergin (1966) notes, some psychotherapists appear to worsen the condition of their patients, even though such practitioners may be presumed to have no less kindly intentions than do those whose therapeutic impact is positive. Further, one could assert that faith in one's ability to give psychotherapeutic assistance to others is at least as morally presumptuous as the self-appointed liberty an experimenter takes in temporarily deceiving subjects in his studies. Certainly, too, the psychotherapist is not free of calculated deceits of omission. The psychoanalytic psychotherapist, for example, depends heavily upon withholding from patients his hypotheses about them until he feels it advisable to reveal them. Nor can such psychotherapists claim to be working entirely for the sake of their patients, with no thought of viewing them as objects of study, for it has been a source of great professional pride among psychoanalysts that they also use their mode of psychotherapy as a method of scientific investigation.

Taking a less contentious approach to sooth the qualms of clinicians, one could evoke some empirical findings about subjects who have been repeatedly deceived in psychological experiments. Thus, Holmes (1967) found that, compared with subjects who had participated less frequently in such experiments, "subjects with more experience evidenced a greater tendency to see the experiments as scientific and valuable as well as to make more conscious attempts to cooperate. Interestingly enough, with more experiences subjects reported fewer attempts to determine what the experiment was about [p. 406]." Such results would appear to lend encouragement to the possibility, raised previously, that people in a genuinely equalitarian society might be able to serve appropriately as experimental subjects — while being both aware and accepting of the fact that such experiments practiced deceptions upon them.

Finally, one could call the attention of apprehensive but scientifically-minded clinicians to the epistemelogical problems posed by the suggestion (Kelman, 1967) that simulated experiments may be utilized to circumvent the ethical dilemmas of deception. But such methodological substitutes cannot be routinely counted upon to accomplish the scientific objectives toward which actual experiments are directed. Attempts to compare the results of actual and simulated experiments indicate that people cannot necessarily produce within themselves, via vicarious empathy with hypothetical conditions, the same intensity of psychological arousal that they would experience if they were actually exposed to such conditions. For example, in a simulated replication of Schachter's (1959) experiment concerning the interactive effects of different levels of anticipated pain and birth order on social affiliation, Greenberg (1956) was unable to reproduce the original results. "Although the differences between conditions was in the predicted direction, none proved to be statistically significant [p. 55]." Yet an actual experimental replication (Sarnoff & Zimbardo, 1961) did give statistically reliable support to Schachter's findings that firstborn children want to affiliate significantly more than later-born when anticipating strong pain but not when anticipating weak pain. Moreover, it should be noted, even simulated experiments of the type conducted by Greenberg involve a deception of omission: a withholding from the subjects of the hypotheses concerning the effects of the simulated conditions on the relevant dependent variables.

But having marshalled all these moral contentions, logical arguments, and empirical data to soften the possible resistance of clinicians to the experimental use of deception, one cannot be at all certain of persuading the dissenter who shrinks away from it. Indeed, in the end, as in the beginning, it must be admitted that the employment of falsehood in human relationships is scarcely consistent with commonly accepted ethical precepts. Yet it must also be recalled that scientific knowledge of human behavior largely hinges on the systematic employment of deception.

Acceptance of this paradox by researchers and subjects alike renders scientific deception amenable to just application. For it properly distributes the social responsibility of its uses, requiring laymen no less than scientists to share the onus of the same ethical decisions. In this equalitarian manner, within a society of realization and under the methodological safeguards previously described, those who conduct psychological experiments and those who participate in them would have the best possible opportunity for humanely coping with the inescapable moral problems of investigatory deception. Anticipating such favorable circumstances, scientific psychologists can at least publicize the existential absurdity that requires the use of deceit in research with human beings, informing both potential subjects and the general public about its indispensable epistemological function and inviting everyone to cooperate in the creation of the decent social conditions under which its employment would be limited, by mutual consent, to the transient conduct of a scientific study.

6 Measuring Independent Variables of Personality

A measuring instrument is an aid to observation that gives observers a convenient and uniform perspective from which to collect quantifiable data pertinent to a given variable. If they had no such instruments, scientists would have to rely exclusively upon their own unaided sensory equipment. Obviously, that restriction would be most damaging to scientific advancement in fields such as biology and astronomy, whose progress has depended very greatly on man's ability to extend the range of his own powers of observation. By contrast, in the field of personality, which now rests almost entirely upon the use of imputed variables of an avowedly fictive character, the extension of man's sheer observational capacity is not so crucial a prerequisite to scientific advance, albeit such devices as the slow-motion film and the tape-recorder may well reveal behavioral nuances that bear vital relevance to theoretical development and evaluation.

Apart from its function in extending man's native observational powers, a measuring instrument produces the simultaneous, if paradoxical, scientific benefit of narrowing and standardizing the particular range of observables that circumscribe the imputation of particular variables. Thus, while the microscope renders the whole underworld of bacteria amenable to human observation, its scientific use with respect to the description of a specific organism requires a researcher to fix his focus at a given level of magnification, to prepare his slides in a special way, and to relate the characteristics of his image of the bacteria to clearly specified points of visual reference. Moreover, unless other observers agree in advance to these and similar restrictions of observational context, they can scarcely expect to replicate each other's observations or to communicate intelligibly about even the phenotypic variables they may wish to define from their observations.

In regard to imputed variables of personality, scientific investigation, replication, and communication also depend on the systematic delineation of the observational context within which particular behaviors are selected, in a particular fashion, for the imputation of quantitative variations in a genotypic trait. At the very minimum, the scientific measurement of a variable of personality requires the detailed description of a replicable situational context, within which carefully defined aspects of an individual's total behavior, designated as indicants of the imputed variable, are recorded by an observer in such a way as to permit their quantification.

For example, a subject could be ushered into a barren room of given physical dimensions and permitted to do anything he wished to do within a specific period of time. Meanwhile, an experimenter could observe the subject's behavior via a one-way optical screen, noting those behavioral instances deemed relevant to the trait of personality he wants to measure and recording his observations in a specified manner. Presumably, all potential subjects could be individually placed in the identical situation, and their behavior could be observed and recorded in the same way, yielding data that could be used to categorize the entire sample with respect to their individual differences in the variable of personality imputed from such a procedure of measurement. This procedure could be followed by other investigators who wished to apply the measure in their own research.

This approach to measurement, while logically adequate, is replete with methodological difficulties. At the outset, a researcher must establish a situational context that is likely to elicit a range of behavior on the basis of which individual variations in the imputed variable can be recorded and quantified. Then he must train himself to make and to score the required recordings with a sufficient degree of reliability to warrant the conclusion that he is, in fact, dealing with behavior that can be accurately and quantitatively discriminated from the totality of behaviors manifested by the subjects. Moreover, as a safeguard against the intrusion of his own wish-fulfilling distortions and as a demonstration of the replicability of his measure, a researcher is obliged to communicate his observational technique to others, suspending decisions about its usefulness until further research shows that it can be applied with equal reliability by other observers; that is, until its reliability is demonstrated as independent of the observational abilities of a *particular* observer, albeit those who test the measure's reliability may have to be specially trained in its application. Finally, insofar as the relevant behavior is presumed to indicate the presence of a relatively enduring variable of personality, it should be shown to be fairly stable from one point in the observational sequence to another, and, ideally, from two or more entirely separate occasions of measurement under the same context of observation.

Since human behavior is extraordinarily subtle and complex, implementation of the foregoing situational approach to personality measurement is extremely time-consuming. It involves not only the training of observers and the assessment of their ratings — assuming one can settle upon a fixed context of observation — but also the conduct of subjects through the procedure of measurement singly, or at best, a few at a time. Any such procedure, which, despite its considerable restrictions of observational context, allows great diversity in the behavior a subject may express, is notoriously demanding on the powers of an observer. Hence, to secure a satisfactory degree of inter-rater reliability — or, indeed, to make the observational task at all manageable — such "open-ended" methods necessitate a severe limitation upon the number of subjects being observed at any single occasion of measurement.

Psychological measures as systematic attempts to focus and, hence, to facilitate scientific observation

It is for all these reasons that psychologists have been motivated to construct measures calculated to focus very sharply the range of observations deemed relevant to the imputation of particular variables of personality. And that sharpness of focus is attained by the simple expedient of seeking to concentrate the subject's potential reactivity upon an exceedingly limited array of stimuli. Instead of permitting a subject to evince his theoretically pertinent behavior in responding to the wealth of situational stimuli present even in a quite empty room, the usual measure of personality consists of a highly delimited set of stimuli devised in advance to evoke particular responses that are theoretically conceived as behavioral manifestations of the imputed variables of interest to the researcher.

In keeping with this conception, the stimuli comprising a measure are exactly reproduced in each copy of it, all copies of the instrument being identical in every respect. For a measure's scientific role is to reveal, among subjects responding to it, quantitative differences on the imputed dimension it operationally defines.

Insofar as the measuring stimuli *per se* are capable of arousing — rather than merely reflecting — psychological variables, including the one they explicitly seek to measure, their fixed format insures that their *inherent* powers of arousal will be kept constant from individual to individual. Hence, assuming adequate reliability and the equivalence of conditions surrounding a measure's administration, quantitative differences in the responses of any given sample of individuals to that constancy of stimulus can be quite logically attributed to like differences in their habitual position on the variable involved.

Of course, measures differ among themselves with regard to the degree to which they attempt to confine a subject's responsivity. But whether they are "projective" or "objective" in format, all these measures share the same working assumption: that quite brief, symbolic replies to equally symbolic stimuli are the kinds of behaviors on the basis of which it is possible to infer different degrees of imputed variables of personality.

On the stimulus side, these measures may be pictures, written materials, or spoken words. The responses requested of subjects may be drawings, writings, spoken words; or merely checks, numbers, and circles registering assent with or dissent from a list of printed statements. Also some of these measures may lend themselves more readily than others to their simultaneous presentation to more than a single subject. In addition, the responses of subjects may be more easy to quantify for some of these measures than for others. And they differ among themselves in ease of scoring and administration, as well as in many other practicalities. Nevertheless, their common scientific intent of facilitating theoretically relevant observation appears to deserve rather more emphasis than it has received in the past from partisans of one kind of personality measurement or another.

Certainly, in their scientific usage, both projective and objective types of personality measures share not only the same general aims but also very similar psychological assumptions concerning the relevance of the responses they elicit to imputed variables. Both types of measures thus assume that people will reveal particular variables of personality if they are required to respond to stimuli considered evocative of the psychological properties of those variables. And the operational differences between the two kinds of measures rest on quite secondary differences in assumptions about the types of stimuli likely to elicit the behaviors most validly indicative of the imputed variable.

The congruence between the construct validity of a concept and that of its operational measure

The question of a measure's construct validity is one which cannot be entirely decided *a priori* on purely logical or psychological grounds. Instead, such validity can only be scientifically determined through cumulative empirical study, involving predictions from the imputed variable to other variables.

No single study can possibly exhaust the host of empirical deductions one can make from the concept underlying a proposed measure (Cronbach & Meehl, 1955). Nor, as has been illustrated in detail, can the validity of measures of Freudian variables of personality necessarily be empirically assessed without recourse to deductions from other, related Freudian concepts, whose measurement and validity are not themselves directly under immediate investigation.

In short, it is literally impossible to disentangle the validity of a concept from the validity of the measure purporting to be its operational definition. For the deductive work of conceptual evaluation can only be carried out through such operational definitions of concepts. Conversely, any proposed measure derives conceptual meaning only insofar as, a variable is imputed from it.

Of course, empirical research may show that a measure predicts to all sorts of variables that its originally imputed conceptualization had not anticipated. In such a case, it will still be scientifically necessary to imagine theoretically what concept the measure is reflecting, given the empirical data. Moreover, for those interested in the original concept, the burden of its scientific utility can be properly borne only by devising a new — and presumably more theoretically apt — measure than the one originally proposed; *and then demonstrating empirically* that the new measure does, in fact, yield the kinds of predictions to other variables that would be expected in the light of assumptions about the concept it is supposed to define operationally. Indeed, unless such empirical proofs are forthcoming, one can scarcely claim scientific utility for the concept in question.

On the other hand, many measures, devised without any explicit semantic statement of the concepts to which their elicited responses may be imputed, may be put to many practical uses, such as the assignment of individuals to various wards of a mental hospital or the assignment of pupils to various classes in a school. And, from the standpoint of the societal *status quo*, such measures may "work" very effectively, selecting with vastly more than chance accuracy, for example, which pupils are likely to do well academically and which are candidates for academic failure.

Nevertheless, such practical effectiveness of measures ought not to be confused with the issue of their scientific validity. For it is one thing to find, empirically, that measure A correlates with outcome X, yet it is quite another matter to tease out the variable or variables for which measure A is, implicitly, the behavioral indicant, and to show, through systematic deductive investigations, that measure A does predict successfully to what its explicitly imputed concept would logically suggest. In the absence of such explication and empirical evaluation of a measure's implicit variable, the measure, however widely used for other purposes, cannot be held forth as a scientifically useful instrument.

Thus, insofar as one regards the ultimate goal of science as empirically supported conceptualization, one cannot properly separate a concept's validity from that of its operational measure. Indeed, once the concept is operationally defined, its empirical evaluation is necessarily bound to that measure, and it can be scientifically assessed only through its operational vehicle.

This is not to say that any particular operational definition can encompass all the nuances of meaning implicit in the semantic definition of the same concept. And it is surely not meant to say that operationalism *ipso facto* resolves the problem of developing an adequate conceptualization of the variables whose postulated empirical consequences one wishes to study. But it does affirm the fact that, in any given scientific study, the particular personality measures employed empirically fix, limit, and single out the behavioral criteria taken to represent the imputed concepts.

The prime importance of theoretical relevance in the choice and development of measures

Since the empirical measure of a personality variable is so inextricably related to the concept it operationally defines, its choice merits the most careful thought on the part of a researcher. All sorts of methodological issues may have to be taken into account in deciding what measure may be most feasible for use with particular populations and under particular investigatory circumstances. But an experimenter's primary consideration should be that of the measure's theoretical aptness, and in devising or selecting his measures that concern should be preeminent.

Thus, if it makes the greatest conceptual sense to observe the behavioral manifestations of a given imputed variable under conditions of measurement defined by a rating scale or an open-ended projective test or a video tape or a physiological recording, a researcher has the maximal scientific incentive for struggling with the methodological problems involved in constructing a reliable measure in any of those relevant media. However, insofar as the variable under consideration lends itself to appropriate measurement through less difficult techniques, such as a multiple-choice questionnaire, an experimenter would obviously be wise to take full advantage of them, rather than needlessly to impose upon himself the problems of more complicated methods.

By assigning unequivocal priority to theoretical appropriateness, a researcher can be most accessible to his own conceptualization. He can thus give himself optimal freedom to imagine methodological innovations suitable to the measurement of variables he wants to study and permit himself a like flexibility in choosing among whatever existing measures may be available for his purposes. In this frame of mind, he may best avoid the pitfalls of blind commitment to any kind of measure as an end in itself.

True, given the institutionalized division of labor that has been so characteristic of modern societies and that is still as prevalent in science as in other fields of work, some researchers have devoted much of their careers to the development of specific measures of personality. It is also true that, having acquired such an occupational vested interest, these test-oriented specialists are understandably inclined to favor the most widespread investigatory application of the measures with which they have become professionally identified.

Some of this psychometric partisanship has undoubtedly stimulated the emergence of measures that would not have been devised without the special enthusiasm and devotion lavished upon them by their originators and developers. This form of specialization has called well-deserved attention to the existence of promising measures of variables for which no instrument of observation had formely been proposed, thus facilitating the scientific goal of the empirical evaluation of concepts. Yet the very desire to promote the general use of a particular measure — apart from an informed awareness and a thorough examination of the investigatory aims of every study in which that instrument may or may not be the most desirable of all possible measures — reflects a tendency to value it for its own sake. Insofar as a researcher becomes deeply involved in such promotion, he may undermine his own activity as a scientist. For he may lose sight of the fact that measurement, as an indispensable implementation to the scientific assessment of concepts, requires the most theoretically relevant operational definition he can find or devise, and that all methods in current use are already incipiently obsolete, their mere existence providing a stimulus for their replacement by more apt and effective ones.

Thus, while the requirement of operational definition may seem to be adequately met by a measure toward whose development a researcher has greatly devoted himself, it may also be accommodated through a variety of alternative operations. Some of these alternatives may be concurrently available, while others may be steadily forthcoming, and unless a researcher is sufficiently receptive to them, he may continue to apply his unreasonably favored measures in a stereotyped manner. Insofar as he ignores or rejects measures that are actually more appropriate to the theoretical objectives of his research than the methods to which he has become emotionally attached, he suffers a loss of intellectual perspective that is obviously detrimental to scientific progress in his area of inquiry.

The scientific versus the practical use of
measures of personality

Devotion to specific measures of personality is both more com-
prehensible and more evident in applied psychology. For here a psychologist is fundamentally committed to the accomplishment of a practical
task, such as selecting managerial employees or diagnosing clinical
patients. Insofar as he turns in a creditable performance — by whatever
criteria he is professionally evaluated — such a psychologist is strongly
reinforced toward the use of any measure he feels has insured his
success. Nor is he likely to be dissuaded from using any such measure
on the basis of empirical research that finds it wanting as a predictive
device in its own right. For he can always conclude that it is *his*
particular use of the test that is crucial, he being the actual measuring
instrument and the "test" merely offering an assortment of stimuli
evocative of the kind of responses from which he is personally capable
of making the decisions and answering the questions required of him.
Indeed, under this approach, the psychologist need not even feel
constrained to employ measures in any standardized fashion; he is
free to vary their order and mode of presentation in any way that
dovetails with his ongoing feelings about what stimuli might be best
utilized to explore his emerging view of various facets of the personality
of the individual being scrutinized.

Of course, every scientific measure is, broadly speaking, dependent
upon human interpretation insofar as its results, however finely and
objectively calibrated, must eventually be affirmed by human perception. But the observational ideal behind the use of a measure is
that of yielding data whose discriminanda are so clear that they virtually compel different observers to perceive them in the same way.
Hence, scientifically viewed, the better the measure, the less its data
are vulnerable to a diversity of perceptions; and insofar as those data
operationally define an imputed variable, they invite such imputations
on the part of all observers.

A scientific measure of personality thus aims to preclude dependence for its meaning upon individual differences in perceptual ability
and interpretive disposition of those who employ it. Instead, insofar
as it can be arranged, such meaning is tied to explicitly given and
quantifiable characteristics of particular responses to particular stimuli

contained in the measure, such characteristics being, moreover, discriminable from all other behavior the individual may show in response to those stimuli.

Thus, a scientific measure of personality aims so to standardize and objectify the collection and quantification of its data as to minimize the impact of its particular administrators and scorers upon its psychological meaning. Surely, such human intervention is mandatory for the requisite observations to be gathered and quantified; and, subsequently, for the processed data to be read and reported to other investigators. But every precaution is taken to eliminate the possibility that individual differences among those who administer and score the measure, rather than the intrinsic qualities theoretically ascribed to the stimuli in the measure and to the responses to those stimuli, may determine either the original data or their imputed conceptual significance.

As previously suggested, this ideal of linking data unequivocally to the instruments of observation used to define imputed variables is tremendously difficult to implement in the study of personality. For measures of such variables are inevitably administered within a broader situational context, which contains a host of other stimuli, including the administrator, that can evoke reactions in the subjects being measured. And, insofar as his responses are confounded by the influence of stimuli extraneous to those that constitute the measuring instrument, a subject's data may not be reliably ascribable to the variable they are meant operationally to define.

Well aware of these difficulties, those who strive to construct scientific measures of personality variables attempt to minimize the intrusion of irrelevant stimuli by indicating as precisely as possible the usual conditions that should obtain during the administration of their instruments, especially the instructions given to subjects. Yet, considering the widely varying circumstances that surround the administration of such measures, control over the confounding effects of irrelevant stimuli, which define a plethora of contextual variables, is actually minimal. For these measures are, in practice, given by different administrators in an equally heterogenous variety of situations. Indeed, the only truly constant features involved in the administration of these measures are the self-contained stimuli and written instructions.

By contrast, in dealing with the categorization and quantification of the data obtained through these measures, much more standardization can be obtained. In fact, such standardization can be made virtually free of the intrusion of extraneous influence by having every relevant response precategorized and prequantified. In these instances, as, for example, with a Likert-type scale (Likert, 1932), every response to every question is automatically given, by prior definition, a position on a continuum for a particular variable; and, to compile a subject's total score on the variable, it is merely necessary for a human recorder — or a mechanical aide, such as an IBM machine — to sum the individual ratings the subject gave to each item that was previously designated by the originator of the scale, however unbeknown to the subject, as comprising the particular variable. Thus, a researcher using the scale need make no personal interpretations in scoring it. In fact, with recourse to computers, he may not even have to score it himself, and his only crucial act of observation may rest upon his veridical reading of the machine's printed figures — a kind of observation about which human beings *per se,* as measuring instruments, may reasonably be expected to have quite common perceptions, assuming they have all learned to read numbers.

Still, however objective the categorization and scoring of data is made to become, it cannot vitiate the intrusion of irrelevant situational evocations that may have occurred when the subjects first registered their responses to the relevant measuring stimuli; and that, rather than the measure itself, determined much of the data, however it may be categorized and quantified on an *a priori* theoretical basis.

As already implied in stressing the desirability of giving first priority to a measure's theoretical appropriateness, behavioral irrelevancies may also be produced by defects in the quality of the stimuli contained in the measuring instrument itself, and in the methods employed for quantifying the responses they are presumed to elicit. Thus, errors of measurement may intrude upon the data from so many sources that one might suppose the very attempt to develop scientifically useful measures of Freudian variables of personality is a foolhardy enterprise. Yet, despite their vulnerability to error, such measures have been emerging with increasing scientific promise. And, as shall be indicated, even very crude instruments have proven effective, their theoretical aptness apparently overcoming their methodological deficiencies.

The essential difference between the scientific and the practical usage of measures of personality has been somewhat obscured by the fortuitous circumstances surrounding the history of such measurement. For the earliest attempts at personality measurement did not arise from the needs of deductive research, whereby a scientist wished to measure particular variables in order to carry forward empirical assessments of theoretically derived hypotheses. Instead, the historical impetus for personality measurement was clinical, generated by a desire to develop psychological instruments (analogous to the tests of blood and urine that are so useful to clinical medicine) for conducting the practical tasks of psychiatric classification, evaluation, and diagnosis.

Thus, it is hardly surprising that one of the earliest of such measures was originated by a psychiatrist, Hermann Rorschach. What is slightly puzzling is the fact that, once introduced, Rorschach's Test has retained its firm place in the repertoire of diagnostic instruments. Yet the very timing of its introduction tended to be preemptive, insofar as clinicians seized upon it as a long-sought aid to their very emotionally demanding work. Moreover, Rorschach, somewhat like Freud, stirred the enthusiasm of a number of gifted and loyal followers, who spread his technique not only in psychiatric settings but also in the academic settings where clinical psychologists receive their basic training in diagnostic testing. Clinicians, having learned to associate their professional effectiveness with the application of this instrument, are greatly inclined to continue with its use — no matter what research may reveal about its predictive inadequacies and no matter what new instruments may be offered as alternatives. Finally, having adopted the practice of regularly using the Rorschach Test, clinical diagnosticians have, in those test stimuli, some common frame of reference within which to communicate about the behavior of the individuals to whom they impute diverse variables of personality. Considering the enormous ambiguities attendant upon clinical work, the existence of any degree of communality of reference is likely to be a valued psychological support, which clinicians might well be loath to renounce.

Certainly, Rorschach (1942) presented some theoretical rationale for the inferences he made from responses to his various blots. Yet he did not deliberately devise his test as an operational definition of particular concepts whose measurement was required for the purpose of conducting rigorous deductive evaluations of their scientific utility. Instead, Rorschach implicitly assumed the validity of whatever variables his instrument purported to measure. Hence, to this day, clinicians using that test are inclined to impute those variables from behavioral evocations to the relevant stimuli, thus preserving the aura of self-contained and self-evident veracity within which the Rorschach Test was originally presented and utilized.

To becloud matters even further, some popular diagnostic instruments, including the Rorschach Test, have been clinically interpreted within theoretical frameworks that differ considerably from those initially offered by their promulgators as a basis for conceptual imputation. Most widely, this shifting theoretical context of interpretation has occurred with respect to the imposition of Freudian rubrics as increasing numbers of clinicians were trained in psychoanalytic theory. A notable example of this trend is Schafer's (1954) book, which discusses the interpretation of the Rorschach Test from a psychoanalytic viewpoint.

Of course, there is nothing scientifically illegitimate about seeking to comprehend any behavioral datum from whatever conceptual standpoint one chooses to view it. And, for the purposes of his work, a clinician is impelled by exceedingly powerful motives to find whatever meaning he can detect in the behavior of those whose lives he is presuming to repair in one way or another. Consequently, if a clinician is convinced that Freudian theory offers the most fruitful avenue to such meaning, as well as to such remedial assistance, he may be expected to rely upon it in both his diagnostic and his therapeutic endeavours. Yet it should be kept in mind that interpreting the Rorschach Test from a psychoanalytic viewpoint merely adds a new set of unvalidated assumptions to that originally proposed by Rorschach. And any presumption that the psychoanalytic categories of interpretation are scientifically adequate measures of the variables they impute is completely unwarranted — no matter how thoroughly it is acted upon in clinical practice.

Still, there is no reason why existing clinical tests cannot be adapted to the objectives of scientific measurement. Indeed, insofar as any such tests happen to contain stimuli that promise to be peculiarly evocative of specifically conceptualized variables of personality, a researcher has the best of scientific reasons to attempt such an adaptation. As shall be illustrated, such adaptations have been made in respect to the operational definition of psychoanalytic variables of personality that were the subject of experimental study.

On the other hand, it may often be much more theoretically apt to devise entirely new measures, which are conceived from the outset as operational definitions of the particular variables of personality one is interested in submitting to scientific investigation. It is true that the task of devising a completely new measure of a personality variable may be a quite formidable undertaking, yet it may also be an inescapable one, insofar as a researcher is interested in variables for which no such measures have been developed. Indeed, this is frequently the arduous prospect now facing scientific researchers in the area of psychoanalytic theory. Unless they are prepared to cope with it, they may have to forgo the possibility of investigating Freudian concepts that are of the greatest interest to them.

Administering measures of independent variables of personality within the context of an experiment

Measuring a variable of personality, we have seen, is not a process identical to that of inserting a calibrated pipette into a beaker and drawing out a given volume of inert fluid. Instead, although such measures deliberately seek to tap particular psychological dimensions, their administration does not for a moment vitiate the extraordinarily reactive character of the human being under study. Indeed, even as a subject concentrates upon an instrument that aims to assess relatively enduring dimensions of his personality, his reactions to it may be greatly affected by other stimuli within the environment, by his unuttered feelings about what he is doing, and by experiences inmmediately preceding its presentation to him. Consequently, in operationally fulfilling an interactive experimental design, the measurement of the designated independent variables of personality should be done before subjects are exposed to the manipulations that induce the independent variables of motivation or cognition. Thus, a researcher can at least preclude the differential contamination of that measuring process by the impact of different antecedent conditions of experimental manipulation.

*Administering measures of independent variables
anticipated as alternative explanations for
predicted results*

Insofar as the measures of plausible alternative explanations deal with demographic variables, they may usually be adequately administered either before or after the experimental manipulations. For one's order of birth within a family or one's place of birth, for example, cannot possibly be affected by exposure to such manipulations. However, if measures of such anticipated alternatives pertain to variables of personality, they should be administered before the manipulated phases of the experiment for the reasons given above.

Of course, there are practical limits to how many measures subjects can be requested to take without developing either antagonism toward the very process of measurement or preoccupation with what is being measured and why. But either eventuality is to be avoided, since it threatens to bring theoretically unwanted and empirically uncontrolled sources of variance into the experiment.

With regard to premanipulative measures of an experiment's independent variables, decisions concerning their optimal number and order of presentation often depend entirely on a researcher's judgment and the findings of his own pilot studies. For there is certainly no existing compilation of empirical data bearing upon the outcome of various orders of presentation for various combinations of premanipulative measures.

A frequently used practice, which seems, pragmatically, to have been effective, is the initial presentation of demographic measures, as a kind of emotionally neutral "warm up" to the measures of personality. However, as we shall soon see, the reverse order of presentation has also been successfully employed.

*Examples of provisions made to measure
independent variables suggested as alternative
explanations in Freudian experiments*

A.   *Coping with alternatives suggested by non-Freudian conceptions.*   Bromberg (1967) administered a number of preexperimental measures of both personality and demographic variables in order to deal with the various plausible alternatives that he anticipated. These specific measures, together with their order of administration and the anticipations decisive to their inclusion, are given below.

The very first "instrument" was a pseudo-measure, designed to support the overall rationale of the experiment and to prepare subjects for similarly constructed measures of theoretically relevant variables. Thus, directly following the opening "warm-up" came the "before" measurement of phobic ideation, one of Bromberg's two dependent variables.

Next, Bromberg measured the nonmanipulated independent variable of castration conflict (CC), which was centrally involved, as shall later be shown, in the subsequent creation of three manipulated independent variables of motivation. Then, the personality variables of manifest anxiety (Bendig, 1956) and social desirability (Edwards, 1957) were measured as empirical controls for the measure of castration conflict. For it could have been argued that the CC scale merely measured a general state of anxiety rather than the particular one imputed to it. Similarly, it could be held that a subject's score on the CC scale was only a reflection of what he felt was a socially desirable way of representing himself.

Last among Bromberg's premanipulative measures were those dealing with presumably relevant demographic variables, which included: age, race, religious affiliation, marital status, socio-economic position, number of siblings, and birth order. The possible effects of some of these independent variables on the experiment's dependent variables was suggested merely by "common sense." For example, given the prevailing social tensions between blacks and whites, a subject's racial identity might have determined his affiliative preference, which was Bromberg's second dependent variable and which he measured only once, after the manipulations. Others of the demographic variables have been suggested for inclusion by the findings of related studies. Thus, it had been shown (Schachter, 1959; Sarnoff & Zimbardo, 1961) that college students who are only or first-born children tend to show a greater preference for social affiliation than do those who are later-born children.

In order to cope with these various explanatory possibilities, Bromberg assessed the extent to which each of their measures might be correlated with his CC scale. Since he found no statistically significant results from any of these analyses, he concluded that none of them could be plausibly maintained as an alternative to the variable measured by his CC scale. And he thus felt it theoretically appropriate to invoke that variable as the one involved in the various predicted consequences of its measurement and juxtaposition with the experimental manipulations.

Finally, while most of Bromberg's subjects had volunteered in connection with the fulfillment of a course requirement at New York University, some subjects were volunteers from another university. To make sure that those two kinds of volunteers did not differ on the CC scale or any of the above control measures, Bromberg conducted the relevant empirical comparisons between the two groups. No significant differences were found between them on any of those comparisons, nor, indeed, did the two groups of subjects differ subsequently in their responses to the experimental conditions.

    B. Coping with alternatives suggested from within Freudian theory.   In planning the previously cited experiment on castration anxiety and the fear of death (Sarnoff & Corwin, 1959), it occurred to the researchers that the hypothesized changes in fear of death might be plausibly explained by the Freudian concept of guilt — under the conditions required to test the hypotheses derived from the concept of castration anxiety. Specifically, it appeared that visual contact with photographs of voluptuous female nudes — the stimuli used to induce a high degree of heterosexual arousal and hence to exacerbate the habitual levels of castration anxiety found among the male subjects — might also arouse guilt for those subjects whose moral scruples would be offended by such viewing. Consequently, since punishment is regarded by Freudian theory as the maximally reductive response to the motive of guilt (Sarnoff, 1962), subjects reacting guiltily to the heterosexual stimuli might manifest their need for punishment in fantasies of injury and death. Hence, for these subjects, an increase in the fear of death might be an expression of the wish to expiate guilt rather than a symbolic ideational representation of castration anxiety.

To cope empirically with this theoretical possibility, the experimental design required a measure of moral scruples against heterosexual behavior (Morality Scale) to be taken prior to confrontation of the subjects with the experimental manipulations. Thus, the ensuing fluctuations in the dependent variable, fear of death, could be analyzed with respect to the interaction of both nonmanipulated independent variables of personality, habitual castration anxiety, and habitual moral scruples against heterosexual behavior, with the manipulated independent variable, heterosexual arousal.

The Morality Scale consisted of 5 Likert-type items that were part of a 22-item "Opinion Questionnaire." This questionnaire also contained the "before" measure of fear of death and it was the first instrument administered to subjects. Following completion of this questionnaire, subjects were presented with the measure of habitual castration anxiety. Then, four weeks later, subjects were exposed to the experimental manipulation and the "after" measure of the fear of death.

Subsequent analyses of the data indicated that, whereas the independent variable of moral scruples tended to interact with heterosexual arousal by yielding an increase in the fear of death, the increase was not a statistically reliable difference from the subjects' pre-arousal level of that fear. In contrast, the same analysis applied to the interaction between castration anxiety and heterosexual arousal showed a statistically significant before-after change in fear of death.

It must immediately be noted that the actual amounts of *experimentally induced* castration anxiety and guilt were not *directly* assessed. Instead, castration anxiety was merely *assumed* to have been differentially triggered among subjects differing on the pre-experimental measure of habitual castration anxiety, while guilt was similarly assumed to have been activated among subjects differing on the measure of moral scruples.

Assuredly, the results of this experiment cannot be regarded as having entirely disposed of the theoretical question that led to the inclusion of the Morality Scale in the experimental design. Nevertheless, it shows how implicitly competing Freudian explanations can be anticipated in the design of an experiment, and how the relative predictive powers of those concepts can be sorted out through procedures of measurement.

Pencil-and-Paper Measures
of Freudian Variables of
Personality

Pencil-and-paper measures are surely the most ubiquitous kinds of instruments used in the scientific measurement of personality variables. Nor is it difficult to undertand their popularity. For such measures contain "packaged" stimuli, whose presentation can be made to subjects in a fixed, standardized, and convenient way; for example, a booklet of pictures to which brief written stories are requested or a list of adjectives to be checked. Moreover, these conveniently packaged stimuli lend themselves to group administration, thus saving a researcher an enormous amount of time and also permitting him to arrange for someone else, even an untrained person, to administer the measure – if that procedure is required by the experimental design.

Insofar as such measures represent appropriate bases for making inferences about the Freudian variables one wishes to study, their utilization is avidly sought by investigators. But to make even the slightest beginnings toward their construction, one must first decide upon the character of both the stimuli and the responses to be included in the ultimate package.

The two central dimensions of format in
pencil-and-paper measures

Broadly speaking, this decision is theoretically contingent upon: a) the degree of ambiguity held to be desirable in the stimuli; and b) the degree of restriction deemed to be desirable in the registration of responses to those stimuli.

Traditionally, projective techniques have tended to be characterized by both the ambiguity of their stimuli and the open-endedness permitted to subjects in responding to them. Conversely, objective

118

techniques have tended to limit both the ambiguity of their stimuli and the degree of restriction with which subjects can respond to them. Nevertheless, it should be apparent that the two psychometric dimensions are quite independent of each other, and that they can be put together in combinations quite different from those that have been conveniently utilized.

Certainly, the terms "projective" and "objective" are highly relative, each being, moreover, quite unclear insofar as they are employed without further specification of the stimulus and response dimensions just explicated. Thus, every stimulus in a psychological measuring instrument is to a greater or lesser degree ambiguous insofar as it can be variously interpreted by various subjects. All "objective" tests that rely upon verbal statements as stimuli are necessarily rife with the ambiguity of language itself; and the words used in such measures may have quite different cognitive and emotional connotations for the different individuals who are requested to respond to them. On the other hand, even the most open-ended of "projective" tests is obliged, in the interest of standardization, to confine the individual subject's responsivity to a given space and time for each item; and, in addition, to require that his responses all be given with a particular medium of expression; for example, words or drawings.

Keeping these cautions in mind, it may be helpful to review some of the most basic assumptions concerning the methodological advantages and disadvantages involved in the employment of relative extremes in the two basic structural dimensions upon which every measure of personality, regardless of its psychological content, is necessarily built: ambiguity of stimulus and restriction of response.

The methodological advantages and disadvantages of highly ambiguous versus highly explicit eliciting stimuli

Highly ambiguous stimuli derive their advantages, first of all, by concealing from the subject what is being measured. True, he may nonetheless react to the procedure of measurement with great defensiveness. But insofar as the stimuli do not indicate the nature of the variables they are designed to measure, it is difficult for even the most defensive subject to anticipate which of his responses may give the observer, via the data obtained, information about whatever psychological tendencies he may be reluctant to disclose.

Secondly, highly ambiguous stimuli, such as ink-blots or drawings veiled in shadows, are likely to be evocative of fantasy. These fantasies, in turn, are assumed, like daydreams, to be indicative of unconscious motives and defenses. Hence, insofar as the eliciting stimuli symbolize the subject being measured and important prototypes in his life history, the fantasies they evoke may bear great relevance to his chronic motivational conflicts as well as to his habitual ways of coping with them.

The potential disadvantages of highly ambiguous measuring stimuli are virtually the reverse of their purported merits. For if a stimulus exceeds a certain degree of ambiguity, its physical character may become so amorphous as to preclude agreement about its perceptible attributes, thus, in effect, depriving investigators of common empirical points of reference to which they can confidently refer the responses evoked by the stimulus. At the same time, responses elicited by such amorphous stimuli may be so heterogenous as to defy confident imputation from them to any presumably specific and stable variable of personality.

Highly explicit stimuli have the obvious advantage of lending themselves more readily to agreement among both testers and subjects concerning their sheer physical attributes, and, moreover, they are likely to elicit a much less heterogenous variety of responses than are provoked by highly ambigous stimuli. Hence, the responses elicited by highly explicit stimuli can more easily serve as a confident basis for imputing personality variables from them.

Concrete comparisons between stimuli of varying degrees of ambiguity, each of which is currently employed for identical evocative purposes, may dramatically illustrate these issues. On the Rorschach Test, Card IV has sometimes been assumed by clinicians, according to specialists in that instrument (Klopfer, B., Ainsworth, Klopfer, W. G., & Holt, 1954; Piotrowski, 1957), to symbolize the prototypical father-figure, and such clinicians are inclined to interpret an individual's responses to that card in accordance with that assumption. But Card IV is, in fact, merely a gray ink blot, and no group of dispassionate scientists could possibly agree that the card's actual physical attributes conformed to a configuration that was plainly recognizable as a man.

Moving to a greater degree of explicitness, Card 7 BM of the TAT depicts two adult males, one discernibly older than the other. Logically, the elder of the two men can be regarded as a symbol of the father-figure. And while objective observers might well disagree about whether or not that symbolic identification is inherent in the physical characteristics of this depiction, they would very likely agree that the image in question is a man and that he appears relatively old in contrast to the man with whom he is paired in the drawing.

Finally, at a yet sharper level of explicitness of stimulus, the Michigan Sentence Completion Test (see the appendix of Sarnoff, 1951) contains a phrase, "My father," which, like similar fragments in the measure, is the opening of a sentence that subjects are requested to complete. Here the stimulus qualities of the item are not only extremely definite but unmistakably specific, evoking reactions not merely to a symbol of one's father but to one's actual father. Clearly, responses to such stimuli can be utilized with maximum confidence as bases for imputation to whatever variables are considered theoretically related to the particular aspects of the subject's behavior that are recorded. In other words, whatever the subject reveals about himself in relationship to his father can very reasonably be assumed to refer to that parent, whom the stimulus unequivocally represents.

These highly explicit stimuli have, however, the methodological liability of clearly suggesting to the subject what realms of psychological concern are being investigated. Indeed, they may, as is frequently the case in self-report questionnaires, by sheer repetition of the same category of explicit items, provoke the subjects to guess what specific variables are defined by those items. Hence, the very explicitness of the measuring stimuli may put the subject so much on the defensive that his responses are based not upon the intrinsic character of those stimuli but, instead, upon his discernment of the psychological dimensions they seek to delineate. For example, his answers to the items may reflect his interpretation of the social desirability of his replies (Edwards, 1957), rather than his genuine feelings about the psychological states and patterns of behavior the items invite him to reveal.

A second possible disadvantage of highly explicit stimuli is their tendency to restrict the play of fantasy by making the subject very acutely aware of the psychological issues upon which such stimuli deliberately attempt to engage his full attention. Thus, these unequivocal stimuli may largely fail to stir the presumably unconscious motives of the individual. Instead, by mobilizing the subject's awareness of his reactions to inescapably definite stimuli, such as "my father," these kinds of items may induce a very cognitive and deliberative orientation,

with the subject weighing and measuring the contents of his consious-
ness before responding. For instance, he may first ask himself, "How
do I feel about my father?," and then reply in terms of that query rather
than letting himself respond without the intervention of a heightened
self-consciousness.

Insofar as these relatively definite stimuli have such inhibiting effects upon the emergence of the unconscious tendencies a researcher
wishes to measure, they may defeat his investigatory purposes. And he
may obtain data pertaining to the operation of the individual's ways
of dealing intellectually with his possible evocations of those tendencies
rather than to the tendencies themselves. Thus, the very clarity of the
explicit stimuli may inadvertently induce an almost reflexive and ob-
scuring defensiveness, introducing confounding factors that their very
lucidity had been designed to preclude.

The methodological advantages and disadvantages
of highly unrestricted versus highly restricted
channels for expressing psychological reactions
to measuring stimuli

Spontaneity is the prime advantage to be gained by maximizing
the lack of restriction upon the manner in which subjects are asked
to reply to measuring stimuli. For it is assumed that, the greater the
spontaneity allowed in the registration of such replies, the more likely
is the subject to reveal the actual impact of the stimuli on him. Moreover,
the less restricted he is in the means of replying, the more likely is he
to reveal the idiosyncracies of his expressive style, including the ways
in which he expresses unconscious motives of defenses.

Thus, if a subject is confronted, let us say, by a TAT card to which
he is asked to write a story, his subsequent written production cannot
but reveal aspects of his habitual psychological functioning, if only in
the characteristics of his handwriting and the structure of his prose.
But it is, of course, further assumed that, given the relative freedom to
say whatever he wishes to say, all the substantive contents of his stories
represent motivated choices among the infinite variety of things he
could have chosen to express. Hence, even if such contents actually
express defenses against his unconscious motives rather than the unconscious motives *per se*, the very fact of their inclusion in the stories

indicates that they are of psychological significance to the individual.

Given these assumptions, the clinician who is primarily concerned with uncovering the relative uniqueness of the individuals he examines may be best able to make psychological capital out of whatever is spontaneously expressed through such unrestricted responses. Indeed, he may even be able to read useful significance in stories consisting of a single word — or in a refusal to reply altogether to a given stimulus for which a story is requested.

But, for scientific purposes, the whole point of administering a standardized package of stimuli in accordance with a fixed set of instructions is to generate data relevant to the variables one has decided to measure. Consequently, *unless it is specifically included in the plan of quantification for a particular variable,* the absence of a response is not a relevant datum for a scientific researcher. Nor may such a researcher be able to make scientific use of a host of the responses that various subjects may choose to give to the same stimulus under conditions of highly unrestricted expressiveness.

Thus, insofar as he does not restrict the responsivity of the subjects, a researcher takes the chance of collecting a lot of protocols that are, however intrinsically fascinating and idiosyncratic, entirely worthless for his scientific objectives. For he cannot use these irrelevant data as a basis for quantifying the responses of the pertinent subjects on the imputed dimension of personality he is seeking to investigate.

This problem cannot necessarily be overcome merely by developing extremely concrete and highly reliable systems of scoring to impose upon such open-ended data. Indeed, the more explicit the scoring scheme, the more it tends to narrow the range of spontaneous productions that may be reliably coded under it. For example, a correlational investigation dealing with the ego defense of identification with the aggressor (Sarnoff, 1951) employed such highly reliable codes (reliability was assessed in terms of interrater agreement in scoring) to quantify the relatively open-ended responses of subjects to various stimuli from the TAT and the Michigan Sentence Completion Test. But an enormous amount of the collected data, representing responses that simply could not be unequivocally viewed as indicative of the personality characteristics under study, proved to be unscorable.

It may be argued, of course, that the scorable protocols contained responses whose genuine relevance to the variables measured was likely to be very high, considering the fact that those responses were spontaneously given to stimuli whose specific measuring objectives for the particular study could scarcely be discerned with any accuracy by the respondents. Yet the attrition of protocols containing totally unscorable data was so great that some of the *a priori* predictions could be tested on only a handful of the many individuals in the total sample of subjects to whom the measures were administered.

As can be deduced from the above example, the clear methodological advantage of highly restricting the responsivity of subjects lies in the possibility, through such restriction, of obtaining the maximal amount of data relevant to the variable being measured. Indeed, by prearranging the limits of response permitted to choices that automatically impute a given amount of the pertinent variable to subjects registering such choices, an investigator can be certain of obtaining a score on the variable for every subject.

By applying such a procedure, a researcher may be able not only to avoid any waste of data but also the waste of time and effort that imposing codes of scoring on more unrestricted kinds of responses requires. Moreover, by building the scoring scheme into the only choices of response available to subjects, the resulting data can be rendered directly amenable to processing by computers, without having to be passed through any intermediary process of categorization and quantification. Finally, the built-in scoring scheme can be arranged to suit various investigatory and statistical desiderata, such as breadth of numerical range. Thus, for very young children, one may wish to use only a two-point rating system, whereas the interests of reliability would warrant a broader scale for older respondents, who can cope with the greater psychological demands of discriminating more finely among gradations in their feelings and behavior.

On the other hand, by requiring subjects to choose among a few highly explicit responses, whose contents were formulated in advance to insure their theoretical relevance to the variable measured, a researcher runs the risk of revealing to the subject the nature of the variable involved. Insofar as the subject does accurately perceive what the instrument is intended to measure, he may respond in terms of his attitudes about expressing the variable — rather than in terms of the degree to which he actually possesses it. Hence, he may be put very much on guard, responding defensively as indicated in previous examples regarding highly explicit stimuli.

In such instances, low scores on measures dealing with variables

considered, for some reason, socially undesirable, may be especially difficult to interpret at face value. Assuming the nature of the variable
measured is equally apparent to subjects, those who score high in the
measure are likely to do so in spite of whatever awareness they may
have about the psychological meaning of their responses. Thus, their
scores can reasonably be interpreted as indicants of the degree to which
they possess the variable *per se*. However, scores on the low end of
the scale may reflect either a relative absence of the variable measured
or a defensive reaction to the measure — or some combination of both
(Adorno, Frenkel-Brunswik, Levenson, & Sanford, 1950).

A related risk inherent in the use of highly restricted channels
for responding to measuring stimuli is that of leading subjects correctly
to guess the hypotheses under investigation in the experiment. For if
the subject is, through such channels, inadvertently induced to perceive
the dimensions of personality they operationally define, he automatically
acquires information about one of the variables in the experimenter's
hypothesis. And he may thus be better able, in due course, to guess
at the intention of the experimental manipulations and to link them
conceptually to the personality measure.

*On selecting the most advantageous format for
a pencil-and-paper measure of a
personality variable*

In the light of the foregoing discussion of the formal characteristics
of pencil-and-paper measures of personality variables, it is evident that
both extremes of ambiguity of stimuli and restriction of response contain numerous methodological advantages and disadvantages. Indeed,
virtually every advantage gained by a given aspect of format is offset
by a disadvantage that its use creates. Therefore, the question besetting
a researcher, is: How can one maximize the advantages discussed while
minimizing the disadvantages attendant upon their application? There
can be no really definitive answers to this nagging query, for the format
of an instrument is contingent upon the substantive content of the
variable being measured, and also upon the overall design of the experiment in which the measure is utilized. But it may be of heuristic
value to illustrate two somewhat different methods that have been used

in the effort to develop or to apply scientifically useful measures of Freudian variables.

The first of these methods may be described as objective-projective and the second as objective. Since their differences will become apparent in due course, their similarities deserve at least a passing mention. First, they are characterized by highly restricted channels of response. Second, they are amenable to group administration, their accompanying instructions being printed directly on them and easy for subjects to follow. Third, they tend to be brief in length. Thus, the format of these measures lends itself to convenient administration and mechanical processing, readily yielding prescored responses for every subject on the variables measured and freeing the experimenter from the burdens of coding.

The objective-projective method of measuring Freudian variables of personality

This method seeks to combine the evocative quality of relatively unstructured stimuli with the practical advantages of a highly restricted set of alternatives for registering responses to those stimuli. With respect to Freudian variables *per se*, the use of this type of measure was greatly stimulated by Blum, whose Blacky Test (1949) consisted of eleven cartoons of dogs, each of which was designed, on the basis of Freudian theory, to represent, in chronological sequence, the various stages of psychosexual development.

One of Blum's students, Goldstein (1952), devised a method of presenting every Blacky card in conjunction with a set of brief pre-written responses. "Goldstein's technique requires the S to rank his preferences for a number of statements which purport to summarize an interpersonal situation which is depicted pictorially. These statements are assumed, on an *a priori* basis, to represent several of the mechanisms of ego defense. By having the same set of ego defenses represented by summary statements which are appropriate to a series of different pictures, it is possible to obtain an indication of the strength of the individual's preferences for any one of the defenses in relation to the others [Sarnoff, 1960b, p. 134]." The registration of a subject's ranking is presumed to be determined by the extent to which the particular defensive alternatives exert an unconscious appeal to him. Thus, his order of preference for the verbal descriptions that hypothetically represent the functioning of the various defenses is assumed to reflect his own defensive inclinations in dealing with the motives portrayed.

The theoretically discrete usage of this kind of objective-projective measure has tended to produce quite encouraging results. For example, in the formerly mentioned experiment on the relationship between reaction formation and cynicism (Sarnoff 1960b), the relevant personality variable, reaction formation against affectionate feelings, was measured through an adaptation of Goldstein's technique to pictorial stimuli regarded as more appropriate than any of the Black cards to the evocation of that variable.

Ss ranked sets of three summary statements in respect to a series of four pictures. Three of these pictures were taken from the TAT (Murray, 1938); cards 10, 6BM, and 7BM. The fourth picture was a TAT-like photograph which is very often seen as a father-son relationship.

Ss were asked to rank, for each picture, three summary statements designed to represent a different mechanism of ego defense against affectionate feelings. One of these ego defenses was reaction formation; the other two were projection and regression. The same three defenses were always represented by the three statements which the Ss had to rank, though the specific content of the statements varied with the picture theme, and the order in which the defenses were represented was varied for each of the pictures. The number of times an S assigned first rank to the statements which had been designed to represent reaction formation was taken as the measure of the strength of his reaction formation against affection. Ss scoring 0 or 1 for all four pictures were classified as low in RF, while those who scored 2 or 3 were placed in the high category. Examples of the statement which represented the defense are given below. Reaction formation is indicated by RF, projection by P, and regression by R; the following set of statements is appropriate to TAT Card 10:

RF.   His affection having been stirred by a chance meeting with his former wife, the man realizes that his reaction is artificial, and he quickly expresses the coldness of his dislike.

P.   After a series of casual dates, the woman confesses that she is deeply in love with the man and wants to put the relationship on a more tender basis.

R. The man's friends consider him to be independent and self-reliant, but when he is alone with the woman, he lays all his problems at her feet and seeks support and encouragement [Sarnoff, 1960b, p. 134].

By varying the order in which the purported defenses against affection were represented from picture to picture, it was hoped both to obscure the variable being measured and to prevent the subjects from developing a "response set," whereby they might begin to anticipate a regular progression in the type of outcome contained in the statements and, hence, rank them in a rather automatic manner. To counteract such an anticipation, the variation in their order or presentation tended to require an individuated reading of each set of statements.

But while pointing out these methodological refinements, it should also be noted that no attempt whatever was made to assess the reliability of this particular measure. It is entirely possible that the failure to obtain more conclusive results than were found in this experiment was due, primarily, to a lack of reliability in this measure of the vital independent variable rather than to the previously discussed possibilities of statistical regression. Certainly, insofar as the measure of reaction formation against affection was lacking in reliability, it would have wrongly classified subjects with respect to their degree of imputed reaction formation. Thus, some subjects classified as High might actually have been Low and vice versa. To the extent that such erroneous classifications were made, they worked against the hypothesis under test and thus prevented the proper juxtaposition of the nonmanipulated and manipulated independent variables specified in the hypothesis. Considering the probably low reliability of the measure of reaction formation against affectionate feelings, the results obtained are quite remarkable. And perhaps they indicate how far theoretical aptness can compensate for methodological crudity.

An even more dramatic instance of such compensation seems to have operated in the experiment on castration anxiety and fear of death (Sarnoff & Corwin, 1959), to which reference has been made in illustrating other principles. In that study, the crucial variable of personality was habitual castration anxiety (CA), which was measured by a *single* item.

When it was devised, this one-item measure of castration anxiety appeared methodologically indicated. For the researchers believed that any additional items of similar content might incur acute defensiveness among subjects presented with them, and that such defensiveness might vitiate the possibility of obtaining a valid measure of whatever degree of habitual castration anxiety the subjects actually possessed. It happens, as we shall presently see, that later research (Bromberg, 1967) showed this concern to be unwarranted.

In any case, owing to its singularity, the CA's reliability could not be assessed, much less reported in the publication of the experiment. Yet its content, described below, seems to have represented such a straightforward and literal operational translation of the variable under investigation that differential responses to it may have been sufficiently prognostic to overcome the measure's inherent shortcomings with respect to reliability.

Ss were presented with the so-called castration anxiety card of the Blacky Test (Blum, 1949). This card shows a cartoon depicting two dogs; one dog is standing blindfolded, and a large knife appears about to descend on his outstretched tail; the other dog is an onlooker to this event. Ss were asked to look at this card and then rank three summary statements which purported to summarize the situation which was depicted. Actually, each statement was composed, on an *a priori* basis, to express a different degree of anxiety, ranging from slight to intense. Thus, Ss attached a score of 3 to the statement they felt best reflected the emotions of the onlooking dog, a score of 2 to the statement they felt fit the situation second best, and a score of 1 for the statement they felt fit the situation least . . . Below are the summaries used for the Blacky card (L represents the Low castration anxiety statement, M, medium castration anxiety and H, high castration anxiety).

L.   The Black Dog appears to be experiencing some tension as he watches the scene in front of him. However, the sight of the amputation has little emotional significance for him, and he views the situation in a fairly detached manner.

M.   The Black Dog is evidently quite frightened by what is going on in front of him. He is afraid that his tail might be next to be amputated. Nevertheless, he is able to bear up to the situation without becoming deeply upset or overwhelmed.

H.   The sight of the approaching amputation is a deeply upsetting experience for the Black Dog who is looking on. The possibility of losing his own tail and the thought of the pain involved over-whelm him with anxiety [Sarnoff & Corwin, 1959, p. 379].

The obtained distribution of rankings was decidedly skewed, with a majority of individuals showing greater preference for L than H. Of course, such findings might have veridically reflected the actual distribution of the variable among the individuals sampled. But the distribution could also have resulted from the intrusion of defensiveness, occasioned by the reluctance of some subjects to give responses that they felt to be in various ways threatening to their personal security. In short, even the single item may have put some subjects very much on guard. Yet such defensiveness would have militated against the possibility of finding empirical support for the hypothesis tested. For it would have led to the inclusion among those classified as Low in castration anxiety subjects who really were High in that variable, but loath to reveal it on the measure employed.

However, analysis of the effects of the interaction between habitual and experimentally aroused castration anxiety on the fear of death strongly substantiated the predictions that had been made. Thus, it would appear that, despite the rather obvious content of the Blacky measure, most subjects were willing to respond quite openly to it.

Indeed, these results were consistent with those found before and after this experiment in regard to the use of a format requiring highly restricted responses from subjects to prearranged alternatives. Seemingly, most subjects are quite willing to respond more or less as they actually feel, given the assurance of anonymity that introduces the measure — and, in fact, the entire study — to them. Moreover, since these experiments rest on comparisons between groups rather than between individuals, they seem capable of absorbing a considerable degree of misclassification due either to unreliability or defensiveness.

On the other hand, insofar as they are not replicated, the results obtained in these studies cannot be taken too seriously as having demonstrated the scientific usefulness of the measures of personality used in them. Thus, the success of the one-item measure of castration anxiety may have been quite illusory, reflecting a lucky occurrence of events, all of which conspired by chance — and despite the aforesaid methodological conditions of the personality measure — to produce confirmatory findings for the hypothesis under test.

It was scientifically reassuring to find, via Bromberg's (1967) subsequent experiment on the psychodynamics of phobia, that a much more refined use of the above procedure for measuring castration anxiety yielded results that not only supported but also extended the ones obtained with the original measure. Indeed, owing to the vastly improved methodology employed in all phases of his experiment, Bromberg was able to demonstrate that subjects differing in habitual castration anxiety did, in fact, experience like differentials in that anxiety when it was triggered through the arousal of heterosexual motives. Thus, whereas, in the first experiment, this differential in experienced anxiety was assumed to have occurred as a prelude to alterations in the fear of death, Bromberg took care to collect data that could show the extent to which that assumption was empirically supported.

Fortunately, in refining the measure of castration anxiety, Bromberg was able to draw on a good deal of psychometric work that Blum had been doing on open-ended responses to his test in the interim since the experiment by Sarnoff and Corwin (1959). Bromberg was also very mindful of the desirability of developing a measure with sufficient items to permit an assessment of its reliability. In this regard, he anticipated that a Likert-type rating procedure, whereby subjects could indicate varying degrees of agreement or disagreement with each item might, by expanding the range of possible responses, contribute to the reliability of the scale. Moreover, before using his tentatively selected items for classifying subjects on the personality variable they presumed to measure, he conducted: a) an item-analysis, aimed at eliminating items that failed to discriminate between high and low scorers on the total scale; and b) a study of the internal consistency of the discriminating items to determine the degree to which they represented a unitary variable.

Thus, using the previously described "castration" card of the Blacky Test, Bromberg presented subjects with nine items purporting to describe the illustrated situation. To counteract the establishment of a response set, one item was worded so that an affirmative reply meant a disavowal, rather than an avowal, of possession of the variable being measured. As matters turned out, two of the original items were ultimately dropped, owing to their failure to discriminate between high and low scorers on the overall scale. The seven items that were finally retained as the CC (castration conflict) measure had an internal consistency reliability of .73.

Of course, an even more reliable CC scale would have provided still more insurance against the erroneous classification of subjects. But Bromberg's work surely indicates that methodological improvement is not incompatible with theoretical appropriateness. Indeed, insofar as the content of his CC scale does conceptual justice to the Freudian variable involved, Bromberg's elimination of its methodological impurities gives that variable a much better chance to exert its theoretical impact than would otherwise have been the case.

The objective method of measuring Freudian variables of personality

This approach to measurement is characterized by both highly structured stimuli and highly restricted channels of response. Consequently, it maximizes the vulnerability of the instrument to detection by the subject of the variable being measured. This seeming vulnerability may well make a researcher wary about using such objective instruments as measures of Freudian variables of personality. And perhaps such wariness is often justified in respect to the clinical assessment of disturbed individuals, who may be as fearfully guarded about trusting the examiner as they are keen to express themselves openly in the interest of obtaining help. But the anonymous conditions of research, especially when voluntary subjects perceive themselves as responding to the same measure as many other people, is quite a different situation. Evidently, under such circumstances, when people are convinced that they have little to lose or to gain personally, they are inclined to respond to measures with sufficient candor to permit an investigator to work on the assumption that group differences among them do mark actual differences in whatever the test measures — and to the extent that it measures the variable reliably.

The Dynamic Personality Inventory

Thus far, the objective measure most widely used by my students has been the Dynamic Personality Inventory (DPI), constructed by Grygier (1961). The DPI is the modification of the Personal Preference Scale (PPS) devised by Krout and Tabin (1954), which was inspired by Abraham's (1927) articulation of the Freudian view that adult character is largely a reflection of how the individual managed to deal with the ontogenetic emergence of his libidinal drives.

Basically, the DPI has divided the PPS subtests into smaller scales, while adding a number of new ones. Now containing more than 30 scales, as compared with ten in the PPS, the DPI purports to offer measures of oral, anal, phallic and other traits pertinent to the operational definition of psychoanalytic variables.

"The items of the DPI 'include objects, concepts and activities which are associated with one or more relevant personality traits, tendencies and defence mechanisms.' (Grygier, 1961, p. 1). Each scale consists of a group of such items. The subject marks his reaction to the items in terms of like or dislike [Stringer, 1967, p. 187]."

Subjects can also leave an item unchecked, if they do not feel either way about it or are not sure about their feelings. However, the instructions to the DPI urge subjects not to "leave too many" blanks.

Thus, the DPI scales represent an attempt to operationalize a number of psychoanalytic concepts through verbalizations of their presumed manifestations. For example, the twelve items in the oral dependence (Od) scale include: 58. Asking others for guidance; and 41. Visiting relatives. By contrast, the eleven items in the anal hoarding (Ah) scale include: 163. Storing many old things in case you need them one day; and 241. Collecting coins. Presumably, a subject's pattern of preferences for such items reflects the extent to which he possesses the traits defined by the various scales.

Grygier has yet to publish separate reliabilities for the various scales of the DPI. However, Zimbardo (1969) is currently collecting such data in a normative study based on large samples of male and female college students. And the use of the DPI in hypothesis-testing studies of psychoanalytic concepts has only recently begun.

Thus far, the principal foci of research in which my students have used the DPI concern the oral and anal areas of psychosexual fixation. In measuring those variables, the investigators have sometimes administered the relevant scales separately, thus precluding the expenditure of time it takes subjects to go through the entire inventory. It appears that either method of administration — presenting the whole DPI or only its pertinent scales — can be equally effective for investigatory purposes.

Naturally, one is making a large assumption in considering that patterns of preference registered to such items represent enduring psychological residues of the pertinent stages of an individual's psychosexual development. And one could argue that these patterns merely represent culturally learned attitudes, which may have been acquired long after the periods of weaning and toilet-training were past. But with adults, it is clearly impossible to do anything but make retrospective and highly circumstantial inferences about the relevance of any of their ongoing behaviors to experiences of early childhood. Thus, the problem becomes one of deriving and testing predictions between presumptive measures of the characterological consequences of various kinds of psychosexual experiences and dependent variables whose hypothesized appearance, under theoretically indicated conditions of experimental arousal, should be affected in specific ways — if, in fact, the measures involved were valid indicants of the personality variables under study.

It happens that the subscales of the DPI, as indicated in the above examples, do contain items whose content is consistent with what psychoanalytic theorists and clinicians have proposed as indicative of subsequent characterological manifestations of various types of psychosexual fixation. Still, the ultimate scientific evaluation of the validity of these scales is contingent upon empirical test.

A. *Findings pertinent to the anal scales of the DPI.*   To date, the anal subscales of the DPI have tended to produce the most supportive results for predictions made from them. The previously described experiment by Bishop (1967) produced a striking instance of such findings, which derived from the use of the Ah scale *per se.* But while Bishop was content to rely upon that single scale, other investigators have been more cautious and have used all four of the anality scales in classifying subjects in terms of degree of fixation at that stage of psychosexual development. And insofar as more than one measure of a variable is available, it does appear prudent, in the absence of any convincing data concerning their relative merits, to include as many of them as is feasible, and to base the classification of subjects on their composite scores rather than on their performance on any one of the measures. On the other hand, such psychometric redundancy may induce a more accurate awareness of the variable measured, thereby evoking greater defensiveness among subjects. Moreover, insofar as the separate measures do not have high empirical intercorrelations, a researcher may have to sample a very large number of subjects before he can sort out enough correspondences among their several scores to obtain the differences in intensity that are theoretically required for a test of his hypothesis.

Using all four of the DPI anality scales, Gordon (1966, 1967) and Pettit (1969) obtained statistically significant correlations between composite scores on those measures and scores on a variety of judgmental and attitudinal measures postulated as concommitants of the "anal character" (Fenichel, 1945). Specifically, Gordon demonstrated and replicated differences in decision making that she had anticipated would differentiate clinicians of different levels of anality. "The results confirmed earlier findings that high anal clinicians have less confidence in their interpretations, make fewer specific predictions, and identify less pathology in patients than low-anal clinicians [1967, p. 477]." Pettit found, as predicted, a positive relationship between anality and a high estimation of the importance of time.

B. *Findings pertinent to the oral scales of the DPI.* The results my students have obtained on the DPI measures of orality are considerably more equivocal. Thus, Conrad (1968) found that, of six scales he assumed might reflect the "oral character" (Abraham, 1927), only three correlated significantly with obesity: Oral-sucking (0), Oral-biting (OA), and Oral-dependence (Od). Indeed, for the other three orality scales — Verbal aggression (Ov), Passivity: liking comfort and mild sensual impressions (Wp), and need for freedom and independence: a reaction formation against oral-dependence (Om) — "the mean scores for obese Ss were actually *lower* than mean scores for normals, although none of these differences was significant [Conrad, 1968, p. 67]." Yet it should be noted that there is certainly no theoretical basis for expecting obese individuals to exceed nonobese ones in reaction formation against oral-dependence.

Lish (1969), expanding the twelve-item Od scale (and thus increasing its internal consistency reliability from .65 to .75) with ten similar items, failed to demonstrate that oral dependency would interact with experimentally induced success and failure to yield theoretically predicted changes in depression and self-esteem.

Nor did Conrad's (1968) *post hoc* exploration of a combined index of three orality scales — O, OA, and Od — yield statistically significant differences in eating behavior, although subjects designated as "high-oral" showed a tendency to eat more than "low-oral" subjects in 11 of the 12 comparisons that were made between those two groups.

It remains for future research to determine more conclusively the construct validities of these and other component scales of the DPI. But the methodological viability of such objective measures of psycho-analytic variables has received at least some support through the studies cited.

Other objective measures of Freudian traits

Scales quite similar to the DPI have also been used to good advantage in empirical studies of Freudian concepts. Two examples of such scales, the first dealing with anality and the second with orality, are given below.

A.   *The Composite Anality Scale (Schlesinger, 1936).*   Pettit, in the reference noted above, found that a high estimation of the importance of time also correlated positively with a measure of anality, the Composite Anality Scale (CAS), which he constructed by selecting 66 items with the highest loadings on 12 clusters of items reported in a factor analytic study by Schlesinger (1963). Examples of the CAS are: "When I see a messy room I have a strong impulse to straighten it out"; and, "I use more toilet paper than is necessary." Incidentally, as one would expect, subjects agreeing with these kinds of items were also inclined to show a liking for the 41 anal items of the DPI, the obtained correlation between the CAS and the combined anality scales of the DPI being .57, which is statistically significant at the .001 level for a sample of 91 subjects (37 males and 54 females).

B.   *The Food Preference Inventory (Wolowitz, 1964).*   With respect to orality, other measures seem to have yielded results more supportive of psychoanalytic hypotheses than have the orality scales of the DPI. Thus, Goldman-Eisler (1956) found a relationship between her measure of oral traits, assessed by a questionnaire, and lateness of weaning, as reported in retrospect by her subjects' parents.

Subsequently, Wolowitz (1964) constructed a self-report inventory of food preferences (FPI), which was designed to distinguish between oral-passive versus oral-sadistic types of psychosexual fixations. Following the model established by Krout and Tabin (1954), Wolowitz assumed that distinctive patterns in choice of foods among adults reflected much earlier vicissitudes in psychosexual development. Thus, for example, affinity for soft and liquid foods would be theoretically consonant with an oral-passive fixation, whereas decided preference for hard and solid foods would be a theoretically expected consequence of an oral-sadistic fixation. And, in its actual format, the 40-item FPI is so designed as to represent oral-passive preferences with high scores and oral-sadistic preferences with low ones.

"Since alcoholics are persons theoretically presumed to be characterized by pathologically intense oral-passive cravings, it was decided they would constitute an excellent criterion group on whom the FPI might be validated [Wolowitz, 1964, p. 652]." And the group of alcoholics studied by Wolowitz did, indeed, demonstrate significantly higher FPI scores than did a nonalcoholic control group. Similarly, Wolowitz obtained positive correlations between the FPI and the Goldman-Eisler questionnaire, thus showing an empirical concurrence between the two presumptive indices of oral-passivity.

Some additional guidelines for the construction of pencil-and-paper measures of Freudian variables of personality

In discussing the nature and use of the objective-projective and objective methods of measuring Freudian variables, passing reference was made to considerations of validity and reliability. And, in dealing with measures of dependent variables, particular points related to the valid and reliable measurement of psychological states shall again be raised. For one can hardly describe any measure and its empirical application without encountering those two fundamental desiderata of all measures.

Naturally, a thorough and systematic coverage of the ways in which those basic attributes may be built into pencil-and-paper measures far surpasses the compass of this book. But since researchers interested in Freudian variables may well be obliged to design their own measures of them, it seems fitting to close this chapter with some psychometric precepts that may be helpful to keep in mind in those circumstances.

A. *Internal-consistency reliability and operational redundancy.* A researcher must expect any measure he develops to be faulty in respect to both its adequacy in reflecting the variable under study and its ability to yield a precise reflection of the subject's position on that variable. In order to minimize these inescapable faults, it is desirable to include more than a single item in a proposed measure of a variable. Since each item represents an attempt on the researcher's part to make manifest the psychological properties of the same personality variable, and since the variable's theoretical definition cannot be assuredly reflected in any given phrasing or depiction, an investigator should present a number of conceived operational instances of the variable in any effort to measure it.

Theoretically, each of these proposed manifestations is formulated and offered as revealing, to the same extent, the same underlying variable. The number of items that can be developed to measure any particular variable chiefly depend upon the ingenuity of the researcher and the need to avoid inducing such concommitants of excessive re- dundancy as boredom, irritation, and defensiveness.

The reliability of a measure is not only contingent upon the theoretical pertinence of its component items, but also upon its length. Hence, to minimize error of measurement *per se,* a researcher needs to generate at least enough items to produce a scale whose internal- consistency reliability is sufficiently high to assure him that he can use the measure for predictive purposes without having to be overly concerned that its degree of unreliability could be plausibly offered as an alternative explanation for the possible failure of his theoretically derived hypotheses.

In regard to this last and extremely important point, researchers tend to vary in the degree of reliability that they demand of their measures of personality prior to using them in tests of Freudian hypotheses. If one is dealing with extremes taken from opposite ends of a distribution obtained by administering a measure to a very large population, one may be willing to rely on a less reliable scale than one might in classifying subjects from a much smaller population. If a researcher wishes to use the entire sample, and not merely extreme scores on a scale, he is certainly well advised to employ measures of the highest possible reliability.

To date, most experimental tests of Freudian hypotheses have tended to employ rather rough classifications of subjects on measures of personality; for example, by dividing them at the median or at upper and lower quartiles into two groups — High versus Low. But insofar as the personality variables involved are conceptually regarded as continua, researchers in this area have the best of theoretical incentives for developing measures of them that are so reliable as to facilitate and to justify the application of statistical analyses, such as the multiple regression analysis proposed by Cohen (1968), that trace the impact of the variable throughout its entire distribution.

B. *Factor analysis as a statistical aid to the operational delineation of variables of personality.*   To be sure, factor analysis offers no magical solution to the basic problem of determining the relationship between a measure and the concept it is meant to operationalize. Ultimately, that relationship is most compellingly determined by predictions from the measure to other observable phenomena, which are theoretically posited as effects of the variable defined by the measure. However, in the initial selection of items, a factor analysis can provide some empirical help in indicating the extent to which items conceived as indicants of the same underlying variable do, in fact, cluster together in a common factor. Insofar as a factor analysis produces clusters that are coordinate with a researcher's *a priori* operational definitions, it suggests that he is empirically circumscribing the pertinent concepts in a manner consistent with his theoretical definition of their discrete properties. Yet since exact correspondences are very unlikely to occur no matter how a researcher may choose to rotate his correlational matrix, the results of a factor analysis must necessarily be subjectively evaluated, with the investigator intellectually comparing a set of factors produced against his concept of the variable they appear to define. Thus, if a factor happens to contain some items not in his original conception of it, he may, in the fresh empirical context, perceive a formerly ignored theoretical correspondence between them and the items with which they are clustered; and he may, therefore, decide to include them in his final scale. Conversely, if a factor excludes items he had first conceived as indicants of the same variable, he may read, in their grouping with quite differently conceptualized items, a different theoretical meaning for them; and he may, consequently, exclude them from his final selection.

Thus, the data of a factor analysis merely offer guides, hints, and clues to a researcher, whose ultimate decisions about those data must necessarily rest upon his judgment about their relevance to the concept he wishes to measure. But a factor analysis can perform the important function of reducing masses of data to more manageable clusters, against which a researcher can apply the intellectual test of theoretical relevance.

C. *Conceptual homogenity and the composition of items.*   Regarding the initial articulation of items intended for inclusion in a unidimensional scale, a researcher should focus, insofar as words permit it, his written statements (stimuli) solely on the dimension to be measured. He would thus spare subjects the problem of being uncertain about the part of a multidimensional sentence to which they are being asked to register a reaction. At the same time, such unconfounded items would spare the researcher the quandary of being unable to show logically that the responses of subjects do indeed refer to the dimension he sought to measure. Finally, it is also advisable to write items of at least rough comparability in length and clarity, thus eliminating such formalistic factors as possible confounding determinants of responses to the measure.

D. *Obtaining the reactions of colleagues and potential subjects to the initially composed items.*   Having composed an apparently promising set of items, a researcher can benefit from the reactions of professional colleagues to them, particularly from those who have had extensive clinical or investigatory experience with the behavioral phenomena relevant to the variable proposed for measurement. Assuming that some items are then discarded or modified in the light of the reactions obtained, the remainder may profitably be administered, for further refinement, to a sample of subjects similar to those with whom the final scale will ultimately be used. Moreover, by interviewing colleagues and a sample of potential subjects carefully, a researcher can often uncover important leads toward improving the wording of items or on removing ambiguities in wording that he may have previously failed to notice. In the same way, a researcher can obtain help in clarifying the tentatively chosen instructions and the format of responses through which subjects are requested to respond to the measuring stimuli.

The potential value of such pilot work is strikingly clear the moment a researcher considers the possibility of applying a measure developed with subjects from one culture to subjects from a different culture. Indeed, even with measures as simply worded as the Test

Anxiety Scale and the General Anxiety Scale (Sarason, Davidson, Lighthall, Waite, & Ruebush, 1960), it was found necessary to hire a British teacher to "translate" some of the items from "American" English to "English" English before they could be properly used with children in London (Sarnoff, Lighthall, Waite, Davidson & Sarason, 1958). Similar discrepancies in the connotations of words may often prevail within the same society among people of different socio-economic classes and ethnic groups. And failure to comprehend a measure as it is intended to be understood can obviously introduce all manner of confounding factors in the resulting scores. It is, therefore, important to assure that subjects involved in a formal test of hypotheses based on a particular measure of personality are likely to interpret its meanings in the same way as they were understood by subjects from whose responses the instrument was refined.

Summary of methodological desiderata in the development of pencil-and-paper measures of personality

Having included many points about the development of pencil-and-paper measures within the fabric of the preceding exposition, it seems worthwhile to summarize them in a succinct list. In presenting this list, an attempt is made to maintain a temporal sequence of the steps a researcher might best follow from the beginning to the end of his work in constructing a measure.

1. The initial articulation of items in terms of theoretical aptness.
2. The wording of items in such a way as to maximize their comprehensibility and unidimensionality, while minimizing the possibility of their generating a response set.
3. The composition of a sufficient number of items to enhance the ultimate reliability of the measure, while requiring minimal time and effort for their administration.
4. The composition of clear instructions concerning the way in which subjects are asked to respond to the items.
5. The checking of items and instructions with colleagues and a sample of potential subjects.
6. The formal administration of the tentatively selected items

to a large enough population to permit a factor analysis.

7. Factor analysis to determine the extent to which the *a priori* theoretical formulation of the tentatively selected items actually circumscribes an empirically common cluster.

8. The item-analysis of the factor-analyzed items, eliminating those that fail to discriminate between subjects at opposing ends of the distribution on the total scale — or that fail to correlate significantly with the aggregate score.

9. Assessment of the internal consistency reliability of the purified items, yielding an estimate of the unitary character of the scale with respect to whatever dimension it purports to measure.

10. The ordering of items in the final measure in a manner designed to offset the emergence of a response set and to minimize awareness by subjects of the variable actually defined by the measure.

Toward the Ethical Manipulation of Independent Variables

The quantitative variations required to test Freudian hypotheses concerning the interactive effects of presumably habitual and presumably transient independent variables are operationally defined through temporally coordinated procedures of measurement and manipulation. First, as already seen, quantitative variation in a postulated trait of personality is *measured* by a standardized scale, within which subjects register their differential responses to a fixed set of theoretically relevant stimuli — or which can afterward be imposed on their responses. Then, as shall be seen, quantitative variation in a relevant state of motivation or cognition is transiently *manipulated* by altering those aspects of an experimental situation that are thought, on *a priori* theoretical grounds, to modulate the intensity with which that state is experienced by subjects.

However, just as the process of psychological measurement is very different from the use of a chemical pipette, so psychological manipulation is not equivalent to the infusion of graded quantities of a particular substance into an inanimate receptable. Of course, in psychopharmacological research, the chemical analogy is somewhat more apt, insofar as alterations in bodily functioning are induced by infusing varying amounts of the same drug into the bloodstreams of people assigned to different experimental groups. But Freudian theory does not posit the use of specific drugs to create variations in independent variables that are pertinent to its concepts of psychological functioning. Moreover, with human beings, even the most somatically oriented of pharmacological investigators now feels obliged to establish experimental control over such psychological variables as suggestion, which, rather than the physical properties of the chemicals involved, might be offered, *post hoc*, as plausible alternative explanations of the observed effects of the administration of the drugs (Russell, R., 1964).

*Ethics and the scientific use of manipulation
in human psychology*

Reich (1949), an early follower of Freud, became an advocate of massage and other forms of direct physical contact between psychotherapist and patient, claiming that a literal "laying on of the hands" was necessary to dissolve the cumulative psychosomatic "armor" built up by long years of ego-defensiveness. And Freud (1949e) himself, while never resorting to such bodily handling, did consider that it might be helpful to some of his patients if it could be arranged for them to experience heterosexual intercourse. Yet he rejected the possibility of actually prescribing such experiences for those patients; and his restraint was based on ethical, rather than on theoretical, considerations.

In much the same way, a researcher must often rest his choice of experimental manipulations on his moral precepts rather than on what might be most effective in creating the psychological states stipulated by his hypotheses. For example, in planning their experiment on castration anxiety and the fear of death (Sarnoff & Corwin, 1959), the researchers had the hypothetical option of creating quantitative variations in the dimension of heterosexual motivation by having different groups of subjects view living nudes and fashion models rather than pictures of these. It might even have been possible to vary the degree of tactile contact required between subjects and live women in those differing conditions of nudity and dress. Thus, the experimental rationale about esthetic judgment could have been extended to include such requirements, saying, with perfectly impeccable logic, that the sense of touch as well as that of sight is often involved in the appreciation of an object's beauty.

Had that tactic been employed, it might have yielded yet more striking results than those that were obtained. And actual contact between subjects and women "in the flesh" would certainly have been in keeping with the kind of confrontation likely to exacerbate whatever habitual levels of castration anxiety the subjects possessed. However, the experimenters dismissed the prospect of using this "live" method of inducing variations in heterosexual arousal because it portended a number of morally unacceptable human consequences: the theoretically indicated tactile contact between the male subjects and the living female "stimuli" might have provoked excruciating anxiety and embarrassment among some of the participants, and noxious reactions of such intensity, occurring in full view of the experimenters, might have exerted permanently negative effects on the self-confidence of those who experienced them. It was to avoid these potentially destructive effects on the quality of many human lives that we chose a symbolic rather than a direct form of heterosexual arousal.

In explaining the ethical considerations involved in choosing manipulations for the above experiment, the moral relativity inherent in such decisions has been implicitly illustrated. For it is not as though the researchers dropped their original idea of doing the experiment. On the contrary, they developed what *they felt* was an ethically justifiable manipulation of heterosexuality, although they recognized that other experimenters might feel differently about it.

Manipulation as experimental necessity and moral dilemma

Since it is no more possible to conduct human psychological experiments without manipulation than it is to do them without making use of deception, an experimenter must be willing to take upon himself the responsibility for deciding how much of an ethical risk he is prepared to incur in return for a given quantum of potential scientific knowledge. Viewed from the standpoint of prospective subjects, the other side of this moral question is: how much of their existing mental well-being are people ready to upset, albeit temporally, in order to participate in the acquisition of the most conclusive knowledge that human beings are able to obtain about their behavior and experience?

Replies to this hypothetical query would, of course, vary greatly among people, depending upon the particular systems of value they uphold. But manipulation is *the* defining attribute of the experimental method of research. Hence, insofar as men wish to put the logical powers of experimentation to the service of their own species, they must permit themselves to be manipulated by their scientific fellows. Indeed, in order to support the experimental approach to knowledge about themselves, men are, at they very least, obliged first to tolerate insult, through deception; and, then, the possibility of a passing emo-

tional injury, through psychological manipulation. This seems to be
asking a great deal of human toleration. But men are, in truth, asking
it of themselves. For experimentation in human psychology could have
neither emerged nor flourished if men had not resolved to know
themselves as objectively as they possibly could.

When psychological experimentation was in its infancy, these
ethical implications and social ramifications of its methodology may
not have been apparent to many people. Nor, to this day, does any
firm consensus about the uses of manipulation in psychological research
exist among either scientists or the general public. But as researchers
and laymen alike become more knowledgeable about the effects of
psychological manipulation, they cannot plead ignorance as a way
of shunting off responsibility for its usage. On the contrary everyone
is — and really always was — equally implicated by any practice put
forward in the name of mankind's common good.

In the present circumstances, a great latitude of freedom is implicitly granted by the general public to experimenters. And, while
such researchers do differ widely in the degree of ethical concern
they show in their choice of inductions, it appears that the prevailing
range of manipulations has not yet exceeded the public's level of
acceptance. At any rate, there are no discernible mass movements to
banish experimental research with human beings.

But with or without codified precepts and regulations, an experimenter carrying forward a freely selected investigatory problem must
inevitably choose among types of manipulation which may differ
markedly in the amount of anguish that they may generate among
subjects. In a word, he has to rely upon his own ethical sensibilities
in finally making these choices.

Still, as Sartre (1947) has justly noted, every action a man performs
is an implicit moral model for all men. So be it. And if other scientists
choose to follow the examples here represented as morally acceptable
techniques of manipulation, they will necessarily be proclaiming their
own ethical positions.

Because each new inspiration for an experiment may pose, in the
contemplation of its manipulations, new ethical conflicts, it is impossible for anyone to lay down a detailed list of prohibitions covering
all imaginable methodological contingencies. Nor is it possible to
anticipate everything that may be learned about the impact of ma-

nipulations whose negative effects are generally considered readily reversible. Indeed, such manipulations may have quite persistent effects on some subjects, despite very conscientious postexperimental attempts on the part of researchers to inform all participants about how and why they had been both deceived and manipulated (Walster, Berscheid, Abrahams, & Aronson, 1967). Consequently, the most realistic and honest approach to the formulation of an ethic of scientific research would seem to require the enunciation of general stipulations from which a researcher can exercise moral judgment as each occasion for it arises. Thus oriented, he has a conceptual basis for using or rejecting this or that or the other manipulation, each decision illustrating the particular lengths to which he will go in matching the chances of harming others against the chances of acquiring for everyone a reliable increment in the scientific knowledge of human psychology.

Experimental manipulation and the values of realization

Yet for investigators genuinely committed to the values of realization (Sarnoff, 1966), these lengths obviously cannot be very great. Indeed, such an investigator cannot envision any manipulation without being immediately torn by inner conflict. On the one hand, experimental investigations promise a desirable furtherance of intellectual values as ends in themselves. In furthering those ends, the experimenter may produce knowledge that, in its constructive application, may improve various aspects of individual and social life, thus upholding humanitarian values. Moreover, in conceptualizing and conducting his study, as well as in communicating to others, the researcher has a chance to gratify his esthetic values, and, in reading his publications, others are able to share the esthetic qualities of his experience. In all those ways, experimental manipulations can be an integral part of a process of fulfilling values that are consistent with man's finest ethical precepts. On the other hand, the knowing infliction of any amount of distress on fellow human beings is no more ethically justifiable than is the deliberate use of deception. For to upset someone in such a manner is to violate one's humanitarian values.

Of course, a researcher can use other empirical techniques for investigating phenomena whose manipulation would be ethically unacceptable. But *any* systematic gathering of psychological data may have an upsetting impact on some of the people directly observed, be it via personality measures, open-ended interviews, or behavioral ratings. Indeed, a nonexperimental study may even disturb people in social contact with its own subjects, as is illustrated by the acute parental anxiety that Himmelweit, Oppenheim, and Vince (1958) unexpectedly engendered while doing a seemingly innocuous survey of childrens' involvement in the watching of television. Thus, the correlational method of research offers the experimenter no foolproof technical solution to his moral dilemma. In fact, the only way a researcher can be sure of avoiding every possible inhumane by-product of scientific investigation is to give it up completely.

The manipulative aspects of psychoanalytic psychotherapy

It may also be worth remarking that the practice of Freudian therapy offers no protective haven for the psychoanalytically oriented experimenter who may seek to shed the moral burden arising from his scientific research. On the contrary, such practice requires, in its operational strategy, that the therapist should manipulate the patient in accordance with the psychological assumptions of psychoanalytic theory. For example, the therapist typically withholds an interpretation of some aspect of the patient's behavior until he feels its articulation will exert the strongest possible emotional impact on the patient.

The therapist thus manipulates all his patients — not merely for a few moments but, frequently, for daily hour after daily hour over years of time. Nor are these manipulations uniformly pleasant in their psychological effects. Rather, their immediate impact is likely to be fraught with anxiety and tension.

Quite naturally, the therapist is inclined to reason that these emotional upsets are inevitable experiences, which the patient must endure in order ultimately to attain a more genuine freedom from distress than he ever had before beginning psychotherapy. But the therapist neither possesses nor can give the assurance that the patient's eventual psychological well-being will amply compensate for the emotional travails he encounters in his therapy. Thus, Lindner (1955) reported that his entire psychotherapeutic practice consisted of patients who had been psychoanalyzed and who had considered themselves — and had been so regarded by their psychoanalysts — as having been so solidly improved as to warrant a termination of the analysis. Nor can any therapist guarantee that every one of his patients will be in better psychological condition after therapy than he was before it began. Indeed, as indicated by Bergin's (1966) previously cited review of studies on the effects of psychotherapy, it appears that the conditions of at least some patients are worsened rather than bettered by psychotherapy.

Unquestionably, although the psychotherapist may be thoroughly humane in his remedial intentions, taking the greatest possible care to minimize the negative effects of his therapeutic manipulations, his attempts to induce desirable changes in the overt behavior and private experience of his patients may sometimes, it would appear, only add to their chronic misery. Hence, for the psychotherapist, no less than for the psychological scientist, humane intentions do not necessarily produce *ipso facto* humane results. Techniques of psychological manipulation, because they are utilized in psychotherapy rather than in exclusively scientific investigation, do not thereby acquire a magical immunity from the capacity to harm those exposed to them. If anything, this capacity becomes all the more potentially destructive the more it is obscured from public view and debate by organized and, indeed, legalized trappings that proclaim an almost unquestionable moral probity. And the gratuitous surgical damage that can be both advocated and inflicted by medical doctors, whose work is institutionally stamped with ethical virtue, has recently been illustrated by Comfort (1968a), himself a physician.

The limits of manipulation advocated by this book

Thus, any presumptively humane individual whose work involves the manipulation of other people is necessarily confronted with the moral challenge of assuring himself that the effects of his manipulations do not undermine the values they are intended to fulfill; that, in short, his means are consonant with his ends. But insofar as he continues doing scientific research in psychology, a humane investigator automatically affirms his belief that, whatever distress he is inflicting on others, his work in sum does more good than ill in the world, and that it contributes more to than it detracts from the values of realization. Yet this belief can easily become a smug, if not a deluded, pretension, permitting the researcher to perpetrate grosser and grosser acts of inhumanity upon living persons in the here and now while justifying his behavior in the name of ultimate benefit to a posterity of unborn men. Nor can one ever be certain that even an apparently uplifting enlightenment of some recess of the human mind will not be misused, eventually, as part of someone else's effort to keep men in dark subjugation.

For my part, I believe that, since the potential benefits of the kind of knowledge science can provide appear, on balance, to outweigh those of total scientific ignorance, men should continue doing scientific research in psychology rather than abandon that activity. I hasten to add, however, that I feel it is vitally important, for humanitarian reasons, to disavow whatever Faustian aspirations may still be circulating among psychological scientists, for too uncritical an emphasis on scientific knowledge as the *only* worthwhile aim of one's life can easily lead to ruthlessness, turning intellectual values into goading agonies that destroy the humanitarian values with which they should rightly be fused, or that use the powers of the intellect merely as a means of pursing self-aggrandizement.

Instead, it would seem more humanely consistent, taking all the values of realization simultaneously into consideration, for experimenters in human psychology to accept a self-imposed and very marked limitation on the amount of scientific knowledge they will strive to obtain through the use of their method of investigation. Such an acceptance means that one is quite content to reject the use of any form of manipulation whose noxious effects he has some basis for assuming may be either extraordinarily painful during the experimental session or enduringly resistant to his post-experiment attempts to restore the psychological and physical *status quo ante* among his subjects. Thus, a humane experimenter would willingly restrict himself to the use of manipulations that satisfy both of these criteria; rather than exceed those restrictions, he would be prepared to use less conclusive, non-experimental methods of inquiry in order to study psychological phenomena whose systematic manipulation might unequivocally and irreparably violate the very values for which he does scientific research.

Even in the most decent society of realization, manipulation would continue, like deception, to be an integral and inescapable feature of experimental research in human psychology. And insofar as people in such a society wished to gain the knowledge of themselves that experimentation can uniquely provide, they would be as willing to tolerate the humane use of scientific manipulation as they would that of scientific deception. And, as in the case of deception, they would expect experimenters, no less than experimenters would expect themselves, to use manipulation in a truly humane way.

Pending the emergence of such a society, it is morally incumbent upon humane experimenters openly and publicly to assure fellow members of the present society of aggrandizement of their resolve to confine their research to manipulative procedures that can, at least, meet the forgoing ethical safeguards. Given this assurance, potential subjects would be able to volunteer with genuine good will in psychological experiments, albeit they would not be informed in advance about the specific content of the manipulations to which they had agreed to expose themselves.

Techniques of symbolic communication as manipulations consonant with a humane approach to scientific psychology

Applying these ethical restrictions to my own experimental research, I have rejected the possibility of testing hypotheses whose manipulated independent variables would necessitate the actual infliction of physical pain — via, for example, electric shock. Nor have I sponsored experiments by students who wished to test such hypotheses. On the other hand, I have both conducted and sponsored experiments involving the psychological manipulation of such emotionally disquieting variables as fear, anxiety, and guilt through techniques of *symbolic communication*, and, in these experiments, systematic attempts have been made to undo their temporarily upsetting effects through postexperimental discussions with the subjects who participated in them.

Thus, as suggested in Chapter 5, the manipulations I have found compatible with a humane view of scientific psychology are those that are essentially theatrical in nature; that is, those involving the staging of an interpersonal confrontation between subjects and whatever settings, persons, sights, sounds, gestures, postures, and verbalizations an experimenter feels will best operationalize the variations in motivational or cognitive states stipulated by the theoretical properties of the particular independent variables whose effects he is interested in studying. Judging from publications in the current empirical literature, this theatrical approach also appears to be the one most widely used by other psychological investigators in their experimental manipulations of human subjects.

Yet the terms "manipulation" or "induction" scarcely seem adequate to convey the actual processes of communicative influence that are involved in this means of creating variations in psychological variables. For example, in the previously cited experiment on castration anxiety and the fear of death (Sarnoff & Corwin, 1959), the theoretically required variations in heterosexual arousal were attained by showing different groups of subjects different photographs, and by placing the subjects into more than fleeting visual contact with the pictures through asking them to write out their esthetic reactions to each one, the entire study having previously been rationalized as "an investigation of some of the psychological factors which influence the appreciation of art [p. 378]."

In contrast, because he wished to create variations in socially experienced rejection, Conrad's (1968) experimental manipulations involved a much more complicated piece of staging. First, having told an assembled group of subjects that part of his study dealt with "how, and on what bases, people formed friendships [p. 49]," Conrad asked each subject in turn to go to the front of the room and give a brief speech about his "personality." Upon the completion of his speech, each subject was rated by the rest of the group on a scale of "likeableness." Collecting all these ratings, Conrad pretended to tabulate them, after which he returned to each subject a sheet of false information, which he had prearranged, giving some subjects the impression of being definitely liked by the majority, some as being definitely disliked by the majority, and some as being either definitely liked or definitely disliked by equal numbers of their peers.

Thus, in both experimental situations just described, subjects were asked to carry out procedures that had been presented to them as having a definite and reasonable scientific purpose, although it was not the one truly under study by the researchers. Yet in the very act of doing that which, in the overall context of their participation in the research, seemed eminently rational and credible to them, the subjects were putting themselves into the psychological states required by the experimenters' hypotheses. In effect, having set the stage and provided the materials for them, the experimenters permitted the subjects to play the roles necessary for experiencing, within themselves, the particular psychological states that defined the relevant independent variables. Hence, as was pointed out in the discussion of deception, the subjects inadvertently became actors, without knowing it, unwittingly performing a play on their own emotions within the scope of the undisclosed purpose of the total drama of the experiment.

The subjects' self-involvement in looking, listening, writing, and speaking were central features of what, for want of better words, have been called "manipulations" or "inductions," although it should be clear from the foregoing examples that the passive connotations of these words are quite misleading. For the subjects are not mere lumps of clay that are molded by the movements of the experimenter's hands, nor are they lengths of electric wire through which current is induced at the flick of an experimenter's finger. Instead, they are continually active participants in a very special scientific theater. And unless subjects are willing to play the roles into which they are cast, an experimenter's "manipulations" are bound to fail.

It is precisely the engagement of this willingness and its channelization into the specific roles theoretically designated as essential to the emergence of different levels of the relevant independent variable that constitutes the theatrical art of the scientist who uses this type of experimental manipulation. But since these manipulations confront subjects with fluid and complicated configurations of stimuli, they cannot help but involve more of the subject's psychological functioning than the single dimension they are specifically intended to vary. Yet for obvious scientific reasons, particular manipulations must be empirically shown to have accomplished their task of inducing those quantitative differentials in the target variable that are needed for a theoretically appropriate test of the hypothesis under study. If an experimenter can demonstrate that his manipulations have produced those required variations, he need not be overly concerned about whatever nuances of additional evocation they may have stirred among his subjects. For given the extraordinary reactivity of people as well as their individual differences in experience, these surplus meanings cannot be entirely precluded, however one may try to purify the stimulus properties of an experimental manipulation. Indeed, even highly explicit measuring stimuli are only relatively free of ambiguity, being open to interpretations that may differ from those attributable to the variable they were operationally meant to define.

In any event, insofar as culturally conditioned human beings are concerned, it is hardly possible to conceive effective and plausible ways of arousing psychoanalytically relevant motives, such as heterosexual ones, without establishing a social situation in which the manipulation can be introduced in a highly rationalized manner. And such an introduction contains, in itself, a host of stimuli to which subjects can react in addition to responding to the subsequently presented sexual stimuli *per se.*

However, to fulfill the deductive logic of his own research, an experimenter would strive to rid his manipulations of formal or substantive features that may plausibly be advanced as alternative explanations of their theoretically postulated effects, or that may be a source of failure to create the conditions required for an adequate test of his hypothesis. Thus, having decided to work within the ethical boundaries given above, and having decided to use theatrical types of manipulation, a researcher would wish to employ manipulations that are of the greatest possible theoretical aptness to the variables whose operational presence within the subjects they are meant to insure. And, if such a manipulation does not exist for an independent variable of interest to a researcher, he is obviously required to develop one before he can mount an experiment involving that variable.

The current dearth of pertinent information regarding the construction of humane experimental manipulations

In regard to the contrivance of quantitative variations in the dimensions aimed at by humane experimental manipulations, the field of human psychology suffers from a dearth of relevant empirical suggestions. Specifically, what it not yet available is a compendium of data gathered from carefully conducted parametric studies that were undertaken to plot the intensity and duration of the kinds of manipulations that could be usefully applied to ethically acceptable experimental tests of Freudian hypotheses.

True, some helpful information has been gradually accumulating as a by-product of experiments that have been conducted on such hypotheses. But it is thereby limited to the variables those experiments happened to concern. And, even for those variables, the manipulations have generally sought to do no more than to create two levels of intensity, usually demonstrated as differing from each other to a degree that is conventionally regarded as statistically significant. Yet both the levels involved might actually fall toward one end or the other of the range of intensity that might be induced by a sample of manipulations designed to map it. Likewise, for the manipulations currently designated as "high" and "low" in inductive intensity, there exist no comprehensive body of empirical — much less replicated — data about the duration of time over which various levels of arousal will maintain their respective strengths. Such information as we do have is spotty and thin, although it comes primarily from experiments that were designed, fortunately, to include independent empirical checks on the effectiveness of whatever manipulations they happen to employ. And all that can usually be most reliably reported about the temporal particularities of these manipulations is that their intended differences in intensity of arousal lasted long enough to be veridically acknowledged by subjects in the contrasting experimental groups.

Certainly, Freudian theory offers no clear theoretical specifications for the operational establishment of such parameters. Thus, in formulating manipulations of independent variables relevant to experimental tests of psychoanalytic hypotheses, a researcher must frequently work without practical help from either the theoretical or the experimental literature. In such instances, he is obliged to decide, mainly on the *a priori* grounds of his own sensibility, in what ways a theoretically required manipulation may be operationally varied to induce larger and smaller amounts of a given independent variable.

A later chapter will consider how it is possible to measure the effects that these manipulations exert upon an experiment's dependent variables. It should be apparent that such measurement involves, in essence, an actual test of the experimenter's theoretically derived hypothesis. But, well before he submits his hypothesis to its formal test, a sensible experimenter would try to satisfy himself that he is bringing to it feasible manipulative procedures, which have been shown to induce the levels of intensity of the manipulated independent variable that he predicts will exert like differences in the dependent variable, and which, in the case of an interactive design, will provide a theoretically appropriate basis for studying the interaction between the hypothetically stipulated levels of the manipulated and the measured independent variables.

Whether or not the differential strengths of the manipulated independent variables maintain their relative intensities long enough to exert their predicted main or interactive effects on the *dependent* variables is, as implied, presently unknowable short of actually running the formal experiment. Thus, the most one can do at the pilot stage is to make those manipulations as strongly differential as he feels is necessary for their impact to be detectable by the measures of the dependent variables which, in the experiment proper, may be variously separated from the onset of the manipulations in both time and whatever intervening activities are required for the best administration of those measures.

From a purely abstract scientific standpoint, the prevailing ambiguity about the essential parameters of these techniques of manipulation is undoubtedly deplorable. Yet progress toward greater certainty will not be made simply by decrying this state of affairs. Nor, surely, can it be of help for potentially interested experimenters to throw up their hands in despair and leave this area of research for one, such as the study of instrumental learning among albino rats, where information about the behavioral consequences of gradations in the relevant manipulated variables is both more abundant and much easier to acquire. Rather, as with so many other ambiguities that now surround experimental work in this theoretical realm, one can decide that the inherent interest of research on Freudian concepts is well worth the price — in terms of time, effort, and ingenuity — one has to pay in developing a viable methodology for it. In regard to the development of experimental manipulations, a researcher must be prepared for many false starts and pilot studies. Yet he may also find that the challenge of creating workable manipulations is an endlessly fascinating one, involving as it does not only a translation of conceptual subtleties into interpersonal relations but also an expression of dramatic skill.

The systematic development of humane experimental manipulations

As is the case for the construction of instruments to measure independent variables, the proper development of manipulations of independent variables usually demands a considerable amount of exploratory effort. Having made many tentative decisions about the structure and ingredients of the drama he hopes will arouse the required psychological state, a researcher would be wise to avail himself of several preliminary means of assessing the impact of his procedural judgments on others. For it is other people who comprise the social reality his methodological calculations are ultimately intended to affect in accordance with his preconceived theoretical assumptions.

First of all, an experimenter can solicit the reactions of professional colleagues who have clinical and scientific experience with phenomena related to the variable he is seeking to manipulate. In addition to describing verbally the procedure he has in mind — a process that may yield some helpful advice in its own right — a researcher can ask colleagues to attend "dress rehearsals" of his proposed manipulations. In these sessions, the consultants may discern unnecessary and awkward aspects that the experimenter had overlooked. Indeed, they may find particulars of wording or pacing that seem, to them, to be having emotional effects directly contrary to those hoped for by the experimenter. And, of course, colleagues attending such "previews" can give the experimenter a feeling for the degree of success he may have achieved in creating situations that induce different amounts of the variable to be investigated.

This last point is particularly crucial, since the logic of the subsequent experiment depends largely on the actual establishment of those quantitative differentials among subjects in the various experimental conditions. Yet it is not sufficient to let the determination of such an important matter rest entirely upon the impressions of a few professional colleagues. On the contrary, realizing that his colleagues are likely to differ considerably in outlook from the subjects with whom the manipulations will be used when his hypothesis is formally tested, the experimenter will wish to try out the manipulations with a group of subjects similar to those that will ultimately participate in the experiment proper.

In this phase of pilot study, the experimenter can find out, first of all, whether the proposed levels of manipulation do yield significant differences between the groups of subjects to which they are applied; for example, whether the designated "high" level of arousal of a particular motive does, in fact, affect the subjects exposed to it more intensely than does the "low" level of arousal, which is applied to a different group of subjects. Moreover, the measure of these differentials can be similar or identical to the one that is subsequently used in the formal experiment as an independent check on the manipulations. And it should be noted, incidentally, that it is usually quite feasible to devote an exploratory study solely to the objective of obtaining a preliminary assessment of the effectiveness of the manipulations, although it may be possible to use the same occasion to obtain data germane to the construction of personality measures and to the refinement of other procedures that will be employed in the experiment. Finally, the pilot subjects, who are representative of the future experimental sample, can also be interviewed, like the experimenter's colleagues, to obtain their suggestions for improving the flow and force of the manipulations; in short, for producing a yet more polished and convincing manipulative performance.

The scientific advantages of flexibility of outlook in developing techniques of manipulation

Regarding the development of his manipulations, an experimenter certainly should not feel confined to the props, manners, and style of the classical theater. Thus, insofar as their use can spare him time and energy, while conveying appropriate and effective psychological impact, modern devices of communication, previously mentioned, merit incorporation into an experimenter's manipulative dramas.

But fascination with electronic and other gadgets can easily become a scientifically mistaken end in its own right, leading some experimenters to strive to employ them even when more conventional theatrical approaches may be more theoretically apt for creating quantitative differentials in a given independent variable. Therefore, as is true of decisions regarding research design and the measurement of independent variables, an attitude of methodological flexibility can best serve the deductive objective of a humane experimental scientist. For this goal requires the contrivance of the most theoretically appropriate, methodologically sound, and ethically acceptable test that he can give to a particular hypothesis. And it is within the scope of these three basic stipulations that he is well advised to be as free as possible from theoretically unwarranted and intellectually stereotyped commitments to one manipulatory prop or another. Certainly, the needed advances in this phase of methodology can be most readily furthered by imaginative experimenters who, appreciating the human communality of art and science, are able to use the esthetics of drama to solve the scientific problems of a humane psychology.

Imagination as a Humane Medium of Experimental Manipulation

Thus far, the basic assumption underlying the use of theatrical forms of experimental manipulation has been taken for granted: the ability of socialized human beings to be psychologically affected by symbolic representations of persons, objects, and experiences. Yet it is entirely *because* they can think abstractly, feel vicariously, and imagine prospectively that human subjects can be induced to attain, through involvement in scientifically planned dramas of manipulation, the motivational or cognitive states relevant to the experimental investigation of Freudian concepts.

These symbolic skills of human beings make it possible for the theoretically crucial contents of manipulations to exert their desired psychological impact, no matter by what sensory medium or combination of media those contents may be communicated. Thus, the motivationally arousing power of nudes depends upon a subject's ability to perceive them not as mere blotches of black and white but, rather, as vividly incarnate and tantalizing objects of his sexual desire; and it is precisely through their imaginative abilities that subjects are able to galvanize symbols presented to them into the psychological states an experimenter seek to establish and to vary.

Accordingly, by exercising his own imagination, an experimenter may conceive ways of powerfully enlisting the imaginations of his subjects. And, among the methodological conveniences that can thus accrue, one of the most versatile stems from the ability of human beings to be motivated not only by ongoing events but also by events they expect to take place in the future. This ability to anticipate imaginatively, and to be affected by those anticipations, can be systematically utilized in the construction of psychological manipulations.

Obviously, the anticipation of events — rather than their actual occurrence — will not be a theoretically appropriate means of manipulating every variable in which an experimenter may become interested. But insofar as it is conceptually apt, anticipation can be both strong in its impact and easy to build into the methodology of an experiment. It can also save the experimenter the work of actually having to create the anticipated event and of having to conduct subjects through it. Finally, and very importantly, it spares subjects whatever pain and trouble might result from the actual experience of those events.

Thus, by using anticipation, an experimenter may succeed in inducing psychological states that he feels ethically constrained from manipulating via direct physical contact between subjects and the anticipated event. Yet by creating a compelling expectation that such events will occur, as in the case of expectedly painful electric shocks, an experimenter can induce the same psychological condition that would obtain if the subjects were required, in fact, to experience the dreaded occurrence.

But even as he seeks to manipulate theoretically relevant variables, an experimenter must strive to prevent the inclusion of confounding ones. In this regard, the fullest exercise of his imagination is also desirable. For if he can successfuly imagine himself as a subject and anticipate how potentially confounding variables may intrude in the sheer process of conducting his theoretically required manipulations, he can preclude their unwanted effects.

Using the kinds of methodological devices mentioned in Chapter 4, a researcher should strive to eliminate whatever inadvertent "experimenter effects" he can visualize as possibly occurring within the context of his manipulative procedure. Likewise, he should envision all possible confounding "subject effects;" that is, all the ways in which subjects may inadvertently influence each other to affect the outcome of his hypotheses. For example, subjects in group manipulations may be able to influence each other profoundly through nonverbal means of communication unless precautions are taken to keep them from visual or auditory contact with one another.

The remainder of this chapter will give detailed presentations of two theoretically and methodologically related experiments that made extensive use of imaginative anticipation in the manipulation of their independent variables of motivation. At the same time, these experiments sought very carefully to eliminate the methodological intrusion of confounding variables in the conduct of those manipulations. Surely, researchers interested in Freudian concepts not represented in these experiments may have to contrive quite different manipulative procedures. However, the examples presented may at least provide some concrete suggestions for the range of possibilities open to experimenters in this area of research.

Anxiety, fear, and social affiliation (Sarnoff & Zimbardo, 1961)

This experiment did not adhere to the type of interactive design previously advocated for the testing of Freudian hypotheses. For the researchers could not confidently deduce from Freudian theory a variable of personality that might be expected to interact predictably with the two manipulated independent variables of motivation whose hypothesized differential effects on the experiment's dependent variable they were interested in testing.

Our point of investigatory focus centered upon the conceptual distinction Freud (1949f) had made between neurotic anxiety, which we referred to simply as *anxiety*, and objective anxiety, which was designated by us as fear. Essentially, Freud conceived neurotic anxiety as arising from the evocation of a repressed motive, and as serving to warn the individual that the consciously unacceptable motive was about to emerge into consciousness. Typically, according to Freud, such repressed motives — and, hence, their concomitant anxieties — are stirred by stimuli that are not, in themselves, a direct threat to the physical safety of the individual. Instead, stimuli capable of arousing anxiety may often be inherently innocuous — or even potentially pleasurable, as pictures of voluptuous female nudes may be for many male viewers. Hence, individuals made anxious by sensory contact with such stimuli are likely to perceive their anxiety as emotionally inappropriate, and they should be reluctant to make their anxieties known to others.

Fear, on the other hand, is presumed by Freud, in keeping with his conception of it as objective anxiety, to be evoked by unequivocal external danger. And, since the arousal of fear tends to be perceived as an emotionally appropriate reaction to environmental threat, most individuals should not feel overly hesitant to let others know about the fact that they are fearful. Indeed, faced with a clear and present external danger, people should want to get together with others to gain support in coping with it and to find cathartic release for their tensions.

It follows from this theoretical viewpoint that people should be inclined to be alone after they have been made anxious. Conversely, people should prefer the company of others after they are made fearful. And our experiment was designed to test the predictions that preference for social isolation would increase as anxiety rose, whereas preference for social affiliation would become stronger with rising fear.

Thus, our hypotheses required the development of experimental conditions in which different groups of subjects would be induced to experience a different degree of anxiety or fear. Specifically, we experimentally manipulated two levels of anxiety, high and low, and two levels of fear, high and low.

In creating the anticipations necessary to arouse each of these motivational states, we employed auditory, visual, and tactile stimuli. Moreover, by using virtually the same quantity of such stimuli in each of the four experimental conditions, the formal characteristics of the manipulatory media were kept fairly well matched. But we systematically varied, of course, the theoretically crucial contents of the objects with which subjects were led to anticipate imminent physical contact of various kinds. Hence, as in a theatre, subjects were required to imagine the outcome of future occurrences suggested by the dramatist. And since they perceived those outcomes as being directly applicable to themselves, subjects permitted their anticipations to act upon their own immediate existential situation, and not simply as expressions of empathy with a dramatically portrayed character.

The subjects were male undergraduate students. And the experiment was rationalized as a physiological investigation of the cutaneous sensitivity of the hand, to the fear groups, and of the mouth, to the anxiety groups.

The specious purpose of the experiment and of the conditions of waiting were further established by marking the experimental room "Sensory Physiological Laboratory" and two nearby rooms "Waiting Room A" and "Waiting Room T." Because of absentees, the size of the groups tested varied from three to five, and was usually composed of four Ss. In order to eliminate the possibility of superficial friendships developing during the experiment, and the Ss reacting to cues from one another or from E, the Ss were isolated in adjacent cubicles, no communication was allowed, and the tape-recorded instructions were presented through earphones.

The experimental conditions and instructions common to all Ss will be presented first. After rolling up their sleeves, removing their watches from their wrists and gum or cigarettes from their mouths ("they interfere with the recording electrodes"), the Ss were told:

"The earphones which have just been attached will enable you to receive instructions which have been tape-recorded. You are to listen carefully to these instructions and not talk or ask questions because the instructions cannot be repeated. This is a control that is necesary so that each subject will hear the instructions in the same way.

"Our experiment falls in the general area of physiological psychology. As you may know, one branch of physiological psychology is concerned with the reactions of the sense organs to various kinds of stimulation. Our present experiment deals with the skin (mouth) as organs of sensation. We are interested in studying individual differences in response to particular stimuli applied to it.

"There has been a good deal of controversy about the relative sensitivity of the fingertips (lips) as compared to the palms (tongue), and upper surface of the hand (palate). Our experiment will help to provide data, upon which we may be able ultimately to draw a detailed map of the cutaneous sensitivity of the human hand (mouth).

"In order to measure your physiological reactions, we are now going to attach some instruments to your arm and finger (corner of your mouth). These instruments are electrodes which are connected to a machine which records exactly the strength of your responses to each stimulus. These electrodes do nothing except measure changes in the resistance of your skin — changes which are so subtle that only a special device of this sort can record them. There will be a brief delay while we attach the recording electrodes to your forearm and fingertips (corner of your mouth). Electrode jelly will be applied first to the area to insure that we get good electrical contact." (The electrodes were then attached by a female laboratory assistant of middle age.)

In order to provide a reasonable basis for asking the Ss to wait in other rooms (and thus, for making the choice of affiliation or isolation), the Ss were told that it was necessary to assess their basal rates of responding prior to the application of the actual stimuli. They were led to believe that their individual sensitivities were being recorded while they viewed a series of slides of a typical subject who participated in the experiment. They anticipated that a waiting period would come after the slides, and then in the second — and purportedly major — part of the experiment their direct reactions to the actual stimuli would be measured. Accordingly, they were told:

"Now that your basal rates have been recorded on our polygraph recorder, it will take us about ten minutes while we tally the data and reset our measuring instruments so that they will be geared to your individual basal rates as you are run one at a time through the rest of the experiment. While we are doing these things, we are going to ask you to wait in other rooms which are available to us. We will come and get you when it is your turn to go through with the experiment. Incidentally, we have found that some of our subjects prefer waiting alone, while others prefer to wait together with other subjects. Therefore, we are going to given you your choice of waiting alone or with others. In either case, you will be ushered to a comfortable room furnished with adequate reading material."

After indicating their preference of waiting alone or together with others, the Ss also indicated the intensity of this preference on an 'open-ended' scale in which 0 represented a very weak preference and 100 a very strong preference. On this relatively unstructured scale, there were as many as 175 points of differences between Ss (from "75-alone" to "100-together").

Presentation of the slides during the experiment served two purposes in addition to the one previously mentioned. The content
of the slides (which was appropriate to each experimental treatment) served to reinforce the Ss differential expectations of the
nature and severity of the stimulus situation. Furthermore, the S
seen in the slides became a focal point for measuring the effectiveness of the experimental manipulations. It was assumed that
a direct attempt (by means of a scaled question) to appraise the
level of Ss' fear or anxiety would be likely to: (a) sensitize them
to the true purpose of the experiment; (b) yield unreliable results,
since the Ss might neither be consciously aware of, nor able to
verbalize, their anxiety reaction; and (c) evoke resistance, since
some Ss might not want to admit to being anxious or fearful,
which would question their masculinity.

Therefore, it was necessary to use an indirect, disguised measure
to evaluate whether the experimental inductions had actually
aroused two levels of both fear and anxiety. Immediately after the
slides had been shown (but before the affiliation choices had been
made), the Ss were told:

"Now before continuing with the experiment proper, we would
like you to stop for a moment and have you make a judgment.
As you may know, an individual shows his physiological reaction
in a variety of behavioral forms. We are interested in seeing whether it is possible to estimate how ill-at-ease or upset individuals are
at the prospect of receiving the stimulation in this experiment.
Recalling the subject whom you just saw in the slides, how upset
or ill-at-ease did he seem to you? Please assign a number anywhere
from 0 to 100 to indicate your feeling. 0 would indicate that you
thought he was completely at ease and unconcerned. 100 would
indicate that you thought he was extremely ill-at-ease and very
concerned about being in this experiment."

Since the subject in the slides was a posed model instructed to
remain poker-faced throughout, it was assumed that there was
no objective difference in his expression. Thus, any systematic
difference in ratings between groups should reflect Ss' attribution of
fear to the model.

However, because the content of the slides was not identical for every group but rather "tailored" to each specific treatment (see below), it was possible that there was an objective difference in the model's expression, that is, he actually looked more fearful in the slides shown to Ss in the High Fear than in the Low Fear conditions. As a control check on this possibility, four additional introductory classes (N=108) served as judges. They were told that the slides were of a typical subject in a recently completed experiment, and their task was to estimate how ill-at-ease and concerned he appeared (on the same scale used by the experimental Ss). Two of the classes saw only the face of the model (the rest of the slide was blacked out) and were told only that he was a subject in a physiological experiment in which stimuli were applied and responses measured. The other two classes saw the entire stimulus field of the slides and were given the same complete description that the experimental Ss received. Since each class of judges rated the slides for all four experimental treatments, their order of presentation was counter-balanced.

After the indirect measure of motive arousal and the measure of affiliation, the electrodes were removed and a measure taken of the Ss' reasons for choosing to affiliate or be isolated. The Ss were also asked to note whether or not they wished to continue in the experiment.

Only one S (in the High Fear condition) refused to remain for the "stimulation" part of the experiment.

The true purpose, hypothesis, design and reasons for the various deceptions (and at a later time, the results) were explained fully to each S.

Motive Arousal. *Fear.* Fear was induced by leading the Ss to anticipate either a series of painful electric shocks (High Fear), or a series of mild, subliminal stimulations (Low Fear) to the hand. The High Fear Ss were told:

". . . A series of electric shocks shall be applied to three different points on your hands. . . . From our past experience with this experiment, we know that some of these electric shocks will most probably be relatively painful to you. However, let me hasten to add that the stimulation will not be strong enough nor long enough to cause any damage or injury to you. Unfortunately, it is just not possible to advance our knowledge in this area without varying the stimulation over a wide range of intensity. Thus, the purpose of the experiment is to correlate the amplitudes of physiological responses of different skin surfaces to several levels of electrical stimulation. I am sure you realize the necessity for the methodology we have adopted, and will therefore bear with us. Each of the shocks will be of two minutes' duration with an interval of three minutes between the shocks."

The female assistant (dressed in a white lab coat, as was E) then attached electrodes to each S's arm and fingertip and strapped his arm onto a cotton-padded board. The leads from the electrodes appeared to go to a polygraph recorder. The recorder was also seen in the series of slides of the typical S and its function explained (this was common to all groups). The other slides showed an enormous electrical stimulator (photographed at the West Haven Veterans Hospital). It was called to the Ss' attention that:

"The four dials shown in the upper right-hand corner of the stimulator enable us to regulate automatically the frequency, duration, delay, and intensity of the shock you get."

The other slides portrayed the S with earphones and electrodes attached (like the Ss themselves), "listening to the instructions," and then "about to receive his first painful shock," administered by E, who could be seen in the background manipulating the dials on the stimulator. A final situational factor which may have enhanced the effectiveness of the High Fear manipulation was that the experimental room housed electrical generators for the entire building, which made a continuous buzzing sound; a cue interpreted by High Fear Ss as the electrical stimulator "warming up," but unnoticed or quickly adapted to by other Ss. An unobtrusively posted sign reading "Danger/High Voltage," present only for the High Fear Ss, gave further credence to this notion.

In the Low Fear condition the word "shock" was never used, and all cues in the situation associated with shock, fear or pain were removed; that is, no white lab coats, arms not strapped to boards, etc. The expectations of these Ss were guided by instructions stating:

"The stimuli in the present study will consist of three mild electrical stimulations which will be felt as tingling sensations. They shall be applied to three different points on your hand. . . . our methodology, then, is to apply a constant stimulus whose intensity is quite low, and which is just sufficient to elicit a measurable physiological response. Thus we can compare the frequency, amplitude, and latency of response on different skin surfaces to the same constant stimulus. Because of its low intensity, in some cases you will be unaware of the stimulus, while generally you will feel it merely as a tingling sensation. Each of the tingling stimuli will be of 10 seconds' duration, with an interval of three minutes between the stimuli."

In the series of slides viewed by these Ss, the imposing electrical stimulator was replaced by a small innocuous-looking apparatus (actually a voltmeter), an E was not seen in the active role as an agent of pain, but in the passive role of recording data from the polygraph recorder.

Anxiety. Anxiety was manipulated by arousing a motive assumed to have been repressed by most of the Ss. The motive we attempted to arouse might, in Freudian terminology, be called "oral libido," a desire to obtain pleasurable gratification by sucking on objects that are clearly related to infantile nursing experiences. The female breast is, of course, the prototype of such objects, but others includes nipples, baby bottles and pacifiers. Thus, to arouse this motive and, hence, the anxiety that should follow its arousal, Ss in the High Anxiety condition were led to believe that they would have to suck on a number of objects commonly associated with infantile oral behavior. In the Low Anxiety condition, Ss expected to put 'neutral' stimuli in their mouths, that is objects not directly associated with infancy, and not eliciting (or requiring, in the Ss' anticipated use of them) the sucking responses.

The High Anxiety Ss were told:

"The stimuli will consist of a series of three differently textured objects which you shall be asked to put in your mouth and suck for a period of time. . . . Of course, individuals differ in their sensitivity to oral stimulation, and, as I have said, we are most interested in studying individual differences. But regardless of the fact that individuals do vary in their reactions, we have never found a single person among the many we have already observed who has not found each of these three objects to be distinctly stimulating. You will suck on each object for a period of two minutes, with an interval of three minutes between the objects."

As the female assistant took the electrodes, to be attached to each S's mouth and arm, from a cart on which they rested, the cart was intentionally pushed close to the S. In clear view on the cart were the following items: Numerous baby bottles, oversized nipples, pacifiers, breast shields (nipples women often wear over their breasts while nursing) and lollipops.

The same variety of stimulus objects was shown arrayed in front of the S in the slides. He could be seen, tongue hanging out, lips puckered, about to suck his thumb (as one of the objects of stimulation) or on one of the other objects. An enlarged close-up of the model's face, highlighting the mouth area, showed him about to suck on a baby bottle. Ss were told that the contact taped to the mouth recorded the direct reaction to oral stimulation, and the arm contact recorded peripheral reactions.

The instructions to the Low Anxiety Ss did not mention "suck" or any stimulation that they would receive from putting the objects in their mouth. Moreover, they were led to believe that they would keep each object in their mouths for only ten seconds. The stimulus objects were not in immediate proximity to the Ss while their electrodes were being attached. The stimulus objects that they anticipated putting in their mouths were shown in the slides: whistles, balloons, "kazoos" and pipes. Since these objects do not require sucking (but rather, in general, blowing), the model's tongue was not to be seen as he prepared to use the stimuli. With this exception, attempts were made to equate the expression and stance of the typical S in the series of slides shown to the High Arousal and Low Arousal Ss [Sarnoff, 1962, pp. 195-201].

The results of the experiment gave empirical support to our hypotheses. For as the arousal of fear increased, so did the intensity of preference for social affiliation, while the increased arousal of anxiety led to a decrease in the intensity of such a preference. Moreover, whereas a large majority of the subjects chose to wait with others following the low arousals of both anxiety and fear, 95 percent of the subjects in the High Fear condition chose the "together" alternative as compared with 46 percent of the subjects in the High Anxiety group.

Incidentally, these findings also appeared to reinforce the scientific utility of the general Freudian assumption, stated in passing in Chapter 3, that every motive, because of its own special psychological properties, provokes tensions that can be maximally reduced only by a behavioral response that is functionally related to those properties. It is further assumed that consciously experienced emotions are epiphenomenal indicants of particular motivational states (Sarnoff, 1962).

Indeed, these were the basic premises permitting us to consider the very possibility that, although social affiliation might well be a highly tension-reducing response to fear, it would not necessarily serve the same function for all motives; and probably not for anxiety, whose imputed psychological properties differ considerably from those of fear. Certainly, these were the central considerations that led us to question the extent to which Schachter's (1959) findings on the relationship between fear and social affiliation could be properly generalized to all emotional states.

The effects of fear and two modes of anxiety reduction on social affiliation and phobic ideation: (Bromberg, 1967)

Bromberg was interested in testing hypotheses derived from the Freudian view of the determinants of phobic behavior and ideation. Very briefly, as Bromberg sorted it out, the Freudian approach to the ontogenetic development of phobias among males assumes, first, the emergence of parentally induced castration anxiety and, then, the displacement of that anxiety onto objects in the environment.

Insofar as an individual has developed a high level of habitual and repressed castration conflict, he should become anxious when he is heterosexually aroused. For it is the imminent intrusion of heterosexual motivation into consciousness that heralds danger to such an individual, given his presumed interpersonal history of having been severely threatened for the overt expression of those desires. And individuals of this kind are likely to have a hyper-sensitivity to the harmful potentials of certain external objects, which are symbolically associated with the threat of castration they had once suffered.

A phobia, therefore, consists of the displaced location of one's underlying castration anxiety. For whereas such free-floating anxiety is felt as an "objectless" state of inner dread, phobic anxiety is attributed to particular environmental objects, which are not regarded with similar apprehension by other people.

> Thus, inherent in phobic anxiety, despite the fact that it, like fear, has a specific external object, is the critical quality of all anxiety: the improbability that the individual is aware of the true source of his emotion, and thus, his tendency to experience his exaggerated apprehension of the external situation as somewhat inappropriate and absurd. This particular relationship between the motive and the emotion should distinguish phobic anxiety (as it distinguishes free-floating anxiety) from fear, by leading to an increasing preference for social isolation following its arousal, as opposed to the increased affiliation preference elicited when fear is aroused. In fact, the preference for isolation subsequent to the arousal of phobic anxiety should be even *stronger* than that following the arousal of free-floating anxiety, inasmuch as an individual's perception of his apprehension relating to an object or event which he *recognizes* as relatively innocuous should be felt as even more inappropriate than the experience of diffuse, unlocalized discomfort [Bromberg, 1967, p. 22-23].

Bromberg was also interested in ideation as a dependent variable, in respect to which some correlational results pertaining to his CC Scale have already been presented. But for immediate purposes it is sufficient to emphasize that he could not have put any of his hypotheses to experimental test without having hit upon a method for juxtaposing two separate manipulations on the same experimental occasion, inducing the independent variable relevant to each and arousing a third independent variable out of their mode of coalescence. Thus, using only two manipulations, Bromberg succeeded, as will be explained, in creating the three motivational states that were essential to a theoretically appropriate experiment on the phenomenon: fear, free-floating anxiety (FFA), and phobic anxiety.

Operationally, it was not overly difficult for Bromberg to devise methods for inducing either fear or free-floating anxiety, since manipulations of those variables had been suggested by the experimental work of other investigators. Specifically, his procedure for manipulating fear had been initiated by Schachter (1959) and subsequently adapted by Sarnoff and Zimbardo (1961). Similarly, Bromberg's arousal of free-floating anxiety evolved from the technique of heterosexual manipulation employed by Sarnoff and Corwin (1959). But Bromberg greatly improved the use of that technique by actually measuring the anxiety-inducing impact of the photographs, rather than merely assuming that their differential sexual inductions would trigger like variations in anxiety among subjects who differed on the CC Scale.

However, Bromberg showed exceptional theoretical and methodological originality in the act of creative reasoning whereby he saw that phobic anxiety could be the resultant of those two manipulations acting upon subjects who were high on his CC Scale; in other words, subjects experiencing high free-floating anxiety following the HAS arousal. For it was just these individuals, Bromberg deduced, who should be most vulnerable to the temporary acquisition of phobic anxiety when they anticipated the onset of a mildly painful (MP) stimulus, rather than a strongly painful (SP) one or a stimulus that is not painful (NP) at all.

On the other hand, Bromberg's deductions led him not to expect much FFA to be induced among High CC subjects who were exposed to the LSA manipulations. Nor did he expect subjects low in CC to develop appreciable amounts of FFA as a result of their exposure to either of the SA conditions, or of phobic anxiety, upon their subsequent encounter with any of the AP conditions. But he did reason that all subjects — whether High or Low in CC or whether previously in the HSA or LSA manipulations — would experience more fear in the SP condition than in either the MP or NP conditions. And

Bromberg employed careful empirical checks following each manipulation, obtaining independent evidence that the three desired motivational states — fear, free-floating anxiety, and phobic anxiety — had been differentially induced in accordance with his expectations, thus meeting the theoretical stipulations for an adequate test of his hypotheses.

It should be pointed out that the establishment of those motivational states implicity constituted an interactive experiment in its own right, since they had been predicted as a consequence of interactions between the nonmanipulated independent variable of personality (CC) and the manipulated independent variables of heterosexual arousal (SA) and anticipated pain (AP). Logically, therefore, Bromberg could have regarded fear, free-floating anxiety, and phobic anxiety as dependent variables, whose differential manifestation he had specifically hypothesized as effects of the above interactions. But he chose, instead, to extend the sequential chain of theoretical explanation, conceiving of those three experimentally created motivational states as independent variables, and predicting their effects, in turn, on the formally designated dependent variables of social affiliation and phobic ideation.

To clarify this exposition, Bromberg's (1967, p. 43) diagram of his research design — which also gives his predictions — is reproduced in Figure 4. In reading this diagram, it should be kept in mind that the three variables labeled "Independent Variable I, II, and III" are those that interacted to produce the three crucial motivational states from which, in fact, Bromberg directly predicted the effects listed under the columns headed: "Dependent Variables." Finally, with respect to the measures represented as operationally defining the ideational segment of the dependent variables, CDPI stands for Castration-Derived Phobic Ideation, whereas PHICON is an abbreviation for Control Inventory of Phobic Ideation (that is, items constructed, and empirically found, to bear less relationship to the variable measured by the CC Scale than those contained in the CDPI). Thus, PHICON represents an empirical control by which to assess the *differential specificity* of the effects predicted for CDPI. For, as can be seen, no changes are expected for PHICON, despite the fact that its items, like those of CDPI, refer to potential objects of fear.

To secure the indicated juxtaposition between his SA and AP arousals, Bromberg needed procedures that would sustain the impact made by the SA manipulations, and that could lead into the AP

FIGURE 4 *Bromberg's Experiment: General Research Design*

Independent variable I, castration conflict (CC)	Independent variable II, sexual arousal (SA)	Motive aroused, free-floating castration anxiety (FFA)	Independent variable III, anticipated pain (AP)	Dominant motive	Dependent variables		
					Preference for social affiliation	Phobic ideation	
						CDPI	PHICON
High (HCC) →	High (HSA) → / Low (LSA)	High (HFFA)	No pain (NP) →	Free-floating anxiety (FFA)	Moderate decrease	Moderate increase	No change
			Mild pain (MP) →	Phobic anxiety	Strong decrease	Strong increase	No change
			Strong pain (SP) →	Fear	Increase	No change	No change
Low (LCC) →	High (HSA) → / Low (LSA)	Low (LFFA)	Strong pain (SP) →	Fear			
			Mild pain (MP) →	None	Control	No change	No change
			No pain (NP) →	None	Control	No change	No change

manipulations in a methodologically smooth manner while, at the same time, being perfectly consonant with the overall investigatory rationale on the basis of which the entire experiment was originally presented to subjects. Let us see how he managed to achieve these required objectives.

The SA manipulations. A visual medium was used to induce two levels of heterosexual arousal (SA): High (HSA) and Low (LSA). As in the experiment by Sarnoff and Corwin (1959), the visual stimuli for the HSA condition were photographs of voluptuous nudes "in highly seductive poses," whereas the photographs employed in the LSA condition were of fully clothed women "portrayed with little suggestion of sexuality or eroticism [1967, p. 74]." And in his preceding investigatory rationale, which had been given to prepare all subjects (male undergraduate students at New York University) for acceptance of the meaningfulness of his subsequent manipulations, Bromberg presented his experiment as a research project on nonverbal communication. "Fine art, magazine illustrations, and photography are all forms of nonverbal communication to the extent that something is being communicated without the use of language. People differ widely in their degree of responsiveness to this form of communication, and evidence, thus far, suggests a relationship between this type of responsiveness and other areas of responsiveness, such as emotional and physiological responsiveness [1967, p. 71]."

The tactile procedures used to sustain the impact of the visual SA manipulations

Having gone through the visual SA manipulations, which included an independent check — via ratings by subjects of the photographs they saw — on the arousing powers of the various pictures, HSA and LSA subjects experienced two different tactile procedures, whose chief purpose was to sustain, for the rest of the experiment, the various levels of SA induced by the photographs. Both tactile procedures were introduced by the same tape-recording, heard and presented in the form of "instructions for the second part of the session which allegedly involved measurement of their 'physiological responsiveness.'" They were told the following:

"As before, please listen carefully, since the instructions cannot be repeated and no questions may be asked until the session is over. The remainder of this session will basically consist of measuring your galvanic skin resistance. Galvanic skin resistance, or GSR as we refer to it, is measured by the instrument you see on the table in front of the room. The measurement consists of two parts. What we do is first take a reading at what is called the resting level; that is, when the nerve cells of the skin are at rest. This reading is then compared with a second reading when the nerve cells of the skin are transmitting impulses. For the first reading, special switching circuits in our equipment allow us to record the GSR patterns of as many as six people at once, on a single record chart. This is done by means of a special pen inside of the polygraph, which is connected to all six circuits but is recording only *one* at a time. Therefore, since the circuits must keep switching from person to person during each unit of recording time, the length of time necessary for the first recording is rather long. Recording electrode #1, which will be used for the first reading, will be held in your hand during the entire period, and will record your GSR pattern at the resting level.

"If you are right handed, the recording electrode will be taken in your left hand; and vice versa if you are left handed. This will enable you to write during the time reading is being taken. What this recording electrode does is to transmit to our polygraph recorder the pattern of nerve cell discharge from the surface of your skin. If you are wearing any rings on the hand which will hold the electrode, I will ask you to remove them *now*, if possible, and put them in your pocket since they may interfere with the recording. A special electrode jelly will then be applied to assure that we get good electrical contact."

Tactile SA Induction

The Tactile SA manipulation was then administered. In the HSA condition the Ss were first informed that the most efficient way we had found to apply the electrode jelly was in a rubber ball used as an applicator. The E then opened a special container and removed a pink rubber ball filled with electrode jelly. The ball was slit along one side, and the edges of the slit were masked with strips of black tape. When manual pressure was exerted by E on the edges of the ball, the slit opened and a small amount of jelly oozed from the opening. The visual impression was strikingly representative of the female genitals surrounded by black pubic hair. While E held up the ball for visual inspection, the Ss were told:

"You are going to insert one at a time, the index and middle fingers of your recording hand into the slit as far as they will go. As you withdraw each finger, the edges of the slit will wipe off the excess jelly. After this is done, recording electrode #1 will be plugged into circuit #1 in the panel next to you, and the circuit will be turned on."

The E then took out the 'recording electrodes' used for the first reading and displayed one to the Ss for demonstration purposes. The electrode which the Ss held in the HSA condition was designed to resemble the size and shape of an erect penis. It was a 6 inch-long, test tube-like cylinder made of hard red plastic, and sealed at its open end by a metal cap. Directly above the cap a wire emerged from the hollow interior of the tube and terminated in a jack plug. Two one-quarter-inch metal bands spaced slightly apart encircled the middle of the shaft and made 'contact' with the treated fingers of the S's recording hand. Each S in the HSA condition was instructed to hold one of these 'electrodes' upright in his fist, with his fingers around the metal band and his arm resting on the desk. Held in this position, the two top inches of the shaft's rounded head were forced to protude from the S's hand and were clearly visible to him during the entire AP induction that followed.

In the LSA condition, the electrode jelly was kept in its original tube and was applied by E directly to the electrode contacts themselves rather than to the S's fingers. The LSA electrode was a three-inch-long, flat-ended cylinder with a broad metal band on either end. These bands served as 'skin contacts' and appeared to connect with a wire and jack plug extended from a terminal at one end. Not only was there nothing 'phallic' in appearance about this electrode, but when it was held in the S's fist as in-

structed, all but the wire was completely concealed from view
[Bromberg, 1967, pp. 75-78].

The transition from the tactile procedures
sustaining the visual SA manipulations
to the procedures needed to induce
three levels of AP

Once the correct position for holding the electrode was demonstrated by E, the electrode jelly was administered, the electrode
plugs were inserted into the #1 circuit jacks on the booth panels,
and the corresponding panel lights were switched on. After
elaborately and carefully checking to see that each S's electrode
was in good 'contact' with his skin and being held properly, E then
walked to the instrument table and switched on the psychogal-
vanometer and polygraph. For the next 60 seconds E made various
sensitivity adjustments in the GSR needle fluctuations, while Ss
followed the activity of the other meter and the changing pattern
of the moving polygraph chart. To make the deception even more
compelling, E 'studied' the instruments from time to time and
made detailed mathematical notations on a clipboard he carried
with him. (This adjustment and notation procedure was repeated
at various intervals throughout the entire recording period).

The Ss were then ready to receive the AP induction. Before
administering it, however, it was felt desirable to allow a brief
resting period for the Ss to digest and to consolidate their prior set
of experiences. It was hoped that an interlude of relative sensory
deprivation would heighten responsiveness to the *internal* effects
evoked by the SA inductions, and that these induced emotions
would thus tend to be more available when the AP manipulation
was presented [Bromberg, 1967, p. 78].

The machines mentioned above were merely electrical props, wired
in advance to show the fluctuations needed to convey a sense of their
authenticity; and to permit Bromberg to dramatize the impressions
he gave subjects of the electric functions. Thus, the devices performed
no measurement, since the electrodes worn by the subjects were not
actually connected to them. Nor were the machines obliged to deliver

any degree of electrical stimulation, as subsequently indicated by Bromberg in the specific introductions to the various AP conditions. Instead, as in the experiment by Sarnoff and Zimbardo (1961), they served only to create an anticipation of different amounts of such stimulation, after which the measures of the two dependent variables were taken and the experiment concluded.

A summary of Bromberg's findings

Bromberg's data almost entirely confirmed his theoretical expectations about how the three independent variables of phobic anxiety, free-floating anxiety, and fear would affect the two dependent variables: phobic ideation and preference for social affiliation. Moreover, in regard to the latter dependent variable, it may be noted that Bromberg's results tend to reinforce those previously predicted by Sarnoff and Zimbardo on the basis of Freud's conceptual distinction between anxiety and fear.

A. *Findings relevant to the dependent variable of preference for social affiliation.* (1) When anxiety was aroused but was not bound to a specific external object (free-floating anxiety), isolation preferences *tended* to increase as predicted; this finding, however, fell short of statistical significance. (2) When anxiety was aroused and was bound to a specific external object (phobic anxiety), the preferred affiliative behavior, as predicted, was social isolation; this preference, as hypothesized, exceeded that following the arousal of free-floating anxiety. (3) When fear was aroused (by an *inherent* threat in the same external object to which phobic anxiety was bound), affiliation preference increased as predicted [Bromberg, 1967, p. 175].

B. *Findings relevant to the dependent variable of phobic ideation.* (1) As predicted, the arousal of phobic anxiety led to an increase in phobic ideation specifically related to the repressed castration conflict which was the source of the anxiety. (2) The arousal of fear, as predicted, evoked a lower level of castration-derived phobic ideation than that evoked by phobic anxiety. (3) The arousal of free-floating anxiety led, as predicted, to an increase in castration-derived phobic ideation; contrary to prediction, however, this increase extended to areas of phobic ideation *unrelated* to the repressed conflict. Nevertheless, the increase in *conflict*-related phobic ideation, as hypothesized, was less than that found for phobic anxiety [Bromberg, 1967, p. 176].

10 Checking on the Effectiveness of Manipulations

After manipulating the theoretically relevant independent variables of his experiment, a researcher needs to know whether and to what extent those manipulations have succeeded in creating their intended variations in psychological states. For the creation of the specific conditions required to test his hypothesis is the *sine qua non* of an experimental — as compared with a nonexperimental — approach to scientific knowledge. And unless an experimenter has empirical evidence testifying to his having met that requirement, he cannot confidently assume that he has put his hypothesis to a theoretically appropriate test.

Without such evidence, an experimenter has no objective basis for dealing convincingly with alternative explanations about the relationship between the results of his tested hypothesis and the actual psychological properties of the manipulations from which they were predicted. Thus, if he obtained disconfirmatory results, he could conclude either that his manipulations were defective or that the theoretical assumptions contained in his hypothesis were erroneous. But even if his findings were positive, he could not empirically discount the possibility that they were determined not by the particular psychological state he intended to create but by some other one that his manipulations actually induced.

Of course, explanatory indeterminacy is much more obvious in the first instance than in the second. But theoretical equivocation is scientifically undesirable, and all the more so when its sources can be readily anticipated and methodologically prevented. Indeed, a researcher chooses to test an hypothesis through an experiment for the very reason that he wants thereby to maximize his ability to draw the firmest possible theoretical conclusions about it.

Anticipating this explanatory problem in advance of his experiment, a researcher can and should include in his methodology a device for independently checking on the effectiveness of his manipulations; that is, for assessing the psychological impact of those manipulations *per se*, entirely apart from whatever effects they may exert upon the dependent variables. For the measure of a dependent variable cannot logically serve both as a criterion of the predicted consequences of the manipulated variable and as an operational indicant of the manipulated variable itself.

But any independently taken checks on the manipulations are, of course, measures in their own right. Hence, their construction, validation, and reliability are governed by the same general principles that apply to the measurement of all psychological variables. Moreover, since they necessarily follow rather than precede manipulations, these checks are further contingent upon the same considerations of format and administration as pertain to measures of dependent variables, which will be discussed in the next chapter.

So, rather than repeat material that has been and shall be presented, this chapter will be devoted to those procedural issues that appear to be of special relevance to measures used as checks on the effectiveness of manipulations. Because of the temporal contiguity between such measures and those used to define dependent variables, it will be necessary to refer to matters that involve both kinds of measurement.

Using checks in interactive research designs

The scientific desirability of providing checks on the effectiveness of manipulations is equally applicable to experimental designs that involve only manipulated independent variables and to those that contain both manipulated and nonmanipulated independent variables. However, even in interactive designs, the checks are intended to measure psychological differences prevailing between manipulated groups, without regard to individual differences in personality within those groups. This focus of intention is logically required, since the manipulated states are viewed as independent variables in their own right, albeit as also capable of interaction with nonmanipulated ones.

Of course, individual differences in personality may indeed mediate the ways in which given subjects reflect the inductions applied. For example, responding to the measure of heterosexual arousal used by Sarnoff and Corwin (1959), subjects high in habitual castration anxiety may have been somewhat less inclined to admit having been sexually aroused than were subjects low in habitual castration anxiety. In that event, the obtained differences in arousal between the HAS and LAS conditions was less than it might otherwise have been. But had those differences between conditions not been obtained, we could not have concluded that the induction had been successful and that the theoretically required independent variable of heterosexuality had been quantitatively varied in accordance with the empirical stipulations of our hypothesis. Thus, the checks were administered and analyzed on the assumption that, despite their individual differences in personality, subjects exposed to a "high" level of arousal would, by and large, experience more of the requisite psychological state than would subjects exposed to a "low" level of arousal.

In this way, checks on the effectiveness of the manipulations also empirically define the independence of the independent variable that those manipulations are designed to create. And, indeed, that independence is the operational counterpart of the conceptual independence the variable is assumed to possess. For such conceptual independence is inherent to the very postulation of a variable. The whole meaning of an interaction between variables rests on the assumption that each of them subsumes its own particular set of psychological properties, which, when brought together, mediate behavior and experience in ways other than those resulting from their separate functioning. Even if the outcome of this mediation is merely an intensification of the relationship between one of the independent variables and a given dependent variable, it could not have occurred in the absence of the mediating independent variable.

The results of interactions between a manipulated and a non-manipulated variable may, in themselves, define the psychological states that an experimenter wishes to induce as independent variables. Thus, his hypothesis may sometimes require that such states be established in order to test their effects upon particular dependent variables. And the theory from which his hypotheses are derived may indicate that the required states can only be induced by arranging for prior interactions among the variables presumed to give rise to those states.

Hence, in Bromberg's experiment, the personality variable of CC had to be systematically taken into account in assessing the differential motivational impact of the SA and AP manipulations. For his theoretical position led him to assume that his three immediately operative independent variables would result from the interaction of CC with *both*

SA and AP; and that, therefore, proper checks on the arousal of those three variables could not be based simply on a comparison between levels of SA and AP *per se*, but would depend, instead, on how HCC and LCC subjects differed in their responses to the interactive motivational consequences of exposure first to the various SA conditions and then to the various AP conditions. Consequently, it was only by systematically including this personality difference in the analysis of the data obtained by his checks that Bromberg could assess, as shall subsequently be described, the effectiveness of his inductions in a theoretically appropriate manner.

*Verbal report as the medium of measurement
most appropriate to checks on manipulations
relevant to tests of Freudian hypotheses*

Because humane experimental manipulations of motivational or cognitive states are necessarily transient in their impact, an experimenter would naturally wish to check on their effectiveness as quickly as possible. Indeed, if much more were known by science about the precise physiological concomitants of different psychological states, an experimenter could apply that knowledge by arranging for the continuous monitoring of his psychological manipulations via physiological measurement. Assuming such measuring devices were sufficiently unobtrusive, the effectiveness of the manipulations could be checked without any intrusion on the procedural flow of the experiment and, moreover, at the very same time that a subject was actually being confronted by the manipulations.

However, the field of psychology has not yet advanced to the point at which physiological measures have validly distinguished among the motivational states whose quantitative variation is typically involved in experimental tests of Freudian hypotheses. Surely, we have on hand no such indices for distinguishing, let us say, between fear and anxiety, much less between phobic and free-floating anxiety. Nor has anyone yet produced a motivationally discrete and scientifically reliable physiological indicant of manipulated variations in monetary privation or social rejection.

Admittedly, nonphysiological measures may also encounter considerable difficulty in registering the motivational nuances that have been theoretically attributable to the subtle psychological differences presumed to differentiate motives such as those mentioned above. However, given our present level of scientific knowledge, we have no reasonable basis on which to prefer physiological measures of those motives to verbal ones. Besides, the verbal measures are more theoretically appropriate to the psychological terms in which those induced motivational variables are conceptualized. Nevertheless, one might argue, some sort of running record could be kept of overt behavior displayed by subjects from the very onset of the manipulative procedures. For example, an experimenter might make a video tape-recording of subjects undergoing the manipulations; and score that tape, subsequently, on one or another aspect of the subject's nonverbal behavior.

However, it can again be said that, as in the case of physiological indicants, no reliably discernible categories of nonverbal behavior have been shown to differentiate among the motivational states previously mentioned; and certainly not under the conditions of observation that generally prevail while subjects are being exposed to experimental manipulations. For the systematic imposition of necessary situational controls over their exposure to manipulations usually involves the placement of subjects in a relatively immobile position vis-à-vis the manipulatory procedure. The range of behaviors they can display is often restricted to fleeting changes in facial expression, alterations in which would now be virtually impossible to categorize as representing, for example, either anxiety versus fear, or one type of anxiety versus another.

Thus, the measures used as checks in experimental tests of Freudian hypotheses have been of the verbal kind, usually of a pencil-and-paper variety, in which subjects are requested to make or to respond to verbal statements descriptive of the psychological states presumed by an experimenter to characterize the inner experience induced by the manipulations. The verbal measuring stimuli may be given in connection with and reference to pictorial material, as in the case of the "projective-objective" types of measures. Or, they may be "objective" in format. Further, subjects may be asked to respond within a prearranged and very restricted system of registration; or they may be offered a quite "open-ended" possibility for articulating their verbal responses. Finally, subjects may be requested to respond directly in terms of their own feelings, or indirectly in terms of how someone else might have felt under similar circumstances.

The general desirability of administering checks
before measuring the dependent variables

Various combinations of these formats have been employed, their choice resting upon what an experimenter considers most suitable to the variables manipulated and the overall conduct of his experiment. And a number of such decisive considerations will be examined later in this chapter. However, all of these verbal checks have in common the facts that they: a) represent clearly perceptible occasions of measurements within the experiment and b) require time and focused attention to complete.

As a result of these two intrusive characteristics, checks on manipulations raise the two methodologically calamitous prospects of either giving away the hypothesis under study or siphoning off too much of the motivational tension that the manipulations had induced. For the very process of verbally expressing the quality and intensity of one's inner psychological state may reduce its tension, while simultaneously leading one to wonder exactly what that state has to do with the purpose of the experiment.

In some cases, therefore, an experimenter may decide, however reluctantly, to delay the administration of the checks until after the postmanipulative measurement of the dependent variable. And that is what Bishop (1965) chose to do, in an example that will be further elucidated in the discussion of measures of dependent variables.

Such decisions are undertaken only with great reluctance, for it is obviously much more logical to check the effectiveness of the manipulations when they are presumed to have maximally induced their intended psychological state. The passage of time *and* interpolated experimental activity may well either reduce the intensity of those states or replace them with theoretically irrelevant ones. And insofar as the tension induced by the manipulations is channelled into discharge via responses to the measures of the dependent variables, the subsequently administered checks may fail to register the psychological differentials that had earlier been present. Hence, an analysis of the data obtained by such belated checks may lead an experimenter wrongly to conclude that his manipulations had been defective.

Thus, it is both logically and psychologically desirable, *if theoretically appropriate and procedurally feasible,* to administer the checks on the effectiveness of the manipulations before rather than after the measurement of the dependent variables. On the other hand, since he is keenly aware of the risks entailed in adhering to those desiderata, an experimenter can be duly careful in the provisions he takes to minimize their hazards.

An experimenter can reduce the hazard of excessive motivational discharge by keeping his checks on the manipulations brief. Indeed, their optimal brevity tends to militate against the possibility of developing any appreciable degree of internal consistency reliability for them, since such reliability is largely contingent on the length of a measure.

But an experimenter can also contrive a variety of devices directed toward the preclusion of undue suspiciousness and defensiveness, whose occurrence might not only invalidate a check's measuring function *per se* but also contaminate the measurement of the crucial dependent variables. These devices depend for their use upon the extent to which they are, in fact, consonant with the theoretical objectives and methodology of a particular experiment. And the examples given below merely indicate what can be done to forestall the inadvertently undesirable effects of the employment of checks on manipulations. If they fit an experimenter's particular situation, they may properly be applied as illustrated. But if they do not, an experimenter obviously needs to determine — as usual, with the help of pilot investigations — what form of check is most suitable for his special purposes, taking into consideration all the other theoretical and procedural matters involved in his study.

Presenting checks in a manner supportive of an experiment's overall rationale

Assuming that checks are administered as the next procedural step following the exposure of subjects to the manipulations, their exact manner of introduction should be a matter of very careful concern. For if they are presented too precipituously and gratuitously, they may call too much critical attention to themselves; and they may lead a subject toward theoretically unwanted puzzlement and conjecture about their actual purpose.

The best precaution against such an undesirable eventuality lies in the compellingness with which the checks are rationalized as a logical and perfectly expectable consequence of the subjects having already experienced experimental procedures. To be sure, the procedure that occurs immediately before the checks will not have been labelled as a "manipulation" to the subjects. Yet that is actually what it is; and what the experimenter will have obscured from the perception of subjects in his presentation of it.

It remains, therefore, for the experimenter to link his checks explicitly to the specific rationale with which the manipulations were previously introduced — and implicitly to the general rationale on the basis of which the subject had been, as it were, psychologically ushered into the experiment. Simultaneously, mindful of the measures and procedures to come, the experimenter can see to it that the checks lead smoothly into the immediately following step in the experimental sequence. Indeed, the checks can be so "packaged" in their administration as to follow directly and logically from material aimed at supporting the rationale for the just-concluded manipulation; and to bring subjects directly and logically into the rationales and measures that come immediately afterward.

The previously mentioned experiment (Sarnoff, 1960b) on reaction formation (RF) and cynicism (CS) contains an example of such "packaging." The manipulations — a "live" and a tape-recorded performance of a play (Saroyan, 1943) — were intended to arouse two degrees of affectionate feelings toward others: High (HA) and Low (LA).

The booklet which the Ss were required to fill out after the experimental manipulations contained these measures in the following order of presentation: a rating scale designed to ascertain whether or not the HA and LA conditions succeeded in evoking different intensities of emotion, the CS, and two open-ended questions which aimed at checking on the content of the emotions which the HA and LA did stimulate.

The measure of the intensity of the emotions aroused by the play or recording was obtained from the last of a series of six rating scales which were contained on a sheet headed 'Empathy Judgment Scale.' The first five scales on this sheet were designed simply to support the rationale which had been given to Ss as the objective of the research. Thus, they required the Ss to judge various aspects of the 'empathic' ability of the actors. The sixth scale, the one actually used to measure the emotional intensity of the affection-arousing stimuli, was introduced on the sheet as follows: 'On the following five-point scale, similar to the ones above, check the point which best represents your judgment concerning the intensity of emotion portrayed by the actors in the scene.' Under the instructions were five points labeled 'Very Weak,' 'Weak,' 'Moderate,' 'Intense,' and 'Very Intense.' Ten equally spaced dots separated each of these labeled points and it was already understood by the Ss that they could place their check marks on any dot along the scale.

The mean rating of Ss in the LA condition clustered near the 'Weak' designation, while the HA mean was close to the 'Intense' designation. Statistically, the difference between these means is significant at beyond the .001 level.

The two open-ended questions which inquired about the content of the emotional reactions of Ss to the affection-arousing stimuli were printed on a sheet headed "Report on Empathy Judgment." These questions were: "1. During the scene from 'Hello Out There,' were you able to get a feel for the characters and their emotions? What did you yourself feel during the scene?" [Sarnoff, 1960b, p. 136].

The written statements yielded by these two questions were eventually coded to determine the extent to which HAS and LAS differed both in respect to having been emotionally stirred and to having experienced affectionate feelings. But it was also necessary to evaluate the reliability of these codes, by having different raters apply them independently to the same protocols.

A high degree of inter-rater agreement, 95 percent, was obtained in the application of the codes devised for each question. And the statistical analyses of the coded responses showed that the HAS and LAS subjects differed significantly — and as experimentally intended — in the amount and the quality of the emotion experienced.

Separate measures of intensity and content of the induced psychological state appeared to be indicated as the best means of supporting the rationale of "empathic ability," which was what the above experiment purported to study. However, those two qualities of an induced state can easily be combined in a single "objective" measure, thus precluding the extra processing of data involved in the coding of replies to "open-ended" questions. Indeed, such a combination of content and intensity in a single item is a far more typical format of current psychological measurement, as employed in experimental work in the areas of personality and social psychology. And when experimental circumstances permit its use, that format can save a good deal of time in administration and response, thus minimizing the risk of overly discharging the specific psychological tensions aroused in subjects by the manipulations.

Such an "objective" and directly self-descriptive measure was employed by Sarnoff and Corwin (1959) in their previously reported experiment, which was rationalized to subjects as "an investigation of some of the psychological factors which influence the appreciation of art [p. 378]." Subjects were told at the outset of the experiment that they would be asked to give their "esthetic reactions" to several pictures, which, of course, constituted the manipulative stimuli. As in the experiment on reaction formation, this check was given following the manipulations and prior to the "after" measure of the dependent variable. Specifically, the check sought to determine the extent to which the differential arousal of heterosexual motivation succeeded in inducing the two levels of intensity — high (HAS) and Low (LAS) — it was intended to create.

In fact, the data provided by the check showed that such differential in intensity of heterosexual arousal had been established. "On a rating scale ranging from 0 (not at all arousing) to 100 (intensely arousing), the HAS Ss had an average score of 59, whereas the LAS Ss had an averaged score of 35. The difference between these means was well beyond the .001 level of significance [p. 380]."

While the internal consistency reliability of so short an "objective" measure, consisting of a single item, is impossible to assess, it is quite reasonably assumed that its scores will almost certainly be read in the same way by people with a common knowledge of simple numbers; and that it is unnecessary to obtain an index of the inter-rater reliability of that reading.

The use of indirectly self-descriptive checks

If well-rationalized and brief, a directly self-descriptive check may not elicit a damaging amount of suspiciousness or defensiveness. But such checks may sometimes inadvertently raise too much self-consciousness about their contents for particular groups of subjects. In that event, it is advisable to devise checks whose object of measurement is less obviously the subject himself. Thus, by permitting the subject to feel less personally exposed in his psychological admissions about the impact- of the manipulations, a more indirect kind of check can, at once, perform its epistemological function and prevent the intrusion of uncontrolled variables from vitiating the remainder of the experiment. The type of indirect check to be illustrated here actually emerged from pilot work in which the more frequently used direct variety was found deficient for the kinds of subjects available for the ultimate experiment. Specif- ically, in doing preliminary work on the development of the methodo- logy for the previously discussed experiment on anxiety, fear, and social affiliation (Sarnoff & Zimbardo, 1961), it was discovered that partici- pants tended to be reluctant, when asked directly, to report any appreci- able amount of apprehension when confronted by the induction of fear. That is, an ordinary six-point "objective" type of item, requesting sub- jects to indicate how ill-at-ease or upset they were at the prospect of receiving painful electric shocks, consistently failed to reveal a stronger response than it revealed among subjects who were led to anticipate only a mild "tingling sensation." Yet interviews with these pilot subjects led us to believe that those manipulations were credible; and that subjects had been considerably more frightened in the High Fear con- dition than in the Low one.

Further thought upon this problem suggested that the students, who lived in the rather Spartan subculture of an all-male college, might have felt loath to admit having experienced fear. For such a direct admission, however anonymously registered, might have been seen by them as a basic vulnerability in their manliness. And the self-disclosure of such a vulnerability might have been more emotionally menacing to the subjects than the physical pain they expected to endure.

As a result of such conjectures, we decided to employ a check that, as described in the last chapter, consisted of having subjects report not on their own reaction to an experimental condition but, instead, on that of a purported subject depicted in photographic slides. And this indirect check did, in fact, differentiate subjects in the various conditions in accordance with the intensity of the apprehension those conditions were intended to arouse.

Such indirect measures require a good deal of special work on the part of an experimenter. First, he must compose a very convincing rationale for showing pictures of a purported subject and for having those pictures rated by the actual subjects. Then, he must prepare those pictures and their mode of presentation. Operationally, this requires a different set of photographs for each manipulative condition. In our experiment (Sarnoff & Zimbardo, 1961), it was necessary to make four different sets of slides to accommodate the expectations induced by each of the four manipulative conditions. Moreover, although the same model is used in all pictures shown to subjects, the mere constancy of his presence does not guarantee control over the possibility that he himself may somehow elicit, in the various sets of pictures, different degrees of the psychological state that the manipulations alone are intended to induce and that the checks are, therefore, intended to measure. Hence, as in the above experiment, it is necessary to do an independent study, with subjects not included in the experiment, merely to be able to rule out that possible source of contamination of the response of subjects to the checks.

Next, the set of photographs have to be coordinated with the channels of response that subjects are requested to make to them. And insofar as the measuring stimuli are indirect, those channels probably can be quite "objective"; that is, prearranged according to a scale within which subjects register the degree to which they feel the model possesses the relevant psychological state. Finally, the administration of these checks must be mechanically smooth, fitting as unobstrusively as possible into the equipment used to carry out other phases of the experiment. For example, in the above experiment, we coordinated the presentation of our checks with the tape-recorder used to communicate experimental rationales and instructions via headsets to each subject in the partitioned group. Thus, as each slide was flashed on a screen before the subjects — from a projector situated behind their partitions — subjects heard a brief commentary describing it. This commentary was, of course, prerecorded on the tape by the same experimenter who made the whole recording and who was seen both in the slides and in front of the subjects in the ongoing experiment.

Subsequent to this experiment, Zimbardo did some research bearing upon the relative efficacy of direct versus indirect checks on the effectiveness of manipulations. And this research reinforces the general assumption, indicated above, that the choice between such checks is a matter largely contingent upon the kind of subjects participating in an experiment. In referring to this research, Bromberg (1967) summarizes its relevant conclusions as follows:

> Zimbardo (1964) presents data from the study by Zimbardo and Formica (1963), that a person's general style of defensive emotional response will determine whether or not a direct measure will be sensitive to the expression of his aroused feelings. Using both a direct and a projective measure of fear arousal, he found that Ss who reported themselves reticent in the expression of their feelings showed greater fear arousal on the projective measure than on the direct measure, while the opposite was true of Ss who reported that they were likely to express their feelings to others [p. 83].

Bromberg goes on to add, however, that both of the checks alluded to by Zimbardo succeeded in differentiating between conditions with respect to the levels of fear they were designed to induce; and that the direct measure employed by Zimbardo and Formica tended to correlate quite highly, .75, with their indirect one, which was the check discussed in the foregoing example (Sarnoff & Zimbardo, 1961).

Problems involved in devising theoretically appropriate verbal criteria for checks on the effectiveness of manipulations

While the indirect checks used by Sarnoff and Zimbardo (1961) were successful, their resulting data were not as unequivocally interpretable as such data should ideally be. True, we were able to demonstrate empirically that both "High" conditions were significantly more arousing than their respective 'Low' conditions. However, we used exactly the same wording in the item that requested subjects to indicate how "ill-at-ease or upset" they felt the model was in the slides they saw. Hence, responses to that item had to apply equally to the imputation of levels of anxiety, on the one hand, and levels of fear, on the other.

But since we had based our entire experiment on Freud's conceptual distinctions between anxiety and fear, it was incumbent upon us to devise a check whose content reflected the different psychological properties attributed to those motives. Certainly, our predictions about the opposing effects of those motives on affiliative preference were deduced from the attribution of such differential properties. Yet the wording of our check offered no means of reflecting the differential inner experiences of fear and anxiety.

Thus, while our hypotheses were supported, it might still be argued that the motivations we manipulated were not necessarily the two we had intended to compare. For example, it could be said that, while the anticipation of painful electric shocks may well have induced fear, the anticipation of sucking on a rubber nipple may have aroused shame rather than anxiety, and that subjects given the latter anticipation may have chosen to wait alone not because of anxiety but because of embarrassment.

Indeed, the phrase "ill-at-ease or upset" could easily describe a variety of feelings, including embarrassment. Consequently, as our checks were worded, they could not yield the data required to answer such plausible alternative explanations of our predicted results.

This situation can, of course, be operationally avoided in instances where the psychological states involved are easily distinguishable in verbal terms; where, that is, the feelings to be measured are clearly connoted by particular words that are not used to express other kinds of feelings. Thus, for example, the semantic representation of hetero-sexual arousal presents no special problems, as indicated by the preceding example of a simple verbal item referring to it. Nor are such feelings as rejection or anger difficult to represent linguistically.

The terms "fear" and "anxiety", however, are exceedingly difficult to represent in unequivocally different semantic forms. For the two terms are often used interchangeably in generic speech — a fact that may well indicate that their common element of apprehension may blur conscious perception of nuances of the psychological difference that Freudian theory attributes to the two motives.

But certainly, we could not have expected our subjects to be so aware of those nuances that they would have found it perfectly meaningful to rate the model twice — once on "how fearful" he appeared and once on "how anxious" he appeared. Nor, given the semantic overlap in the generic use of those terms, could we have safely concluded that the responses of subjects to them were valid indicants of the theoretical differences those terms define in their technical usage with respect to the Freudian concepts under investigation. Besides, the presentation of two such measures might well have given subjects an indication of the variables involved in our hypotheses, thus inadvertently introducing undesirable sources of contamination in their responses to the checks themselves and to the subsequent measure of the dependent variable.

It is apparent that, while verbal checks on manipulations involved in Freudian experiments are now preferable to physiological or non-verbal behavioral ones, the psychological states induced by such manipulations may sometimes be extraordinarily difficult to operationalize in linguistic terms. Yet these difficulties are not necessarily intransigent. Rather, the very shortcomings of one experimenter's attempt to cope with them may stimulate another to develop a more adequate technique.

That is what happened when Bromberg adapted the indirect checks used by Sarnoff and Zimbardo (1961) to his experiment. He used two indices of the psychological state induced by his manipulations of phobic anxiety on the one hand, and fear on the other. The first was a six-point scale on which subjects were asked to indicate how concerned or ill-at-ease the purported model appeared to be. And, essentially, that item was, in content, the same as the one we had employed. In addition, Bromberg included a second item, also on a six-point scale, which requested subjects to indicate how *justified* was the concern shown by the model.

In asking the additional question, Bromberg verbalized a conceptual property of anxiety that we had operationally neglected: its tendency to be inwardly perceived as unjustified by the objective nature of the external stimulus that provokes it. For such perceived inappropriateness of anxiety is, from a theoretical viewpoint, one of the psychological characteristics that distinguishes it from the conscious experience of fear.

As a result of using both items, Bromberg's checks permitted him to assess, with greater theoretical precision than we had been able to do, the effectiveness of his manipulations in arousing phobic anxiety versus fear. For he could rely upon the measure of unjustified apprehension as a quantified index of a verbalized experience assumed to be more readily induced by anxiety than by fear.

Checking on a sequence of manipulations within the same experiment

It will be recalled that Bromberg's experiment also called for a check on the third of his manipulated independent variables: free-floating anxiety. The check on this variable had to be administered before those pertaining to phobic anxiety and fear, for two levels of free-floating anxiety were assumed to be induced by the exposure of subjects high and low in castration conflict to two levels of hetero-sexual arousal; in short, from an interaction between the nonmanipulated CC variable and the manipulated SA conditions. The resulting two levels of free-floating anxiety were then expected to interact with the three manipulated levels of AP, leading HFFA subjects to experience more phobic anxiety than the LFFA subjects when both anticipated the onset of mild pain, and permitting HFFA subjects under that anticipation to represent the phobic anxiety group, whose responses to the dependent variables were compared with those of the year (HFFA-SP and LFFA-SP) and free-floating anxiety (HFFA-NP) groups to test the experiment's hypotheses. Of course, each of the above groups had its own control group, as indicated in Figure 4 of Chapter 9.

Thus, the checks on free-floating anxiety had to be administered after the SA arousals and prior to those of the AP. At the same time, it was necessary to check on the impact of the SA conditions *per se*, since a theoretically appropriate imputation of anxiety related to castration conflict among males requires any measure of such anxiety to be specifically linked to the prior arousal of heterosexual motivation.

Accordingly, following the SA inductions, Bromberg obtained checks not only on the intensity of heterosexual motivation aroused but also on the degree of free-floating anxiety presumably triggered, in turn, by those arousals. Both these checks were presented in the form of seven-point "objective" scales of a direct variety, the subjects being asked to report upon their own feelings. This particular procedure had,

like all the checks, been thoroughly and convincingly rationalized to
the subjects. The check on SA read: "This print tends to be sexually
stimulating," whereas the item checking on the induction of free-floating
anxiety was worded: "It is difficult to feel completely relaxed and
comfortable while looking at this print." And since the SA materials
consisted of three cards — three voluptuous female nudes in the HSA
condition and three clothed women in the LSA condition — the same
two items were administered with each card, yielding a range of
intensity scores from three to twenty-one.

Analyses of these data showed that the HSA and LSA differed
significantly and, as intended, in their intensity of reported sexual
stimulation; and that the high CC and low CC subjects likewise differed
in the degree to which they reported it was difficult "to feel completely
relaxed and comfortable" while viewing the HSA prints. Moreover,
Bromberg found that the HCC and LCC subjects did not differ on
the check of the sexual stimulation aroused *within* either HSA or LSA
conditions. He was thus able to conclude: "Consequently, any greater
level of FFA (the degree of discomfort associated with viewing the
HSA pictures) that may be shown by HCC Ss, cannot be attributed
to their being more *sexually aroused* than the LCC Ss. The same finding
would also make implausible any attempt to account for differences
on the dependent variables between the FFA, phobic anxiety, and
fear groups as due to uncontrolled variation in the 'take' of the SA
induction between the HCC cells themselves (pp. 94-95)."

Finally, to obtain empirical assurance on the ability of his tactile
procedures to sustain the levels of arousal induced by the SA manipulations, Bromberg included a last check, following his checks on the
AP inductions of phobic anxiety and fear. Thus, after subjects had
rated the model on his amount of concern and its degree of justification, they were asked to indicate on a six-point scale their response
to this item: "The person in the slide appeared to be sexually aroused."

Analysis of the data pertaining to this item showed that subjects
previously exposed to the HSA condition and its subsequent tactile
reinforcement attributed significantly more sexual arousal to the model
than did the contrasting LSA subjects. Moreover, in accordance with
the findings of the initial check on the SA manipulations, the data
from this last check indicated that there were no differences in the
intensity of attributed arousal between HCC and LCC subjects within
the HSA or the LSA groups.

*The special problems involved in attempting
to check on manipulations employing
subliminal stimuli*

All of the preceding examples have dealt with manipulations whose theoretically pertinent stimuli are well above the subjects' threshold of recognition. During those manipulations, subjects were not given the actual scientific reason for being asked to have a sensory confrontation with particular stimuli. Nor, in the relevant cases, were they told what the stimuli were meant to symbolize, above and beyond their purported experimental function. But, in every instance, subjects certainly were aware of the manifest content of the manipulations in which they were involved. Indeed, it was the whole intent of the manipulations to make a subject's exposure to their crucial stimuli as explicit as possible.

The explicitness of these supraliminal stimuli was indicated by theoretical considerations. Quite simply, it was necessary for the creation of the conditions required to test the hypotheses involved. But a researcher may be interested in testing Freudian hypotheses that concern the intrusion of stimuli below the threshold of consciousness; stimuli which, while being consciously unrecognized, may nonetheless exert predictable effects upon an individual's behavior or experience. Indeed, one might even argue, as Silverman (1967) has done, that such stimuli, because they presumably do not arouse ego-defensiveness, may sometimes have even greater effects than perceptible stimuli.

Given an hypothesis that requires its use, subliminal stimulation is obviously what should be conveyed by an experimenter's manipulations. And the differential levels of intensity in the arousal variable may be contrived, for example, by presenting to different experimental groups subliminal stimuli whose content, at a level of recognition, can be reliably judged as differing quantitatively on the dimension they are meant to evoke.

The extremely thorny methodological problem that has tended to limit the experimental use of subliminal manipulations arises from the difficulty of presenting evidence concerning the effectiveness of such manipulations to create the states of motivation or cognition they are intended to induce. For if a person cannot even recognize a rapidly passing flicker of light, how can an experimenter conclude with any confidence that the person has not only been affected by it, but affected in precisely the manner and to the degree required by the experiment's hypothesis? Yet, even if he can so privately persuade himself, how can an experimenter, in the absence of relevant empirical data, publicly demonstrate the effectiveness of his subliminal manipulations?

Insofar as an interested experimenter cannot provide such data, his experimental use of subliminal stimuli leaves his research open, at the very outset, to the kind of indeterminacy that is not only scientifically undesirable, but that is, in fact, preventable through the use of supraliminal manipulations. For if he fails to gain support for his hypotheses, he certainly cannot rule out the distinct possibility that he failed to create the conditions essential to a theoretically appropriate test of those hypotheses. The whole scientific point of manipulating a variable is to obtain empirical control over it, and if a researcher embarks on an experiment *knowing* that he has built into it no way of demonstrating such control, he fails to make minimally adequate empirical use of the very method of inquiry whose logical advantages he seeks to gain.

On the other hand, in such circumstances, there is nothing very reassuring in positive results about a hypothesis that concerns the impact of a subliminally manipulated independent variable on any dependent variables. For, if there is no separate empirical check on the psychological impact of the subliminal stimuli, it is quite conceivable that their effect on a dependent variable is not a function of the psychological property theoretically attributed to them by the experimenter but, is instead, a result of some other property contained by the particular set of stimuli employed. For example, an experimenter may use two apparently appropriately contrasting sets of drawings for the subliminal creation of his experimental conditions. Yet those sets may contain some differential contents, which, rather than the ones assumed by the experimenter, may, quite fortuitously, produce effects wrongly attributed to other contents — and hence to the wrong independent variable.

Silverman (1967) has attempted to cope with the challenge of devising independent checks on the impact of subliminal manipulations by having subjects give free associations to supraliminal presentations of the manipulative stimuli after an experiment is concluded. Certainly, such associations can establish motivational differences evoked by sets of contrasting stimuli as viewed at the level of full recognition and awareness of their contents. However, differences in such su-praliminal associations cannot reasonably permit one to conclude that the same motivational differences were aroused when those stimuli had been subliminally presented, and when subjects were unable to discern the very appearance of those stimuli, much less substantive differences among them. Yet unless a researcher can produce some evidence (even that based on retrospective recall) *of feelings at the time of the subliminal presentation* to show that subjects exposed to the varying stimuli were, in fact, differentially aroused by them, he has no logically compelling empirical basis for claiming that he had succeeded in experimentally creating the conditions required to test his hypotheses.

Until appropriate methods can be devised for objectively dem-onstrating such success, experimentation using subliminal manipula-tions must necessarily be surrounded by the burden of doubt that has been described. And it is to be hoped that experimenters interested in hypotheses involving such manipulations will become equally keen on developing the techniques needed to assure both themselves and others that those hypotheses are adequately tested.

Measuring Dependent Variables

Having experimentally created the conditions necessary for testing a hypothesis, a researcher must observe the extent to which they exert their predicted effects. But to make such observations, he has to specify in advance the empirical phenomena that will serve as operational indicants of those effects. Just as measures and manipulations of independent variables objectify the imputed determinants of consequent effects, measures of dependent variables operationally define the imputed consequences of those hypothesized determinants.

Measures of dependent variables, therefore, are no different in their scientific meaning from checks on the effectiveness of manipulations or personality scales. All scientific measures are meant to be empirical manifestations of concepts, either phenotypic or genotypic, and, ideally, every measuring instrument should reliably reflect the particular properties theoretically attributed to the concept it operationally defines. Since it follows that the same set of psychometric desiderata are generally applicable to all measuring instruments, what has already been said regarding the construction of measures of independent variables need not be reiterated in discussing the measurement of dependent variables. However, many experiments may contain important methodological considerations that militate against the fullest possible application of those principles to measures of the dependent variables involved in them. But before turning to these issues, several very significant points should now be added to what has already been presented on the validity of measuring instruments.

Construct validity and measures of dependent variables

Research on *any* measure's construct validity actually brings into question the construct validity of at least two measures in every such

202

study: the instrument designated, for the time being, as the indicant of the independent variable and the measure likewise designated to represent the dependent variable. The hypothesis that stipulates the causal relationship between the two variables is, of course, theoretically derived, explicitly and principally, from the psychological properties attributed to the independent variable. But the hypothesis also implicitly includes attributions about the properties of the dependent variable it employs; for example, a researcher must make assumptions, although he may not articulate them, about the capacity of the dependent variable to be affected and about the ways in which those effects may be empirically manifested. And the hypothesis is actually tested by bringing the measures of the independent and dependent variables together in the manner prescribed by the experimenter's theoretical deductions.

Conventionally, a researcher may refer to measures of dependent variables as "criteria." And so they are, given the deductive reasoning that governs their empirical placement in studies that happen to regard them as reflecting the effects of antecedant determinants on the variables they are intended to measure. But merely by calling a measure a "criterion" does not *ipso facto* validate its ability to reflect the concept imputed from it. Indeed, such a term may obscure the fact that its status as a criterion is *assigned* to it by the researcher treating it, within the design of his particular study, as a dependent variable. So, while it may be assigned the empirical task of providing data germane to the evaluation of a predictive concept, a measure of a dependent variable can itself be properly validated only by studies in which predictions are made *from it* to measures of other variables. Moreover, as is true of the scientific relationship between *every* variable and its measuring instrument, the validity of a variable that happens, for a specific study, to be regarded as dependent is inextricably tied to the validity of the measure purporting to define it. Hence, every study on the construct validity of such an instrument is also, necessarily and simultaneously, a study of the scientific utility of the concept it is supposed to measure.

There is, in short, an inevitable element of explanatory ambiguity latent in the simplest of scientific studies. For though the predicted relationship between two variables can be observed only through the operational indices of each, both measures may be deficient in the extent to which they succeed in empirically articulating their respective

variables. Thus, failure to observe the predicted empirical relationhips
may stem from the operational shortcomings of either or both measures.
Lacking a sufficient fund of relevant information from other studies,
in which the validity of the measures involved had been tested through
predictions made from *each*, an experimenter might be quite unable
to rule out — as would be scientifically desirable — defective instru-
mentation as a plausible reason for not having obtained results that
support his hypotheses.

Naturally, if a researcher has access to measures whose construct
validity has an impressive empirical history, he would be wise to use
them as indices of both independent and dependent variables, but
insofar as such measures are still scarce for a researcher interested
in testing Freudian hypotheses, he has to make use of the best that
he can find, constructing the theoretically relevant ones that may not
yet even exist. Thus, in finding and constructing measures that appear
most appropriately to express the concepts whose hypothesized relationship he wants to study, a researcher is obliged to tolerate the connotative uncertainties attendant upon their experimental application.

To be sure, in his pilot work a researcher can attempt, in ways
already indicated, to preclude deficiencies of measurement that stem
from unreliability and the mechanics of administration. He may even
gather correlational data that separately bear upon the construct
validity of the measure of his proposed independent and dependent
variables. But short of conducting a whole program of validational
research devoted to studies in which *each* of those measures is conceived as a predictor, an experimenter must usually be willing to
test his hypotheses with measures that may not adequately manifest
the conceptual characteristics of the variables under investigation.

A researcher often cannot escape the prospect of dealing with
dependent variables that have not yet been operationally defined by
a measure of proven construct validity. In other words, he may have
to employ, as criteria, measures of dependent variables whose own
construct validity is actually as unknown as that of the measure of
the Freudian variable he is intending to assess. When this is the case,
he might logically be tempted to suspend his test of assumptions
concerning a Freudian independent variable of personality until he
develops a valid measure of the dependent variable that can serve
with solid empirical — as well as with good theoretical — justification
as a criterion. But if he were to undertake such validational research

as a prelude to the formal testing of the hypotheses of interest to him, an investigator would immediately be confronted by the very ambiguity he had sought to reduce, for every validational study involves the test of an hypothesis. Thus, the researcher might well have to make predictions from the unvalidated criterion measure to measures of other variables whose construct validity was equally unknown. Such preliminary validational studies might yield data no less indeterminant than any the researcher is likely to obtain in using the unvalidated criterion measure to define the dependent variable in the experiment he originally planned to conduct. To be genuinely useful, such preliminary validational studies would require as much methodological care as a researcher would have to give to his formal experiment, for they are governed by precisely the same principles of deductive logic, which impose equally rigorous demands for their empirical articulation.

"Face" validity and the measurement of dependent variables

As matters now stand, therefore, "face" validity may be the only kind of validity an experimenter can call upon in choosing or devising his measures of dependent variables. Of course, he can and should bolster his own impressions of a measure's "face" validity through pilot studies with professional colleagues, as well as with subjects similar to those expected to be included in the actual experiment. In addition, as in the case of personality measures, an experimenter can seek to insure, again via exploratory studies, that his measures of dependent variables are optimally reliable and free from flaws of administration.

Many potential dependent variables readily lend themselves to operational definitions for which the claim of "face" validity can be compellingly made. For example, asking individuals to indicate whether they want to be alone or with others would seem to be a compellingly literal operational translation of the variable of affiliative preference.

Insofar as a researcher uses such straightforward measures of dependent variables, he has at least a very good logical basis for relying upon them as criteria for evaluating the predictive power of any Freudian concept he seeks to test.

Reliability and the experimental use of measures
of dependent variables

Being limited, in advance of his experiments, in regard to what can be done about the empirical validity of any of the measures he proposes to employ, a researcher might be all the more inclined to safeguard their reliability. However, the experimental use of measures of dependent variables is frequently such that the desiderata of reliability may directly conflict with those required to support the rationale of the manipulations, to prevent the hypotheses from being inadvertently disclosed, or to capture an effect that is theoretically presumed to be highly evanescent. Sometimes all three of these considerations are involved, pitting the psychological realities of human reactivity against the mathematical stipulations of psychometrics, and inclining a sensible researcher to choose a less than optimally reliable measure of his dependent variable rather than risk the possibility of undermining his entire experiment. For it would do him no good to insist on a purity of measurement that may foul all the work preceding it.

Naturally, when such a scientifically distasteful choice is not at issue, a researcher would be absolutely foolish not to honor his own labors with as reliable a measure of his dependent variable as that of his independent variable, thereby completing the experimental chain of logic with as methodologically sound a link at its end as its beginning. But when, for example, a lengthy attitude scale of high reliability might clearly jeopardize the maintenance of the deceptions he has painstakingly contrived — and thus abruptly dissipate the predicted effects of the manipulated independent variable — an experimenter would be more than foolish if he did not employ a brief and, hence, in all likelihood a less reliable, measure of the same dependent variable.

Procedural contingencies governing the
experimental usage of less than optimally
reliable measures of dependent variables

A clear instance of such a procedural contingency may be illustrated by reference to studies already cited. In three experiments that were concerned with various motivational determinants of affiliative behavior (Schachter, 1959; Sarnoff & Zimbardo, 1961; Bromberg, 1967), preference for social affiliation was employed as a dependent variable. Following exposure to their particular manipulations, each of those experiments sought, via an essentially one-item scale, to assess whether and to what degree a subject felt inclined either to affiliate with, or to isolate himself from, other subjects.

From a purely abstract perspective, such an inclination could have been measured by a scale consisting of sufficient items to yield a high order of demonstrated reliabiliy. When attitudes are presented to subjects in measures that call for the manifestation of general and longstanding dispositions, which, moreover, are perceived as bearing no consequence for immediate action within the experimental procedure, they can be sensibly queried by a variety of items, each of which is worded in a slightly different manner. But under the actual conditions created by the manipulations of the above experiments, the use of a scale with more than one item was strongly counterindicated by several psychological realities.

Above all, it would have been preposterous to have asked subjects more than once to indicate their preference for waiting with others or alone. For in the context of the deceptions employed, the question was not raised as a general and hypothetical one but, instead, as pertinent to a specific and immediately required decision about an imminently occurring event. In fact, in their replies, subjects perceived themselves as having decided how they would be behaving very shortly, thus permitting the experimenters to conduct them to the appropriate waiting room.

From the viewpoint of a subject, therefore, the query concerned a concrete decision, which was to be put directly into effect; having once stated his preference, a subject expected it to be acted upon by the experimenter who had asked him to express it. Indeed, under the deceptions employed, the experimenter had promised to accommodate whichever choice the subject might make, so that, after the subject had registered his choice, the question soliciting it was exhausted of relevance. Any further questioning along the same lines would have been senseless. Moreover, to have pursued such senselessness would have flagrantly contradicted the very aura of immediate decisiveness and applicability with which the measure had been rationalized to the subjects; it would have made that rationale suspect, and the subjects would have become suspicious about the measure itself. Under those circumstances, the subjects might have reacted defensively to it, their replies reflecting this sudden and uncontrolled defensiveness rather than the impact of the independent variables involved in the experimenter's hypothesis. Indeed, given the unwanted intrusion of such defensiveness, many subjects who otherwise would have registered a preference for isolation, might have indicated a desire for affiliation —primarily to air their suspicions about other subjects.

Redundancy of measurement, so important to the attainment of reliability, may be procedurally inappropriate for use with other kinds of dependent variables. Thus, one of Conrad's (1968) dependent variables concerned the subjective feeling of hunger, while another was the actual amount of food consumed. In both instances, "one-shot" operational measures were predicated by the rationales needed not only to introduce these measures but also to make them intellectually consonant with everything else subjects were requested to do before and after their administration. Oriented toward the immediate present, a question inquiring about one's state of hunger can hardly be repeated without seeming ridiculous and, moreover, calling unwanted attention to the role of that variable in the actual but dissimulated purpose of the experiment. Nor, of course, would it have made sense for the experimenter to ask subjects to eat again, just after they had finished eating as much food as they wished to consume.

Theoretical contingencies governing the experimental usage of less than optimally reliable measures of dependent variables

As previously pointed out, experimental work on Freudian hypotheses is currently obliged to go forward without much solid information about the temporal parameters of the effects induced by manipulations of relevant independent variables. Consequently, an experimenter must usually guess at how long such effects are sustained within subjects exposed to his manipulations. Operationally, in empirically articulating these guesses, an experimenter has to apply his measures of dependent variables in time to register the predicted effects before they dissipate themselves. And he also has to use instruments that are sensitive enough to reflect whatever effects are still ongoing at the time he seeks to measure them.

Thus, an experimenter must plan to employ, as measures of his dependent variables, operational indices that are likely to capture rather fleeting effects. Moreover, those indices must be capable of detecting those relatively slight differentials in impact that are predicted for the different levels of arousal in the manipulations employed. For while these levels may be labelled "High" versus "Low," their actual difference in intensity usually cannot be made as great as might be possible if an experimenter were not restricted by his ethical commitments.

When these various considerations prevail, quite brief measures are the safest ones for an experimenter to use in operationally defining his dependent variables. Their very brevity tends to be a guarantee that the effects induced can be detected before they fade out; that is, before subjects are too far removed, in space and time, from the experimental stimuli that are supposed to exert the theoretically predicted effects upon the dependent variables imputed to those subjects.

Yet the brevity of a measure tends to run counter to the statistical requirements necessary for the achievement of reliability. Hence, once again, an experimenter may be forced to sacrifice reliability of measurement — this time, in the interest of using a measure that is suitable to the theoretically presumed nature of the effects whose observation it is intended to permit. For without such theoretically appropriate observations, the experiment's hypothesis cannot be properly tested; and the whole purpose of the experiment would be vitiated.

It was, therefore, for theoretical as well as for procedural reasons that Conrad (1968) employed a one-item measure of psychogenic hunger, one of his dependent variables. He could not be sure that the subjective feelings of hunger differentially induced by his manipulations would last long enough to maintain their differential intensity over the period of time, however short it might appear to be, required by a questionnaire of reliable proportions. And certainly, he could hardly have had any theoretical grounds for taking any subjective measure of hunger *after* subjects had eaten, which was an activity whereby he measured another of his dependent variables, eating behavior.

Theoretical considerations were also vitally involved in Bishop's (1965) decision to employ only a single item to measure her chief dependent variable, subjective feelings about finding an experimental task either enjoyable or boring. To be sure, the use of this particular measure was needed insofar as a similar one had been used in the

experiment (Festinger & Carlsmith, 1959), whose essential methodology
Bishop sought as fully as possible to replicate. But in both experiments
the same theoretical issue indicated the use of a very brief measure
of the dependent variable. For it was assumed that changes in the
pertinent attitudinal variable would reflect a means of reducing the
dissonance induced by prior experimental manipulations. Hence, having
responded to an item tapping his attitude, a subject may have failed
to contribute to the differences in effect predicted for groups of subjects
in which different levels of dissonance were aroused.

Actually, lacking any theoretically derived measure of dissonance
per se, neither of those experiments could have assessed how much
residual dissonance might have remained following the post-manipulative administration of the one-item attitude measure. Nor is the theory
of cognitive dissonance sufficiently refined to permit an extrapolation of
the *precise* amounts of dissonance likely to be aroused by given manipulations, or reduced by given responses subsequent to those manipulations. Therefore, Bishop had no reason to think it would be theoretically
appropriate to utilize a lengthy measure of her dependent variable,
while having a good deal of reason to employ a short one.

*Coordinating measures of dependent variables
and checks on the effectiveness of
experimental manipulations*

The need to detect promptly the presumably quite transient effects
of a particular manipulation on the relevant dependent variable becomes
all the more acute in instances when checks on the effectiveness of the
manipulation are likely to siphon off some of the manipulative impact
that might otherwise contribute to manifest changes in the dependent
variable. Of course, such a likelihood could be precluded by arranging
to administer a check after, rather than before, the measurement of
the dependent variable. Yet such a procedure is not logically ideal,
since the check would not be as temporally contiguous as possible with
exposure to the manipulation. Moreover, if the check were to follow
the measurement of the dependent variable, it might be contaminated
by the subject's reaction to all the procedures intervening between
the onset of the manipulation and completion of the measure of the

dependent variable. Indeed, the measurement of the dependent variable might be so reductive of the motivational tensions induced by immediately preceding manipulations that any subsequent checks on the effectiveness of the manipulations might fail to show the differentials in arousal that the manipulations had actually created.

As is true of every aspect of methodology, however, final decisions about procedure should reconcile the requirements of logic with the "psychologic" presumed to be operative in the determining of the phenomenon under investigation. Thus, if it made more theoretical sense to have the checks follow rather than precede the measures of dependent variables, a researcher would be adhering to a crazy sort of reasoning if he were to permit entirely formalistic considerations of logic to overrule his scientific objective of creating the best possible conditions for testing his psychological hypotheses.

In Bishop's (1965) case, the previously described theoretical assumptions about the reduction of cognitive dissonance suggested that it would be best for her to apply the checks on the effectiveness of her manipulations of privation after her measurement of the dependent attitudinal variable. If she had followed the reverse procedure, subjects might well have used the checks as a channel for the reduction of their dissonance. In that event, the differentials in attitude predicted by her hypotheses might not have had an opportunity to become manifest through her measure of the dependent variable, and she would not have established the observational conditions required for a theoretically appropriate test of her hypotheses. Under such conditions, negative results would have been a quite misleading basis for concluding that her hypotheses had been in error.

Actually, the checks on her manipulations of privation yielded corroborative data on the effectiveness of those manipulations. Whatever reduction of tension was occasioned by the response of her subjects to the preceding measure of the dependent variable evidently did not entirely dissipate whatever differential feelings about privation were differentially aroused by her manipulations of it. Perhaps she might have obtained essentially similar results if she had followed a more purely logical procedure, applying the checks immediately after the manipulations and then administering the measure of the dependent variable. However, in extrapolating as faithfully as she could from the relevant assumptions of dissonance theory, Bishop was being scientifically appropriate in letting the most plausible psychological deductions from that theory serve as a basis for the procedural sequence she actually employed.

Bromberg was faced with a similar methodological problem. He did not want subjects to discharge their experimentally induced tensions prior to the measurement of his dependent variables, yet, for reasons already discussed, it was imperative for him to check on the effectiveness of each of his manipulations directly after exposing subjects to it. However, some of those checks contained items whose content was psychologically similar to that represented in both his measure (CDPI) of the dependent variable of phobic ideation and in his measure (PHICON) of fears that served as an empirical control on the effects predicted for the CDPI. For example, in responding to the check on level of absolute apprehension induced, the subjects might have reduced the amount of anxiety or fear the AP manipulations had aroused. For in stating how "ill-at-ease" a purported participant in the experiment appeared to be, subjects might have been siphoning off the tensions of either of those motivational states. And insofar as they did discharge such tensions, subjects may have approached the subsequent CDPI and PHICON measures with insufficient tension to reflect the differential strengths of the effects predicted from the manipulations.

Bromberg sought to minimize the occurrence of these eventualities by using as few items as possible in his intervening checks. Moreover, by establishing very compelling manipulations, including the previously described tactile procedure, he insured the likelihood that the theoretically required motivational states would persist long enough and strongly enough to be detectable on the ideational measures.

On maximizing the sensitivity of measures of dependent variables

A. *Detecting short-lived effects.*   Although an experimenter may decide, for procedural or theoretical reasons, to use a brief measure of his dependent variable, brevity alone does not necessarily guarantee the registration of the differential effects of his manipulations. For while those effects may be present, they may also be relatively weak, subjects exposed to one level of a manipulation being not greatly more affected than those exposed to a contrasting level. Yet checks on the differential effectiveness of the manipulations may yield significant differences that an insensitive measure of the dependent variable may fail to reveal. In such an event, an experimenter is, of course, obliged to reject his hypothesis. Yet his rejection may actually reflect not so much on the fallacies of theory involved in the hypothesis as in the crudeness of his observational method.

To forestall such an unfortunate eventuality, an experimenter can attempt to increase the sensitivity of his measures of dependent variables. For instance, regarding graphic scales, there are various devices by means of which subjects can be led to respond with a greater range of individuality. Thus, a researcher can use a totally unmarked and unlabelled line, anchored only at both ends by polar opposites of reaction to a statement to which the scale refers. The subject may then be asked merely to place a mark anywhere along the line, in accordance with his feelings about the statement. Subsequently, a researcher can literally measure the distance marked from one of the poles, using the resulting figures as expressions of the amount of the variable imputable to the subject (Conrad, 1968).

To save the time involved in applying, as it were, measures to measures, a number of variations of this technique may be helpful. For example, Bishop (1965) employed what was basically a six-point linear scale — 0, 10, 20, 30, 40, and 50 — each point of which had a verbal description beneath it. But, between each point, the scale was divided into ten demarcated spaces, like a ruler, and subjects were instructed to "place a check mark at any point on the scale that seems best to express the degree of your attitude or feeling [Appendix E]."

In effect, these scales had a range of 51 points, making them far more sensitive to nuances of individual reactivity than would have been the case in an ordinary six-point scale. Moreover, since Bishop's scales contained no neutral mid-point, all subjects were required to express themselves one way or another, albeit to varying degrees on each of the variables measured.

Young children, admittedly, may not be able to make any finer discrimination in the expression of their subjective experiences than is implicit in a two-point scale. But adults, long trained in translating the subtleties of their feeling into verbally mediated quantitative gradations, may be quite meaningfully approached with items for which considerably more points of psychological discernment are provided.

B. *Detecting relatively strong effects.*   Assuming that the effects of the arousals are sufficiently longlasting to endure for more than a few minutes beyond the process of checking on the manipulations, the sheer quantity of items employed in a measure of a dependent variable may insure that whatever differential changes have been induced in it will be detected, if not by some items, then by others. And the use of a fairly wide rating scale, such as a six-point one, in connection with those items, is a further guarantee that fine quantities of an effect may not be lost, as they might in the case of a narrow rating scale.

In this instance, happily, the requirements of reliability and theoretical appropriateness go together; each may be pursued without undermining the other. Certainly, with adult subjects, there appears to be no difficulty in using a rating scale with six alteratives, applied to a series of items defining the dependent variable (Sarnoff & Corwin, 1959; Sarnoff, 1960b). In those cited instances, the actual substance of the rating scheme, which made no provision for a neutral or noncommital answer, was suggested by the one originally employed by Adorno *et al* (1950) in their studies of the authoritarian personality. Thus, subjects indicate degrees of agreement to items by inserting, in spaces beside the items, +3, +2, or +1, whereas equivalent amounts of disagreement are indicated by −3, −2, and −1. The signs attached to these numbers are intended merely to connote the emotional tone associated with like or dislike. Similarly ,while using different notation, Bromberg (1967) used a six-point rating scale in connection with the 71-item questionnaire that included both the CDPI and his PHICON.

A fairly long measuring instrument may also be able to detect subjective effects that take some time to "sink in" following the application of manipulations (such as the ones Bromberg employed) whose psychological properties hold forth threatening implications. Thus, it may take subjects a little time to recover from the initial onset of some manipulations against which their first reaction may have been a defensive denial of the imminence of the threat. Under these conditions, subjects may not fully admit their fears into consciousness for some moments. Their first responses, for example, to an ideational measure of a dependent variable may not adequately reflect the effects set into motion by the manipulations; those effects may not become manifest until such subjects have completed their responses to a number of items in the measure.

However, without detailed sequential anlyses of the data obtained by various segments of various measures under various conditions of arousal, one can do no more than keep these possibilities in mind in making decisions about the format of a particular measure of a dependent variable. But insofar as the theoretical properties of the variable, the procedures of the experiment, and the presumed endurance of the manipulations permit their usage, it would be prudent to employ multi-itemed and sensitively-scaled measures of dependent variables. Of course, they can be made quite reliable, thus offering the additional advantage of ruling out unreliability as a plausible basis for failing to observe the effects predicted by one's hypotheses.

The post-manipulative measurement of variables germane to alternative explanations of the predicted changes in a dependent variable

Measuring dependent variables requires careful thought about what additional measures, if any, should be applied as empirical controls for the *specificity* of the alterations expected to occur in the dependent variables *per se*. In such cases, a researcher must strive to show that the prediction made by his hypothesis is restricted to the particular dependent variable involved in it, and that those effects do not extend to dependent variables that other theorists may contend bear the same functional relationship to the manipulated independent variable. Insofar as he can show such discrete discriminatory power for his guiding concept, a researcher demonstrates that its constituent assumptions are, indeed, empirically fruitful, however less theoretically parsimonious they may be than those contained in the empirically discounted alternative.

Bromberg (1967) had to make such a provision to control for the possibility that his AP arousals might exert *general* ideational effects rather than the specific one he postulated would occur as a result of the interaction between his nonmanipulated independent variable (CC) and *both* of his manipulations (SA and AP). For it could plausibly be argued, from the standpoint of concepts of conditioned learning, that his AP manipulations *per se* would elicit a generalized response of fear, and that his measure of castration-derived phobic ideation merely defined one among many manifestations of fear that would be induced by exposure to the AP manipulations.

To handle this perfectly reasonable possibility, Bromberg included his PHICON measure of fears, which, he presumed, were not functionally related to castration conflict and hence would not be affected by the interactions from which he derived his predictions of differential changes in castration-derived phobic ideation, as measured by the CDPI.

Measuring more than one dependent variable in the same experiment

A combination of theoretical and procedural factors may frequently permit the measurement of only one dependent variable in a single experiment, even though the experimenter may well be interested in other effects of the particular independent variables than those to which he has temporarily confined his empirical study. On the other hand, considering the effort involved in conducting an experiment, a researcher may naturally wish to extract as much theoretically relevant information as he possibly can from it. And it is sometimes quite possible for him to observe systematically more than one type of theoretically postulated consequence of a manipulated independent variable, or of an interaction between a manipulated and nonmanipulated independent variable.

Actually, the necessity of providing empirical controls for a measure of a dependent variable, as just illustrated, involves the measurement of more than one possible effect of an independent variable — albeit a researcher undertakes the observation of such potential additional effects to cope with explanatory alternatives to his own hypotheses. It may even happen that the same experiment will include not only measures of dependent variables, suggested by those alternatives, but also measures of more than one dependent variable suggested by the concepts from which his hypotheses were derived.

However, the measurement of more than one dependent variable immediately confronts an experimenter with methodological decisions, which, as usual, cannot be properly made without careful consideration of their theoretical implications. Of course, if an experimenter had a sufficiently large number of subjects available to him, he might often be able to cope logically with his theoretical uncertainties by using a counterbalanced administration of his postmanipulative measures, having equal numbers of subjects in the various manipulative conditions take those measures in different orders of presentation. For example, if two such measures were involved, an experimenter would have on hand data to show what difference, if any, is made by their order of presentation *per se*. He would thus have imposed a satisfactory empirical control on an otherwise uncontrolled variable, the effect of responding to one postmanipulative measure on succeeding measures.

As has been noted, it is entirely possible that even the sheer passage of time may contribute to the dissipation of psychological effects set into motion by a manipulation. In such instances, those measures that are furthest removed in time from a manipulation will be at the greatest disadvantage in detecting effects predicted for the dependent variables they operationally define. It is conceivable that they will fail to reflect those effects for that reason, and not because of any inherent deficiency in the concept from which they were deduced.

Yet the deferment in time of the administration of a postmanipulative measure may give it a fortuitous advantage over preceding measures insofar as the effects induced by the manipulations take a while to "sink in" and be expressed. The counterbalancing of postmanipulative measures, when it can be appropriately arranged, is an obviously desirable method of replacing such conjectures as the foregoing ones with empirical data, for insofar as it is empirically found that it does or does not make a difference to apply given measures in one order of presentation or another, such findings can become a more scientifically appropriate basis for making subsequent decisions involving the use of those measures.

But a researcher does not always have available sufficient numbers of subjects to arrange for all the combinations of presentation required by a particular set of measures of dependent variables — even if counterbalancing of those measures were otherwise indicated by the specific theoretical and procedural considerations involved in his experiment. Such considerations may well militate against counterbalancing, even if enough subjects were available to permit its arrangement.

In Bromberg's experiment both such considerations were involved in his decision to use a fixed order of presentation of the measures of his dependent variables. Thus, Bromberg always administered his CDPI measure (together with its PHICON control) *before* measuring the affiliative preferences of his subjects.

In arriving at this decision, Bromberg was guided, theoretically, by the assumption that the ideational effects might be most vulnerable to dissipation by the passage of time and preoccupation with any activities of measurement that might precede his attempts to detect them. On the other hand, it would not have made procedural sense to offer subjects the immediate choice of waiting alone or together — the measuring stimuli needed to observe the responses attributed to the variable of affiliative preference — and then present the ideational questionnaire to them.

Using more than one measure of the same dependent variable in a single experiment

As with the measurement of pertinent traits of personality, an experimenter may sometimes be at a genuine theoretical loss to decide which of several conceivable operational measures of a predicted effect may best reflect the dependent variable involved in his hypothesis. In such an instance, he may wish to apply more than one such measure, on the assumption that he thus minimizes his chances of failing to observe the predicted results because of having selected an insensitive technique of observation. But the very addition of a means of observation may alter, in various ways previously described, the effects induced by the manipulations. Hence, what is done on behalf of one observational technique may vitiate the usefulness of observations that are subsequently made through another technique.

In any event, the use of more than a single index of the same imputed dependent variable raises exactly the same problems that have been discussed in regard to any multiplicity of measures that follow experimental manipulations. Hence, their application is necessarily governed by the same theoretical and procedural implications.

It should be pointed out that, short of literally reproducing the identical measure, any attempt to devise more than one measure of the same variable involves the specification of alternative seats of observable behaviors from which the variable may be imputed. To be sure, these alternative behaviors may, operationally speaking, actually refer to identically registered marks on a piece of paper. Yet those marks refer, of course, to different experiential or behavioral possibilities, thus avoiding a total redundancy of observation.

But since, by operational definition, the referents of the measuring stimuli *must* be different to provide alternative measures of the same variable, the possibility always exists that the responses made to those stimuli actually reflect somewhat different psychological tendencies of the individual. This possibility is both desired and cultivated in constructing measures of variables assumed to be conceptually different, but insofar as it may be an empirical reality in instances when it is neither wanted nor sought after, it works against the attainment of psychological equivalence between alternative measures of the same variable.

Such questions of construct validity, equally applicable to measures employed to define independent or dependent variables, can only be sorted out with scientific appropriateness through the kinds of predictive studies that have been described. And it should also be kept in mind that those questions may be as justly asked of two presumably alternative measures of the same variable as of two measures of presumably different variables.

Conrad's (1968) experiment provides an interesting example of how even an apparently easily observed dependent variable — eating behavior — may profit from two measures of its possible manifestation. Moreover, while both of these indices were predicted, of course, to show the same effect of the pertinent independent variables, they did reflect slight differences in sensitivity to the ways in which that effect was expressed by obese as compared with nonobese subjects. As will be seen below, these differences were very much on Conrad's mind while deciding upon the operations to be definitive of each index:

This variable presented a measurement problem because four types of food substance were offered to the *S*s: crackers, cookies, milk, and water. The main reason for offering four types of food was to maximize the possible range of amount of food consumption. Had only solids been used, eating would have been increasingly inhibited as the session progressed, since both the cookies and the crackers were dry, and most of the crackers were salty. Two solids and two liquids were offered for a more specific reason. Cookies and milk are both considered to be very 'fattening' foods, and it was anticipated that some of the obese *S*s would be dieting. These *S*s could concentrate on the crackers and water, but still ingest a large amount in terms of ounces. On the other hand, it was expected

TESTING FREUDIAN CONCEPTS

that obese *Ss* who were not dieting would prefer the cookies and milk, and that offering only crackers and water would have inhibited their eating, since the type of food they characteristically choose would not have been available. In similar fashion, offering only the rich cookies might have inhibited the eating of the normal *Ss*, since it was felt that they would be more likely to prefer crackers. In general, the choice of foods was intended to make the eating situation as natural as possible, within the limits of accurate measurement of amount consumed, and credibility in terms of the market research rationale.

It was possible to define amount consumed in various ways: number of crackers and cookies, number of bites or oral acts, total weight consumed, or total calories consumed. The author felt that no single measure was fully adequate for use in a study of obesity, and he therefore utilized the two measures which were considered most relevant:

a. *Total ounces consumed.* This measure seemed most relevant to the phenomenon of compulsive eating, and to the frequent accounts by obese individuals that they tend to eat until they are "filled up."

b. *Total calories consumed.* This measure is, of course, the most important with regard to the cause of fat accumulation in the body and the development of obesity [pp. 29-30].

Both of these indices yielded results in line with Conrad's theoretical expectations. The difference in amount of food eaten by obese versus normal subjects was far greater under the condition of social rejection than under that of social neutrality. Indeed, following rejection, normals actually ate less food than they did following the neutral manipulation, whereas the opposite was true of obese subjects.

These findings were even more striking for the index of total calories consumed than they were for total ounces consumed. Thus, the average amount of calories consumed by the rejected obese subjects was significantly greater than any other group, whereas that was not the case for ounces consumed, in which the rejected obese subjects ate significantly more than obese subjects in the neutral condition but not significantly more than obese subjects in the accepted condition.

Precautions against the intrusion of "experimenter effects" during the actual measurement of the dependent variables

The desirability of precluding the confounding intrusion of inadvertent "experimenter effects" has already been emphasized with regard to the methodological precautions that can be taken against them during earlier phases of the experiment. But it should be apparent that the actual measurement of an experiment's dependent variables also presents a most crucial time for preventing such effects. Certainly, an experimenter would want to assure himself that the responses of subjects to the measures of the dependent variables were not simply a reflection of his inadvertent influences upon them at the time they were filling out such measures. He may be able to gain that assurance by employing some variation of the methodological devices illustrated below.

A. *Administration of the measures of the dependent variables by the subjects themselves.* From a purely logical standpoint, the direct intrusion of "experimenter effects" on the process of measuring the dependent variables can best be prevented by not having the experimenter physically present during that process. If he is entirely absent, he can hardly be accused of inadvertently communicating with subjects in any manner!

However, even assuming that all measures of the dependent variables were perfectly suitable for self-administration by the subjects, an experimenter might find it quite difficult to give the subjects a convincing rationale for his absence. Moreover, his absence might inadvertently arouse apprehensions and suspicions that could as powerfully affect the responses of subjects to the measures as any unuttered hypotheses the experimenter might have communicated if he had remained in the company of the subjects. Finally, by totally removing himself from the scene of measurement, an experimenter loses the chance to monitor what actually happens during his absence. For instance, if the measurement occurs in a group context, he can never be sure that the subjects had not taken the initiative, contrary to their instructions, to communicate with each other.

B. *The use of an observational surrogate for administering measures of the dependent variables.* It may often be better for an experimenter to enlist the aid of an observational surrogate rather than leave subjects entirely alone during the crucial measurement of the effects of the manipulations on the dependent variables. And an experimenter can take care to avoid passing on any of his own unuttered influence through the person of his surrogate by enlisting someone who is unfamiliar with: a) the specific hypotheses under investigation; b) the particular manipulations to which subjects have been exposed; and c) the position of subjects on whatever trait of personality may have been previously measured as an independent variable in the experiment.

Of course, while an experimenter can and should always impose the latter course of ignorance upon himself until the completion of an experiment, he can scarcely keep himself in the dark about his own hypotheses. Nor can he usually arrange his manipulations in such a way as to be unaware of what manipulations are being performed in a given experimental condition.

Thus, a properly uninformed surrogate can stand between the experimenter and the subjects, preventing them from being inadvertently influenced in a manner favorable to the hypotheses. And while, as Rosenthal (1966) has noted, such surrogates, despite their temporary ignorance of the experiment, may inadvertently communicate hypotheses of their own, those hypotheses are very much less likely to be identical to the ones being tested. Moreover, the administration by an observational surrogate of the measures of dependent variables could be easily and convincingly rationalized to subjects by presenting him as an assistant, which is what the person would, in fact, be for that time. An experimenter could readily explain to his surrogate both the necessity of deferring an explanation about the experiment until its completion and the mechanics of properly administering the measures of the dependent variables.

But the introduction of a surrogate immediately after the manipulations might cause a jarring break in a mood or emotional state just created, and such an eventuality could vitiate the effects that the manipulations might otherwise exert upon the dependent variables.

While reducing the possible intrusion of "experimenter effects" favoring the hypothesis under study, such a procedure might well undermine the conditions necessary for a fair test of the hypothesis, and the experimenter might actually fail to give his hypothesis a theoretically adequate chance to reveal its empirical potentials.

On the other hand, the use of an observational surrogate may not prevent the possible intrusion into the postmanipulative situation of whatever inadvertent influences an experimenter may have imparted prior to leaving the scene. For subjects continue to perceive themselves as being involved in the same experiment. Hence, inadvertent "demand characteristics" (Orne, 1962) already absorbed by subjects may extend beyond the experimenter's absence, influencing the responses of subjects to the postmanipulative measures administered by the surrogate.

C. *Appearing to bring the experiment to a close and measuring the dependent variables in a different context.* To cope with the last possibility, an experimenter can contrive to make it appear as if the experiment had come to an end prior to the postmanipulative measurement of the dependent variables. Then, in cooperation with confederates, he can arrange in advance for subjects to anticipate participation in an entirely different study, conducted by a different investigator. Upon their arrival at their new location, subjects can be presented with a measure of the dependent variables applicable to the original experiment — under the guise of the collection of information relevant to the investigatory purpose of the second one.

But since this kind of procedure takes considerable time to implement, plus a sizeable amount of instructional rationalization and actual physical movement from one locale to another, it is clearly not appropriate to experiments in which the predicted effects of manipulations are theoretically presumed to be quite transitory and fragile. Nor would it be easy to apply such a procedure with groups of subjects, for they would have to be ushered singly from one location to another without being given any opportunity to communicate with each other in any way, since such communication would represent yet another possible source of uncontrolled social influence on the responses of subjects to measures of dependent variables. Finally, it should be apparent that the specific deception involved in this procedure would preclude its use in before-after designs, since the "after" measure could not be credibly presented as the initial measure in a completely new study.

However, the rationale of an "unrelated" investigation was appropriately and successfully employed by Festinger and Carlsmith (1959) in respect to the measurement of the attitudinal effects they predicted from manipulations designed to induce varying levels of cognitive dissonance. In her modified replication of that experiment, Bishop (1965) adapted their technique to the practical limitations that constrained the conduct of her study. Quite simply, she did not have available the financial resources to hire the surrogates necessary for carrying out the elaborate deception that is required by this methodological device. Consequently she developed a technique, which, while containing the essence of that deception, permitted her to administer the postmanipulative measures without the assistance of a surrogate. Moreover, since her subjects were conducted individually through the experiment, Bishop could absent herself while they were filling out their responses to the measures of the dependent variables.

Masking the repetitive measurement of the dependent variables in "before-after" experimental designs

Owing to the tendency of human beings to be altered in the very process of being observed, there is no foolproof technical solution for eliminating the possibly confounding consequences of mere repetition of measurement *per se*. On the other hand, an experimenter can attempt to minimize such consequences in "before-after" types of experimental designs by striving, in ways indicated below, to attenuate the awareness of subjects to the repeated administration of measures of the dependent variables.

A. *Interposing fairly extended intervals of time between the "before" and the "after" measurements of the dependent variables.* An experimenter can attempt to interpose the largest possible amount of time between the "before" and "after" measures, working on the reasonable assumption that the sheer passages of time will dim the memory of subjects sufficiently to make them forget precisely how they responded to the "before" measure. Hence, the more extended the interval between measures, the less firm a cognitive hold is the "before" measure likely to have on subjects.

However, in many instances, the dependent variable involved is one that could be markedly affected by fortuitous, uncontrollable, and extraexperimental conditions that take place between the "before" and "after" sessions. For example, if the dependent variable were an attitude toward a particular ethnic minority, it could be altered by the occurrence of an event that tended to place that minority in either a more favorable or a less favorable light.

In addition, there usually exist quite stringent practical limits on the amount of time that can be allowed to elapse between two occasions of measurement. Thus, subjects may forget about, lose interest in, or become otherwise distracted from, participation in the "after" session — if it is too long deferred.

B. *The use of measures whose format makes it difficult for subjects to recall precisely how they responded to them.* Conrad (1968) used such a measure in detecting before-after changes in one of his dependent variables, feelings of rejection. He wished to study the differential effects of eating on rejection among obese and normal subjects.

Specifically, Conrad employed an unmarked linear scale of 18 centimeters, anchored only at the two extremes: "Not rejected or spurned at all" versus "Extremely rejected or spurned." Several other exploratory variables — anger, boredom, and fatigue — were also measured in the same manner. Conrad regarded the absence of other than anchoring markings as crucial to the detection of changes in these variables. "No cross-hatches and/or terms denoting increasing intensity were provided along the scales. The scales were constructed in this manner because of E's interest in obtaining measures of several variables before and after eating. It was felt that the use of cross-markings and intensity terms along the scales would result in some Ss marking the 'after' scales at the same position as they remembered having marked the 'before' scales [pp. 28-29]."

It should be added that Conrad's concern was particularly apt because only a very short period of time — 35 minutes — intervened between the preeating measurement of these variables and their posteating measurement. He was also mindful of the possibility that subjects high in oral dependency, which the obese subjects were expected to be, might be more inclined to "cling" to any position they took on the scales than would be the case for the presumably less orally dependent normal subjects. Thus, the ambiguity of the unmarked line was strongly indicated by a variety of theoretical considerations.

C. *Attempting perceptually to disassociate the "after" measure from the "before" measure.* Regarding attempts to dissimulate the fact that the "after" measure is a repetition of the "before" measure, the most subtle device involves the use of two actually different forms of the same measure. Assuming that the correlation between two such forms is virtually perfect, they can with considerable reason be regarded as truly interchangeable. Alterations on the "after" form can be interpreted as reflecting the same changes as might have been found if the "before" form had actually been given twice.

However, it is very difficult to develop two almost perfectly correlated forms of measures of the dependent variables likely to be at issue in deductive tests of psychoanalytic hypotheses. Moreover, the development of such equivalent forms is largely contingent on the initial formulation of sufficient items to permit the empirical demonstration of an extraordinarily high degree of internal consistency among them. Yet reliable measures of such length are often counterindicated by the theoretical or procedural contingencies involved in a particular experiment. Finally, and almost by definition, highly intercorrelated alternative forms are bound to share so much common content as to raise the very awareness of repetition they are intended to obscure.

One could, of course, seek to hide the fact of an identical repetition by embedding the "after" measure in a different context of measurement. Thus, it could be part of a larger questionnaire, surrounded by theoretically irrelevant or "filler" items, whose whole objective is to reduce the possibility of recognizing the existence of the previously experienced measure among them. But this altered context may, in itself, become a source of uncontrolled influence on the responses of subjects to the "buried" measure of the dependent variable. Indeed, insofar as that measure is discernible — and its literal, if camouflaged, repetition would appear to guarantee such discernment — subjects are likely to react with a degree of suspicion that might be much more disastrous to the hypothesis than any consequence of a forthright and undisguised "after" presentation of the "before" measure.

D. *The combined usage of several devices to reduce the recall of a "before" measure.* Bromberg's (1967) experiment contains an example of a procedure that is a compromise between the use of a measure's format — in this case its sheer length — and deliberate dissociation in an effort to counteract its repeated administration. Thus, after the description of his manipulations and the checks on their effectiveness, his dissertation continues as follows:

"The CDPI and PHICON inventories were then administered as a 'slightly revised' version of the 71-item Emotional Responsiveness Index. . . . The Ss were instructed that we were trying to perfect this index of fear, and since there were differences between the two versions (which actually were identical except for the new heading 'Revised Form M-71'), it was especially important that they treat this as a brand new measure and answer each item as spontaneously and sincerely as possible [p. 86]." And the fact that several weeks had intervened between that presentation and the first administration of the questionnaire insured that a literal remembrance of all 71 items was hardly to be expected for any subject. Hence, the deceptive introduction of the "after" measure as a "slightly revised" version of the "before" one could be plausibly given without taxing the credulity of the subjects.

12 The Postexperimental Inquiry

Assuming it had been preceded by a check on the effectiveness of the manipulations, measurement of the dependent variable would bring an experiment to its operational conclusion. An experimenter would then have on hand the empirical data required to test his hypothesis, and it would only remain for him to disabuse the subjects.

However, the literal completion of an experiment raises the problem of how to introduce the process of disabusing subjects. Despite his having checked on the effectiveness of his manipulations, an experimenter may want further assurance of the credibility of his methodological rationales and of his success in excluding inadvertent "experimenter effects" and "demand characteristics." Finally, he may wish to gather exploratory data germane to his theoretically postulated reasons for the ways in which subjects respond to the postmanipulative measures of various dependent variables, for such reasons may help to shed some light, albeit *post hoc,* on the relative merits of competing theoretical formulations of the determinants of the responses under investigation.

A postexperimental inquiry, instituted upon completion of the crucial measures of the effects predicted by an hypothesis, can be devised with a view toward meeting all these needs simultaneously. Such an inquiry can be designed to form a psychological bridge between the end of the experiment proper and the start of the disabusing process. By raising a series of questions about why subjects behaved as they did and what they believed the experiment to be about, the inquirer can gradually prepare subjects for the ultimate revelations of the deceptions that had been practiced upon them. Thus, by the time those disclosures are openly made, they are not likely to be as abruptly unsettling as they might have been if the inquiry had not preceded them. At the same time, the data yielded by the inquiry can be applied toward insight into the residual issues that an experimenter wants to explore.

Of course, such inquiries can be conducted on a quite informal and oral basis, an experimenter posing questions and subjects replying insofar as they feel inclined to talk. However, the informality of such a procedure, while possessing the virtues of spontaneity and directness of contact between experimenter and subjects, precludes the systematic recording of data from all subjects in response to the same set of questions. Moreover, if groups of subjects are orally queried within the same session, they can obviously communicate with each other and thereby exert uncontrolled mutual influences in replying to the questions posed.

For these reasons, it is best to conduct the postexperimental inquiry in the same standardized fashion in which other psychological measures are administered throughout the experiment. Thus, if those measures had been of a pencil-and-paper variety, the inquiry can easily be presented in that same type of format.

Of course, the postexperimental inquiry is, basically, a collection of measures. Hence, its measures are vulnerable to all the sources of invalidity and unreliability that have been examined in previous chapters. Moreover, since it comes at the end of an experiment, the inquiry ordinarily cannot be a very protracted one. And, because of its unequivocally exploratory objectives, the postexperimental inquiry may not stimulate a researcher to do much pilot work toward its psychometric refinement. However, insofar as he were to do such work, an experimenter would be helping to improve the quality of the data his inquiries may provide for him.

Substantively, the contents of the questions comprising a postexperimental inquiry are largely determined, of course, by the particular manipulations and rationales employed in the experiment to which it refers. So, any example must be taken merely as an indication of how the general purposes of such an inquiry may be implemented.

Rather than presenting a variety of brief examples, most of this chapter will give a detailed exposition of the postexperimental inquiry used by Bromberg (1967), whose experiment has already served to illustrate a number of other aspects of experimental methodology. Thus, it will be possible to exemplify an inquiry in the most meaningful way possible — within the context of familiarity with the theoretical issues its questions seek to elucidate. Furthermore, the results obtained by those questions will be reviewed, concretely showing how the data of a postexperimental inquiry may contribute to an appraisal of the extent to which one's procedures have succeeded in operationally articulating the concepts and conceptual relationships under study.

Introducing the postexperimental inquiry to subjects

It will be recalled that affiliative preference was the second and last of the dependent variables to be measured by Bromberg. Having presented his procedure for measuring that variable, Bromberg describes the introduction of his postexperimental inquiry as follows:

After the measure of affiliative preference was completed, the Ss then responded to a questionnaire concerned with the importance of various reasons that might have determined the choice they had just made. This questionnaire consisted of 20 structured items (ten for each of the two affiliative choices), each S answering only those ten items bearing upon his own waiting preference. The 20 items comprised a modified version of the questionnaire designed by Gerard and Rabbie (1961), and were introduced with the identical rationale used by Sarnoff and Zimbardo (1961). The Ss were told:

"Please listen carefully. An associate of ours who is a social psychologist, has become interested in the fact that some of our participants prefer to wait alone while some prefer to wait with other people. He has asked us to get some information for him about this preference and the reasons underlying it. Here is what you are to do. If your choice was any degree of preference to wait *together with other people,* turn now to Page 13 in your questionnaire booklet. (Pause) If your choice was any degree of preference to wait *alone,* turn now to Page 15 of your questionnaire booklet. (Pause) On the page you have just turned to and the page following it you will see 10 items which relate to various motives that may have determined your waiting preference. Please circle the one choice beneath each of the 10 items which best estimates the importance of that particular motive in determining your preference. Please keep in mind that a person's preference may be dictated by more than one motive, so that your answer to each of the 10 items should be independent of your answers to the others. You may now begin [1967, pp. 88-89]."

Questionnaire for assessing the reasons given by subjects for preferring to wait together or alone

The two sets of items to which Bromberg referred are listed below, under their respective instructions. In the actual questionnaire, each item was followed by six verbal labels that described the degree to which the item was important to the individual.

It should be kept in mind that the "second GSR procedure" mentioned in many of the items refers to the anticipated electrical stimulation, varying amounts of which were expected by subjects in the three AP conditions.

I. *The ten wait-together items:*

If your choice was any degree of preference to WAIT TOGETHER WITH OTHER PEOPLE, please answer *these* ten items. Circle the one choice under each item which best describes the importance of *that* particular motive in determining your preference.

1. I am not sure I am reacting the same way as others to the prospect of the second GSR procedure, and would like to compare my feelings with theirs.
2. I feel very worried about the second GSR procedure and would like to know to what extent the others are worried too.
3. I want to be distracted in order to take my mind off the second GSR procedure.
4. I typically prefer being with others to being alone.
5. I am worried about the GSR procedure and feel that talking to someone about it would get it off my chest.
6. I am curious to see what the other participants in the study are like.
7. It would be clearer in my own mind as to how I feel about the second GSR procedure if I could express my feelings to someone else.
8. I anticipate that others will offer reassuring comments.

9. I want to be with others to assure myself that I am not the only one who was singled out for the second GSR procedure.
10. I hoped that perhaps we could somehow figure out a way to avoid this second GSR procedure [pp. 211-212]."

II. *The ten wait-alone items:*

If your choice was any degree of preference to WAIT ALONE, please answer *these* ten items. Circle the one choice under each item which best describes the importance of *that* particular motive in determining your preference.

1. I want to be alone to think about personal affairs and schoolwork.
2. I am worried about the prospect of the second GSR procedure and would like to be alone to try and relax.
3. It would be clearer in my own mind as to how I feel about the second GSR procedure if I could think about it myself.
4. I prefer to be alone because I don't want to find out that the others may be more at ease than I am about the prospect of the second GSR procedure.
5. I prefer to wait alone because I am a little embarrassed at being worried about the prospect of the second GSR procedure.
6. I typically prefer being alone to being with others.
7. I am worried about the prospect of the second GSR procedure, and I feel that others might look down on me because of this.
8. I am worried about the prospect of the second GSR procedure, and feel that being with others in the same situation will just add to my nervousness.
9. I am worried about the prospect of the second GSR procedure and prefer to keep my feelings to myself.
10. I am worried about the prospect of the second GSR procedure, and want to be alone mentally to prepare myself for it.

Upon completion of their responses to the ten relevant items in the above questionnaire, subjects were ready to fill out the last part of the postexperimental inquiry [pp. 213-214].

Questions concerning the credibility and demand characteristics of the experiment

As the final measure administered, the demand characteristics of the experiment were assessed by asking the Ss to describe the study as if they were talking to a friend. This procedure was designed to elicit any hypotheses Ss had about what was really going on, and to determine their degree of suspiciousness about the manipulations. The Ss were told that we wanted to get their feelings about the research, and that their description of the study could only help us if they were as candid and sincere as possible. Two open-ended questions (on separate pages) were used to get at these issues, and read as follows:

'If a friend asked what this study was all about, what would you tell him?'

'If the same friend asked if there was something *more* to the experiment than what you were told, what would you say? Explain in detail.' [p. 89]."

Fusing the end of the standardized inquiry with the beginning of the process of disabusing subjects

After the subjects wrote out their replies to the last two questions, Bromberg proceeded to free subjects from the apparatus involved in the manipulations they had experienced. Such a release would have been necessary if the subjects were to have gone to their preferred waiting rooms. He took the occasion to obtain more information about the credibility of those manipulations. Yet while still seeming to be carrying out procedures consistent with the false rationales he had previously presented, Bromberg was actually easing subjects into a state of preparation for his revelations about the real scientific objectives of the experiment. Thus, his own description of this interlude continues as follows:

The instruments were then turned off, and the Ss allowed to

release their grip on the electrodes, clean the electrode jelly off their fingers with paper towels, and remove their headphones. As a final check on the effectiveness of the deception, they were then asked if they were ready to accompany E to the waiting rooms they had selected. When all Ss had responded affirmatively (albeit, some quite reluctantly) they were casually asked about their feelings about the second GSR procedure that ostensibly awaited them on their return. When it was felt that a maximum degree of spontaneous expression had occurred, the Ss were informed that the experiment was actually over and that the remaining 30 minutes would be devoted to a discussion of its true purpose and to answering any questions they had [pp. 89-90].

Preparing the data obtained in an inquiry for statistical analysis

Since each of the 20 items in the above questionnaire was accompanied by its own six-point scale, the scoring of those items presented no problem to Bromberg. For the items were, in effect, scored by the subjects themselves in the very process of responding to them. Hence, those scores could be used directly in analyzing the reasons given by various experimental groups for preferring either social affiliation or social isolation.

However, the raw data yielded by the two open-ended questions concerning the experiment's demand characteristics had to be coded in order to yield a dimension of credibility on the basis of which various groups of subjects could be quantitatively compared. Moreover, it was necessary for Bromberg to conduct an empirical assessment of the reliability with which that dimension could be quantified by different observers.

Bromberg devised a system for scoring the degree of "skepticism" reflected in the answers to each of the two open-ended questions. And that system, whose scale ranged from one to six in ascending amounts of skepticism, was separately applied by Bromberg and an independent judge of a stratified sample of 72 protocols, which were randomly selected from each of the experimental conditions. Bromberg then correlated his ratings with that of the judge, finding these reliability coefficients for the two questions: $r = .73$ for Question 1 and $r = .85$

for Question 2. Considering these coefficients satisfactory, Bromberg used the ratings he gave to all subjects in the experiment as a basis for analyzing the amount of skepticism they may have harbored.

Results of the questionnaire dealing with reasons given for preferring to wait together or alone

The data produced by this questionnaire could, of course, have been analyzed in a variety of different ways, given the abundance of measures of individual and situational differences that Bromberg had on hand. However, he was primarily interested in trying to track down the reasons associated with the three manipulated motivational states: phobic anxiety, fear, and free-floating anxiety, for these were the variables on the basis of which he made his differential predictions about affiliative preference.

Like every other experimenter, Bromberg had to limit the focus of his hypothesis-testing effort; while his experiment was designed to test the predicted affiliative outcomes of those three motives, it did not permit a direct test of the theoretically presumed differences in mediational processes by means of which the inductions were psychologically translated into the manifest preferences. For example, it did not use as a dependent variable the "need for emotional comparison" which Schachter (1959) had indicated might be the most salient subjective mediator of social affiliation under every condition of emotional arousal; the more so the more intense and novel the emotion aroused. Nor did Bromberg employ as a dependent variable the "need to avoid showing one's inappropriate apprehensions to others," which both he and Sarnoff and Zimbardo (1961) had postulated as a crucial factor in leading anxious subjects to prefer isolation rather than affiliation.

Data bearing upon such mediational differences as were suggested by the above investigators are very pertinent to the acquisition of a commulative empirical perspective about the scientific merits of their alternative conceptions of the determinants of those preferences, and, insofar as it obtained such data, Bromberg's questionnaire made a contribution to the ongoing development of such a perspective. The following excerpt, therefore, is taken verbatim from Bromberg's discussion of the data from that questionnaire, as separately analyzed for each of the three motives manipulated in his experiment. The reasons numbered in the text refer to the appropriately numbered items of the previously reproduced questionnaire. And, in reading these findings, it should be remembered that Bromberg had, through independent empirical checks, demonstrated the effectiveness of his manipulations in establishing each of the motives involved.

Reasons for waiting alone or with other people

Phobic anxiety. . . . none of the ten affiliation reasons (including emotional comparison) proved to be significantly more important to the affiliators in the phobic anxiety condition than to the affiliators in the MP control condition. This finding is consistent with the demonstrated *decrease* in affiliation preference following arousal of phobic anxiety, and supports our view that the effect associated with the anxiety motive, although intense and novel, does *not* increase the need for a social comparison response.

Three of the ten isolation reasons proved to be significantly more important to the isolators in the phobic anxiety condition than to the isolators in the MP control condition: (2) Feels worried and would like to be alone to relax; (4) Doesn't want to discover that others are less worried; (9) Feels worried and prefers to keep feelings private.

These findings lend direct support to our basic position that (a) the increased isolation preference elicited by phobic anxiety is a function of apprehension evoked by a threat attributed to the conflict-related external event. (b) The intensity of this apprehension tends to be experienced as *inappropriate*, leading to preference for behavior which will reduce the possibility of social exposure and potential criticism. In this regard, it must be mentioned that Isolation Reasons 5 and 7, which deal more directly with embarrassment and avoidance of criticism, were *not* reported as significantly more important to the phobic anxiety isolators. It is not too difficult, however, to understand the reluctance of these highly anxious subects to acknowledge in writing the existence of precisely what they hoped to conceal by their behavior.

Fear.   The affiliation reasons discriminating the fear Ss clearly show that an increased need for emotional comparison (Reason #1) is not the *only* variable determining increased affiliation preference. The affiliators in the fear condition also indicated that the emotion associated with this motive led to affiliation as a means of reducing tension by distraction and catharsis (Reasons 3 and 5), thus replicating similar findings by Sarnoff and Zimbardo. The data further suggested that their hope of increasing cognitive-emotional clarity may have depended in part upon the anticipation of being able to discuss these feelings with other people (Reason 7). Inasmuch, however, as this reason had failed to distinguish the affiliators in Sarnoff and Zimbardo's high fear condition, and since Schachter (1959) had demonstrated the fear-affiliation effect in Ss who anticipated *no* opportunity for verbal expression, the general importance of this factor in eliciting a social comparison response is unknown. Thus, as far as these data bear upon the adequacy of social comparison theory to account for the increase in affiliation preference evoked by anticipation of strong shock, they provide additional support for our view that the need for emotional evaluation does not mediate a general relationship between intense novel effect and affiliation preference, but rather that social comparison is merely one of several appropriate responses that are instrumental in reducing the tension associated with the motive of fear.

Further support for this view is provided by the data from the few fear Ss who chose isolation. The one reason distinguishing this group from isolators in the MP control condition (Reason 9) was also shown to be differentially important to the *majority* of Ss in the phobic anxiety condition — a desire to avoid revealing an emotion they experienced as inappropriate. Logically, this is quite plausible since it takes into account the well known need of some men (especially in this age range) to feel *any* strong apprehension of pain as inappropriate to their sex, regardless of the fact that a high degree of pain may be *inherent* in the threatening situation. In other words, although it is the *phobic* individual who *typically* prefers isolation (because *phobic* apprehension is more *likely* to be experienced as inappropriate), to the extent that certain people experience *any* apprehension as unjustified they may choose to isolate regardless of the motive with which the apprehension is associated.

To test this hypothesis we compared the mean levels of unjustified discomfort reported by those fear subjects who subsequently chose affiliation (mean=3.68) and those fear subjects who subsequently chose isolation (mean=2.89). The difference between these means was significant by t-test beyond the .001 level, and demonstrated that the isolators in the fear condition felt significantly less justification for their apprehension than did the fear Ss who chose affiliation. Since their respective levels of *absolute* apprehension did not differ significantly by t-test, the possibility is ruled out that the fear Ss who chose isolation did so because they were feeling less *intense* apprehension.

The implication of this finding for *Schachter's* position is, of course, obvious, since it has been shown once again that affiliative preference is not simply determined by the *intensity* of a novel emotional experience. This finding, however, is also salient to our own viewpoint, since it emphasizes the fact that while a person's response to an intense emotion may indeed be a function of the properties of the motive to which the emotion is functionally related, there are many individual difference factors which modify the experiential effects of these properties. These individual difference factors (e.g., sex, defensive style, etc.) must therefore be investigated to determine the extent of their influence upon the probability of response alternatives evoked by the dominant motive aroused.

Free-Floating Anxiety.   Neither the affiliators nor the isolators in the FFA condition attached a greater level of importance to any of the listed reasons for their choice than did their respective counterparts in the MP control group. For the affiliators, this finding is not too surprising, inasmuch as the FFA induction tended to *reduce* rather than increase affiliation preference.

For the FFA *isolators,* however, it is difficult to arrive at a clear interpretation of why *none* of the reasons were indicated as differentially salient to their waiting choice. The problem is, that even to the extent that a weak but meaningful tendency toward increased isolation *can* be inferred for this group of subjects, it would be most improbable that they could specify the reasons for their behavior. Assuming that their primary reason for isolation *was* the hypothesized need to avoid revealing inappropriate affect, it must be remembered that the anxiety experience for this group was induced by a *prior* event (The SA manipulation) which for them was unrelated to the anticipated GSR procedure. Thus, though their preference for isolation may *indeed* have reflected an increased desire to avoid revealing an emotion felt as inappropriate, the questionnaire was not able to tap this motivation because it dealt with concealment of feelings only with regard to the *anticipated* event. In other words, to the extent that the isolation choices of the FFA Ss *were* motivated by anxiety, the emotion would have been felt as inappropriate, but unrelated to a specific source. Unfortunately, our questionnaire was unable to assess this because in our preoccupation with the distinction between fear and *phobic* anxiety, we failed to list any isolation reasons that had to do with feelings of discomfort or tension that "seemed to come from nowhere."

One might have anticipated, however, that the FFA Ss, when confronted with the motivation questions, would have shown a greater tendency than the MP control Ss to *rationalize* their isolation preference by attributing greater importance to some of the more 'neutral,' less specific, isolation reasons offered; e.g., opportunity to think about personal matters, typical preference to be alone, etc. This, however, was not found to be the case, and must speculatively be attributed to the inability of *any* of the presented isolation reasons to tap the weak FFA effect [pp. 142-147].

Data bearing on the two open-ended questions concerning the demand characteristics of the experiment

Generally speaking, the data from these two questions gave Bromberg empirical assurance that his deception had been successful and that he had not inadvertently conveyed his hypotheses to the subjects. Once again, to demonstrate how the data from this aspect of the postexperimental inquiry may be systematically analyzed, recourse is made to a verbatim extract from Bromberg's thesis. The quotation given below starts just after he finishes describing his procedures for assuming the inter-rater reliability of the coding system he applied to score the above questions on the dimension of skepticism.

Three-way analyses of variance were then performed on the scored responses to each question. The only significant effect found in either analysis was from Question 1, between levels of anticipated pain ($F = 3.93$, $p < .05$). When the mean skepticism ratings of the Ss in each AP condition were compared, it was clear that this significant effect was due to the SP mean (1.67) being greater than the MP (1.17) and NP (1.00) means.

In each group, however, the mean skepticism level was at the extremely low end of the six-point scale, and in only three cases out of the total sample of 72 was *any* awareness shown as to the true purpose of the experiment.

On Question 2, slightly higher skepticism means were found for all groups as compared with Question 1, which is reasonable in light of the deliberate arousal of suspicion by Question 2. Due to the homogenizing effect of the induced suspiciousness, the previous AP difference found in Question 1 was no longer significant ($F = 2.63$, $p > .05$). As with Question 1, the means for all groups were low (NP $= 1.67$, MP $= 1.62$, SP $= 2.21$), and the increases in *every* case were due solely to heightened *skepticism*, with no increased awareness as a function of greater suspiciousness.

Nevertheless, the higher skepticism mean of the SP Ss remains to be accounted for, since it could suggest that the experimental rationale was less believable to the SP Ss. Judging, however, from the significant SP finidngs on the absolute apprehension measure, this was apparently not the case. The most likely interpretation of the finding became apparent to us from the *nature* of the skepticism shown in the protocols of the SP Ss, and from remarks of a similar nature made by several SP Ss during the postexperimental interview. In an effort to reduce their apprehension, many SP Ss had attempted to convince themselves that the strong shock would not really bẹ administered; i.e., the experiment was a "hoax." The phobic anxiety Ss could not, of course, utilize this mode of defensiveness since *objectively* they were led to expect only a "mild tingle"; i.e., there was nothing to repudiate which could reduce their apprehension since it was generated largely from *internal* conflict. The fear Ss, however, tended to amass all sorts of "evidence" to support their rationalizations, which despite their efforts, typically failed to reduce their emotional response to the induction.

A few sample quotations from SP "skeptics" may serve to illustrate this point:

> "The part where the tape recording mentioned the use of a strong electric shock that would hurt made me laugh a little. I don't really know if they would go through with it or not, but just to get the students' reaction on the GSR to it; *I guess the fact that I challenged the thought of pain made me feel quite at ease.*"

> "The threat of electrical shock — and even though I feel it is just a device to see how we would react to the threat of pain, was used to measure our emotional reactions to pain in the GSR. *Though I intellectually am convinced that there will be no shocks, yet I still felt fear.*"

It must thus be reasonably concluded, that to the extent the experimental manipulations were not equally credible to each motivational condition, the effect was too slight to influence the take of the inductions, and that the only obtained difference in skepticism related more to defensive operations against the induced motive itself than to any real penetration of the deception [pp. 103-105].

Concluding remarks on the use of postexperimental inquiries

In introducing his postexperimental inquiry, Bromberg sought to encourage candor among subjects by telling them that the questions they would be answering were of interest to another investigator rather than to himself. In this respect, his procedure was similar to the one used by Bishop (1965). Indeed, Bishop appended her inquiry to measures of the dependent variable and the effectiveness of the manipulations, and all of those measures were taken by subjects after they had been led to believe that the experiment proper had been concluded and that all the questions asked of them were of no concern whatever to her.

These kinds of precautions are aimed, of course, at precluding the possible intrusion of "demand characteristics" as determinants of responses to the very measures intended to assess the roles those characteristics may earlier have played in affecting the outcome of the experiment's hypothesis. For, since the postexperimental inquiry is an occasion of observation, it is vulnerable to the same sorts of "experimenter effects" as may inadvertently influence the responses of human subjects whenever they perceive themselves as being scientifically observed.

Theoretically, the effort to forestall such inadvertent influences could be carried out infinitely, involving inquiry upon inquiry, each seeking to evaluate the extent to which subjects were suspicious of the purported scientific purpose of every immediately preceding one. However, any measure attempting to assess the credibility of the postexperimental inquiry *per se* is very likely to be regarded with both suspicion and ridicule by subjects. Hence, it would defeat its observational objective.

Thus, once his experiment is over, a researcher is clearly limited in what he can do to recapture the state of a subject's consciousness during the experiment. Moreover, since the postexperimental inquiry is retrospective, an experimenter cannot be sure about the extent to which the replies given by subjects reflect, in fact, whatever they actually thought or felt about the aspects of the experiment covered in the inquiry. For example, a subject may not recall very precisely why — in terms of consciously experienced reasons — he responded to a measure of a dependent variable in the way he actually did. Nor may a subject have had any consciously perceptible skepticism about the experiment until he thought about it in responding to its measure in the postexperimental inquiry.

However, since an experimenter cannot, as it were, peer unnoticed into a subject's mind, and since he obviously cannot conduct the postexperimental inquiry until after the experiment is over, he has no empirical alternative but to rely upon a retrospective instrument of whatever format is procedurally and conceptually appropriate. An experimenter would be wise to regard such instruments as vulnerable to the various sources of erroneous measurement that have already been discussed. And with respect to their assessment of inadvertent influences on the responses of subjects to the experiment, negative data obtained by postexperimental inquiries may fail to reveal influences that did occur; or that, indeed, affected the inquiries themselves.

But such data can at least provide *ex post facto* reassurance that the procedures to which they refer were accepted by subjects with the ostensible meanings an experimenter intended them to convey. And when those data are viewed in the light of similarly assuring ones, such as results supporting the effectiveness of the manipulations used, an experimenter has an additional basis for concluding that his methodology was adequate to its investigatory purpose.

On the other hand, negative findings from these inquiries, which point, for example, to widespread skepticism and, moreover, to an accurate perception of the hypothesis under study, can surely not be blithely rejected as inconsequential. Indeed, such data necessarily raise serious doubts about the success with which the procedures involved have created the conditions required for a proper empirical evaluation of the hypothesis.

In such instances, an experimenter would be exercising appropriate scientific caution if he were to drop from the statistical test of his hypotheses the data of subjects whose replies to postexperimental inquiries clearly indicated a knowledge of what was theoretically at stake in the study. Naturally, if a great many subjects give such indications, the entire experiment may have to be scrapped. But so drastic a misfortune is not likely to occur if an experimenter has done the pilot work necessary to establish the effectiveness of his manipulations, as well as the smoothness and rationality of his entire procedure.

Still, information about a particular experiment may conceivably have reached a subject from previous participants in it. Or, some subjects may possess sufficient general familiarity with the concepts involved to guess at the purpose of the specific deduction under investigation in the experiment for which they have volunteered. In any event, it is not uncommon for an experimenter to find it necessary to drop from his study a few such subjects. For example, in previously reported experiments, Conrad (1968) was obliged to eliminate the data of 13 subjects whose inquiries showed they correctly perceived that he had contrived the sociometric ratings that, during the experiment, he presented as indicating the degree of acceptance or rejection each subject had received from his assembled peers. Likewise, Bishop (1965) could not use the data of eight subjects for whom the deceptive rationale of the manipulations was evident. And she had to drop one subject who remarked, in the postexperimental inquiry, that he falsely answered the personality inventory (DPI) from which the nonmanipulated independent variable of anality was quantified.

A researcher should report all the subjects he is obliged to drop from the crucial statistical analyses of the data pertaining to his dependent variables. And he should also note the reasons for dropping them. Finally, when pertinent, a researcher should indicate any significant clustering of such subjects — in terms of a particular manipulative condition, a particular measure of personality, or both. For this information may help to clarify theoretical issues that are related to the hypothesis.

13 Disabusing Subjects

Regarding the ethical desirability of disabusing subjects upon the conclusion of their participation in an experiment, nothing can be added beyond what has already been said in regard to the moral dilemmas posed by deception and manipulation. That discussion may be summarized very briefly: Assuming his scientific endeavors to be both a reflection and an implementation of the values of realization, a researcher has as great a moral obligation to restore the psychological *status quo ante* of his subjects as he does to conduct his experiments in the most theoretically appropriate and methodologically rigorous manner he can contrive. Thus, a researcher would not knowingly employ any deception or manipulation whose psychological impact he could not completely undo.

The four basic postexperimental steps required of a researcher in fulfilling his moral obligations to subjects

On the affirmative side, this precept requires that an experimenter make provisions for that restoration; there can be no morally acceptable excuse for failing to do so, however hard-pressed he may be for time. To be true to himself and to the fellow human beings who have voluntarily subjected themselves to his research, an experimenter must simply arrange to put forth the time and effort needed to: a) reveal the nature of his deceptions and manipulations to the subjects; b) inform the subjects of the relationship between those experimental procedures and the hypotheses they are designed to test; c) solicit and truthfully answer all question the subjects may have about the theory and methodology of the experiment; and d) permit the subjects fully to vent their feelings about their experimental experiences — including their reactions to the experimenter.

245

It would also be in keeping with the intellectual aims of science for the experimenter to promise — and, in due course, to provide — subjects with a report on the results of the experiment. The stipulation is quite easy for an experimenter to fulfill. Although not an indispensable aspect of the disabusing process *per se,* it is a token of thanks, expressing an experimenter's gratitude more perscnally than can any small monetary payment he may also have agreed to give the subjects in return for their participation. For the preparation of a report about his results involves the experimenter directly, whether he presents it in person (if circumstances permit an assemblage of the former subjects) or, in written form, by mail.

But whereas the feedback of his experimental findings may be regarded as a highly desirable moral option, the first four steps are ethically mandatory. Yet little is known about the most effective ways of discharging those obligations — methods, that is, which are most likely to free subjects from all undesirable effects of the deceptions and manipulations they experienced during their participation in the experiment.

Of course, no person can ever be exactly the same as he was before going through an experiment. At the very least, he may be expected to have learned something new, and, hopefully, his total experience — from the outset of his recruitment through the postexperimental confessional — will be a source of intellectual stimultion and emotional insight to him. But while an experimenter may seek to maximize these humanely positive outcomes of a subject's experimental experiences, it is the undoing of any negative ones that demands his principal concern.

So, the question is: How can an experimenter thoroughly disabuse subjects in such a way as to leave them psychologically unscathed by the scientific lies he has told them and by the scientific ploys he has imposed upon them? Clearly, the handling of such delicate matters calls for honesty, sensitivity, tact, resiliency, and humor. For it is not easy to convince a person of one's truthfulness after one has just admitted to gross falsehoods and connivances. Nor is it less difficult to demonstrate one's adherence to humanitarian and equalitarian values after having just harassed subjects under conditions that clearly put them in a submissive relationship to oneself.

Paradoxically, too, the very process of disabusing subjects may incline them toward disillusionment and cynicism rather than toward the intellectual enlightenment and respect for knowledge that presumably motivated the experimenter to do his study. And it would be ironical in the extreme if the net and inadvertent result of an experimenter's confessional were to alienate subjects from any future participation in psychological experiments.

The need for systematic development of methods for insuring the success of disabusing procedures

Despite their crucial importance, the actual methods employed in disabusing subjects are usually never described in detail in published reports of experiments. Nor do we possess a body of empirical information on the relative effectiveness of the various methods that have been used. In reporting the results of their previously cited follow-up study on the effects of "debriefing," the researchers (Walster *et al*, 1967) gave no operational description of the precise means by which they sought to restore the psychological *status quo ante* of their subjects. While their study properly calls attention to the fact that currently employed techniques of "catharsis" and "dehoaxing" may not be as effective as those who use them would like to believe, it does not contribute to knowledge about the impact of one such technique as compared with another. However, their investigation should alert experimenters to the possibility that they may not be effectively coping with the consequences their "debriefings" are intended to vitiate. It is to be hoped that experimenters will respond to this warning by conducting carefully planned studies of the effectiveness of various procedures for disabusing subjects, taking adequate account of the interactions between those procedures and both the manipulated and nonmanipulated variables in the experiments that are studied. In this manner, humane experimenters can apply their most intellectually congenial epistemological method to a resolution of the very ethical problems its use creates.

Indeed, when the slightest doubt exists concerning the adequacy of one's technique of disabusing subjects, it would appear desirable for an experimenter to attempt a follow-up study of the kind done by Walster and her colleagues. For even if an experimenter cannot systematically vary such techniques within the compass of a particular experiment, he can at least try to find out what residual effects of his deceptions and manipulations may still be affecting subjects after he has done his best to disabuse them.

Insofar as he discovers such residuals, an experimenter can attempt to dissipate them among the affected individuals. Undoubtedly, such an attempt may be subject to many practical hazards, such as the inability of the experimenter to obtain further measures from the ex-subjects or to induce them to meet with him again for further disabusing. Although it surely would be preferable to do a thoroughly effective job of disabusing the subjects in the immediate postexperimental situation, given our present state of knowledge, repeated efforts to disabuse subjects may sometimes be the only appropriate means of fully discharging one's moral responsibilities to them.

No matter how many times an experimenter feels it necessary to attempt to disabuse subjects, he still needs to have some idea of how to go about that task. In general, it appears that experimenters do it through a fairly spontaneous and direct social interaction with subjects, starting with a few leading questions at the conclusion of a formally administered and standardized postexperimental inquiry.

The sensitivity and sincerity of the experimenter as crucial to any disabusing process

During the ensuing discussion, an experimenter has to depend completely on his ability to gauge the timing and articulation of his various revelations, taking care to avoid shocking subjects even more than did any of the experimental manipulations. While discussing the actual scientific purpose of the experiment and its relationship to the deceptions and manipulations employed, he must remain sensitive to unuttered feelings subjects may have in response to his disclosures, and must seek in every possible way to elicit their overt expression. At the same time, he should discard his past scientific aloofness by showing the depth and genuineness of his regret at having deceived the subjects, and, if they had been put under stress during the manipulations, at having upset them. Finally, an experimenter needs to show sincere and strong concern for the psychological wellbeing of the subjects, convincing them of his desire to hear them out and to repair any malaise he may have caused them.

Implicitly, therefore, the most generic of currently used techniques of disabusing subjects aims at removing the experimentally required distinction between experimenter and subjects, between the observer and the observed. Presumably, having restored the bond of trust that comes with equality, the experimenter can help his fellow human beings to shed whatever impact may have resulted from his exercise of the social power they had temporarily permitted him to assume. Just as the assumption of that power makes it possible to deceive and manipulate others, the postexperimental renunciation of that power makes it possible to undo those deceptions and manipulations. Insofar as an experimenter is truly humane, that undoing is as necessary for the alleviation of his own guilt as it is for the relief of any discomfort he may have induced among subjects.

If, in fact, the restoration of trust is essential to the restoration of the psychological *status quo ante* for all concerned, its achievement is contingent not only upon the application of an experimenter's "interpersonal skills" but also upon his deeply felt commitment to equalitarian values. If such a commitment is lacking, an experimenter may not succeed in thoroughly disabusing subjects, however well-polished may be his clinical manner.

While clinical experience may well contribute to the sensitivity and skill with which an experimenter disabuses subjects, it cannot *per se* imbue him with an unequivocally equalitarian outlook. Indeed, clinical work is typically carried out within the context of an implicitly authoritarian social relationship, the "therapist" or "counselor" being accorded greater status than the "patients" or "clients" he "treats" or "counsels." Hence, clinical experience is not necessarily an appropriate qualification for learning how to disabuse subjects.

On the desirability of avoiding individual stigmatization in disabusing subjects

Human sensitivity is so fine that no amount of established mutual sincerity, concern, and trust may be able to prevent the inherent psychological pain that could be induced by certain kinds of disclosures. Specifically, people are likely to be terribly upset by learning that they have *individually* performed in some way that they consider highly undesirable. And, of course, such information is likely to be especially disturbing when it pertains to measures of presumably habitual variables of personality that are associated with socially prevalent conceptions of psychopathology. For if people learn that they have scored "poorly" on those measures, they may be stricken with lasting distress, feeling that they possess deepseated and previously unsuspected vulnerabilities that they are powerless to remedy. If an experimenter were to impart individualized results to subjects, he might easily provoke much more severe and enduring emotional havoc than any his earlier experimental deceptions and manipulations could possibly have induced. However, since experimenters are actually interested in testing hypotheses that rest upon comparisons between groups, they can in good conscience withhold from subjects information about their individual performances. Accordingly, experimenters can restrict their disabusing revelations to explanations of the variables involved in the relevant comparisons between groups without feeling morally compelled to divulge to a subject how he himself responded to any of the manipulations or measures on which those comparisons are based. By attaching only an identifying number to each of the measures taken on subjects, an experimenter can preserve the annonymity of individual subjects throughout every postexperimental process by means of which their data are scored and statistically analyzed. Indeed, insofar as he needs it as a control upon his own handling of those data, the experimenter can arrange to keep the individual identities and performances of subjects unknown to himself.

The use of technical terms versus euphemisms in disabusing subjects

Regarding the way in which the substance of an experiment is articulated to subjects, care must be taken to use language that is plainly understood, for the excessive use of technical jargon may befuddle subjects more than no explanation at all.

On the other hand, an experimenter may wish to employ euphemistic translations of conceptual terms whose literal meaning may evoke the kind of anxiety noted above in regard to information about individual performances. Thus, for example, words such as "castration anxiety" and "anality" may, in themselves, be quite upsetting to subjects, albeit that they are not given their individual scores on measures of those variables. For subjects can infer that, since such variables were studied, they obviously are presumed to possess them, and although not knowing their scores, they may conclude that the possession of any amount of "castration anxiety" or "anality" is a "bad" — that is, a psychopathological — sign of their psychological condition.

Of course, an experimenter, informing subjects about such variables in the exact conceptual terms in which he viewed them for his study, can address himself to whatever anxieties or misconceptions his use of theoretical language may inadvertently provoke. And he can repeatedly stress the general premise that applies to all psychoanalytic traits of personality, namely, that every such trait is assumed to be held in one degree or another by everyone in the population.

Still, in his exposition of the Freudian concepts under study, an experimenter will necessarily have to invoke a number of more generic terms for the purposes of clarification. For example, in discussing the theoretical implications of psychosexual fixations for adult behavior, an experimenter would have to give examples of the characterological traits presumed to reflect those fixations. As in Bishop's (1965) disabusing session, to be given later in this chapter, an experimenter can phrase his explanations entirely in terms of those traits, omitting mention of the specific psychosexual fixation theoretically presumed to have determined them. Bromberg (1967), as shall also be seen, followed a similar tack in disabusing his subjects. Thus, he did not use the word "castration anxiety" *per se*, feeling that its usage might well perturb some subjects beyond his ability to reassure them completely about whatever personal concerns the very mention of that term might elicit.

Since researchers do not possess any reliable information about the emotional effects of the use of psychoanalytic terms in disabusing subjects about experiments designed to test their scientific utility, the employment of conceptual euphemisms now depends exclusively upon an experimenter's judgment. Thus, if he feels such euphemisms can truthfully communicate the theoretical essence of an experiment, while, at the same time, preventing inadvertent and unmanageable upset to subjects, he will naturally be inclined to use them.

However, euphemisms do tend to distort the original meanings of the words for which they are substituted. Unless a researcher is very careful about the euphemisms he selects, he may actually introduce fresh deceptions in the very process of trying to banish previous ones. True, these euphemisms may only be "little white lies," intended solely to spare subjects the inadvertent anxiety they might experience if the same general information were differently labelled, but lying of any variety is precisely the kind of interpersonal inequity that the experimenter would hope to eliminate in his postexperimental relationship with subjects. A researcher would only be deceiving himself if, in attempting to disabuse subjects about an experiment, he continued, in actuality, to keep them uninformed of the study's scientific objective.

So, before using euphemistic language to disabuse subjects, an experimenter must weigh the risk of inadvertently deceiving them with linguistic distortions against that of inadvertently disturbing them with technical terms. In balance, it appears wise to minimize the use of euphemisms, since the whole purpose of disabusing subjects is likely to be undermined in direct proportion to the amount of euphemistic substitution that is employed.

Three examples of disabusing procedures described in experimental dissertations

Although articles in journals generally report nothing further about the process of disabusing subjects than that it was undertaken, doctoral dissertations sometimes elucidate that process in at least sketchy detail. So, to indicate how experimenters have dealt with the basic issues raised in this chapter, descriptions of three different disabusing procedures, extracted verbatim from dissertations already cited, will now be presented. They differ in their reported degree of candor, ranging from a quite extensive use of euphemisms to untampered frankness. Hence, the reader will be able to evaluate, albeit only subjectively, the adequacy of the disabusing technique employed in the light of his knowledge of the measures and manipulations that had preceded it. The commentaries begin, of course, following a description of the procedure involved in administering the postexperimental inquiry.

A. *Bishop's (1965) "Catharsis and Dehoaxing."*   When both questionnaires were completed, each S was asked if he had any questions about the experiment. The answer was invariably affirmative. He was then asked to sign a pledge to secrecy on the grounds that any leak to potential Ss would change the conditions, and perhaps the frame of mind with which future Ss might engage in the experiment, and hence, vitiate results. He was offered one dollar to 'seal the bargain' for signing the pledge . . . all Ss agreed to sign, but a few refused to take the dollar, despite extensive urging.

After that, Ss were offered as full an explanation as possible, congruent with their interest and understanding of dissonance theory.

Although they were also informed that the study dealt with personality variables (and this invariably came as a surprise), to avoid arousal of anxiety nothing was said about Freud. They were apprised that attitudes toward the tasks covered a widely divergent range, depending upon personality types. Some wished to know how they stood in relation to control groups, and were told data had not yet been entered and no baseline established from which a correct answer could be derived. If they queried about their personality type, the answer usually was that the full personality profile had not been scored, but from what was available, they tended to be logical and consistent (high anals), or willing to do things other than for the sake of money (low anals).

In general, E took S into her confidence, with the emphasis less on what was said than on permitting S to release his feelings. Many comments from incoming Ss tended to corroborate the belief that the pledge to silence was fully kept [pp. 74-75].

In the above excerpt, the surprise evinced by subjects was caused by the fact that the experimental phase of the experiment had been, in their perception, entirely disassociated from their earlier measurement by the DPI, which had been administered by colleagues of the experimenter and in connection with presumably completely different investigations. On the other hand, the queries subjects made about their performance refer to the rationale Bishop had given them as a pretext for inducing them to make a dissonance-arousing recording, in which they were asked to describe the experiment as enjoyable and interesting — although it had been, in fact, tedious and boring. Presumably, this recording was to be played to an incoming subject in order to assess the effect of such motivating information upon his performance on the experimental tasks.

Concerning the content of her disclosures, it is evident that Bishop was extremely cautious, being reluctant to utter the word "Freud," much less his concept of "anal fixation," which was so centrally involved in the hypothesis tested. And while she used characterological euphemisms to describe her measure of anal hoarding, she does not indicate the extent to which she informed subjects, however euphemistically, about the theoretical relationship of the mentioned personality traits to the mediation of cognitive dissonance. Even when directly asked about it, she did not inform subjects of the fact that their performance on the experimental task was not relevant to the hypotheses and, hence, would not be scored. Instead, she led them to believe falsely that the requested data "had not yet been entered and no baseline established from which a correct answer could be derived."

Perhaps Bishop's caution in the disabusing process — even to a continuation of some aspects of her experimental deceptions — was ethically justified by the vulnerability of some of the subjects to extreme upset by uncensored revelations of the experiment's measures and manipulations. On the other hand, she might have been considerably more frank without unduly disturbing the subjects, for most of them were likely to have had some intellectual familiarity with Freud and his theory prior to participating in her experiment, and it is unlikely that they would have trembled at the sheer sound of his name. Nor is it very likely that they would have panicked at learning the truth about the irrelevance of the quality of their performance on the experimental task, although that information may well have angered them. But it is necessary for an experimenter to accept — and to help in dissipating — such resentments as part of the mutual catharsis attendant upon his confessions to subjects.

It must be added that these retrospective comments illustrate the unremitting self-criticism that is involved in attempting to make a proper application of humane precepts to specific procedures for disabusing participants in specific experiments. For, as sponsor of Bishop's dissertation, the author found her procedure consonant with his moral sensibilities in 1965, even though by the time of this writing he had begun, as indicated, to have serious doubts about their ethical adequacy.

B. *Bromberg's (1967) disabusing procedure.*   The theoretical basis of the study (without specific mention of castration anxiety), the hypotheses, design, manipulations, and reasons for the various deceptions, were fully explained. The open-ended 'therapeutic' technique employed by E at this point tended to promote a high level of participation on the part of the Ss in the discussion, and allowed them maximum expression of their feelings (within their individual limitations). It is felt that an effective job of anxiety and hostility reduction was accomplished during this 30-minute period of 'catharsis' [p. 90].

Apart from his reluctance to mention castration anxiety *per se,* a decision that may well have saved many subjects from agonizing doubts regarding how that intrinsically disquieting term applied to themselves, Bromberg seems to have been quite impeccably frank in his revelations about the experiment. On the other hand, we cannot be certain that explicit reference to castration anxiety would really have been any more upsetting than whatever euphemisms Bromberg may have used as a linguistic substitute for it. Nor can we be sure that the venting of anxiety and hostility to which Bromberg alludes was sufficient to restore the emotional equanimity of subjects. Thus, for example, considering the theoretical and methodological complexity of the experimenter, I have wondered, again in retrospect, whether 30 minutes was a sufficiently long period of time to accomplish both the informational and emotional objective that Bromberg set for himself in the disabusing period.

C. *Conrad's (1968) "Catharsis".*   At this time, E explained the entire experiment to Ss, including every deception and rationale for using it. It was of course essential to explain that the popularity and friendship ratings were 'rigged' and false, so as to dispel the induced social rejection. However, in the pilot study Ss seemed rather unconvinced, possibly suspecting that this was yet another deception. Kelman (1967) has pointed out this danger when multiple deceptions are used in a single experiment. In order to leave no room for doubt, E instructed all Ss to take out their "Individual Summary Sheets" and see if the ratings they received were in accord with the standard ratings for each arousal level, which E then proceeded to read aloud. E also explained that the deceptions were practiced upon them not simply for market research purposes, but because this was a serious study of an important health problem. After fully explaining the meaning and techniques of the entire study, E made a strong appeal for absolute secrecy, since some of the Ss classmates were scheduled for later sessions [pp. 60-61].

In this statement, the remark about market research refers to the overall false rationale on the basis of which Conrad had presented his investigation to the subjects. Conrad does not refer to the emotional reactions of the subjects to his disclosures, nor does he indicate how long a period of time he devoted to these "cathartic" sessions. While we obtain a clear picture of his having shunned euphemisms entirely, we are given no hint concerning the emotional impact of his candor or the emotional state of the subjects at the conclusion of his disabusing interactions with them.

Thus, in Conrad's case, as in the others cited, the description of the disabusing process tends to be cursory and lacking in sufficient detail to be as useful as it might be to other investigators. Hopefully, however, all of us who do research on human behavior will give increasing attention to both the conduct and the reporting of that process, having become aware of its significance to the development of a humane science of psychology.

*On helping subjects who participate in
experiments because of acute
emotional disturbances*

In all of the preceding material, attention has been focused on the problem of undoing whatever psychological upsets may have been induced by an experiment, and of preventing the further and lasting induction of distress that may be inadvertently produced by ethically mandatory attempts to inform subjects about the deceptions that had been practiced upon them.

However, an experiment may attract some individuals who want to participate in it *because* they are already acutely distressed about a particular aspect of their psychological functioning. These people may wish either to gain immediate insight into their personal problems or to bring them to the attention of someone whom they believe may be able to help them.

Certainly, the desire for self-insight is a commendable one that may well be a principal motive for the participation of many subjects. And the desire to alleviate one's personal anguish is also one with which a humane experimenter can readily empathize. But the experimental situation *per se* is not and, indeed, cannot be directed toward the individualized remediation of the torments a subject may bring to it. Still, an experimenter can and should be responsive to such unhappiness when it is brought to his attention. Owing to the formal structure of the experiment *per se*, individuals searching for help usually are constrained from expressing their needs until they are invited to talk freely about their reactions to the experiment during the disabusing process. And, having begun to voice their personal difficulties, albeit initially in the guise of venting their feelings about the experiment, such individuals may virtually plead for special attention from an experimenter. Indeed, in some instances, they may linger after their fellow subjects have gone in order to disclose their problems privately to him.

In such circumstances, the experimenter should, of course, not only hear the person out but also be prepared to refer him, if a request for a referral unfolds from the interview, to appropriate agencies that offer help for personal problems. And if an experimenter cannot conduct a private interview with the individual immediately after the disabusing session, he is morally behooved to do so at the earliest mutually convenient time.

Of course, an experimenter may occasionally be confronted with a subject whose acutely erupting emotional conflicts burst forth in the midst of the experiment proper; or whose need for help is so evident that it cannot be forestalled. Naturally, in cases of this kind, an experimenter would wish to give his chief consideration to the distressed individual, and, as may be necessary, interrupt the experiment altogether or cancel other appointments in order to care immediately for the individual involved.

14 Suggestions for Future Experimentation on Freudian Concepts

A productive future for the experimental testing of Freudian concepts depends, of course, upon those who have an interest in Freudian theory as a scientific account of human behavior and experience. For the theory could continue to develop, as it began, primarily on the basis of inductive reasoning. Thus, alterations in the theory could be made almost exclusively through the ruminative construction of conceptual inferences, which would then be disseminated through processes of personal and social persuasion. In this way, as in the past, new psychoanalytic concepts might evolve and proliferate without ever having withstood the deductive empirical tests that are essential to the scientific development of a psychological theory.

Happily, however, even the official organ of classical psychoanalysis has begun to show signs of a readiness to consider how the scientific future of psychoanalytic theory may be assured. Thus, a recent edition of the *International Journal of Psychoanalysis* contained a paper by Lindzey (1968), who discusses various ways in which psychoanalytic theory might best be changed and improved. After considering five other possibilities, including that of merely continuing the theory's traditional and almost exclusive reliance on inductive processes of thought, Lindzey (1968) affirms: "The sixth and aesthetically most pleasing alternative is introduction of *change on the basis of clear and relevant empirical findings* that imply specific shortcomings or ambiguities in connection with identified segments of the theory [pp. 659-660]." And, later in the article, in reiterating this point, Lindzey stresses that it requires the accumulations of "well-controlled, relevant and replicated findings [p. 660]."

258

This ideal has been amply seconded in this book. And it is to be hoped that psychoanalysts throughout the world will applaud Lindzey's affirmation and do whatever they can to facilitate its implementation.

Regarding the ways in which such research should be conducted, this book admittedly represents only one person's perspective — the examples described here are the merest of flawed beginnings, whose very offering solicits empirical improvement. Still, having had the temerity to present a host of methodological precepts, it now seems appropriate to conclude by suggesting some substantive guidelines for future experimentation on Freudian concepts.

The desirability of placing investigatory priority on evaluating the component variables of Freudian theory rather than on its assumptions concerning the relationships among those variables

The whole of Freudian theory consists of two sets of assumptions: those concerning the intrinsic psychological properties of its component variables and those concerning relationships among those variables. To test hypotheses concerning relationships among Freudian variables, it is first necessary to have on hand measures of the variables involved. The more valid those measures, the more scientically meaningful such tests can be.

With respect to positive findings, the scientific role played in these tests by validated instruments is not so apparent as it is in regard to negative ones, for supporting outcomes obviously do not cast doubt on the hypotheses tested. Hence, the measures employed are not likely to be put forward by a researcher as alternative explanations for the success of the very hypotheses they helped him to test. But the use of valid measures can be crucial to the interpretation of negative findings, without which no scientific theory can ever expect to change or to improve. Speaking directly to this point, Lindzey (1968) has said:

> What we need, of course, are instruments that can be used for something more than demonstration studies — where negative findings, in effect, reject the instrument rather than the theoretical

prediction. We need validated instruments where negative findings introduce a readiness to say the theory is infirm and that with further failures of confirmation should be amended to conform with what is regularly observed under well-controlled conditions [p. 660].

We have already seen that the process of assessing a measure's construct validity cannot be empirically divorced from that of evaluating the scientific utility of the variable it presumes to define. From the standpoint of a Freudian trait of personality, the attainment of a high degree of validational consensus would also mean that its imputed variable is accorded the same amount of scientific usefulness. In short, the psychoanalytic assumptions concerning the properties of that variable would have passed empirical muster as a contribution to scientific knowledge. And those particular aspects of psychoanalytic thought would have stood the test of deductive research.

On the other hand, having failed to survive such validational scrutiny, no unvalidated measure of a Freudian variable of personality could provide much help in sorting out the negative results obtained in studies that sought to test assumptions about its relationships with other Freudian variables. Unless a valid measure of the variable in question could be developed, the psychoanalytic assumptions concerning the intrinsic properties of that variable could not be regarded as scientifically supported.

However, insofar as any measure of a Freudian dimension were to gain widespread empirical support, its scientific deployment would, presumably, shift away from designs calculated to test the assumptions contained in the psychoanalytic conceptualization of its own imputed variable and move toward those focusing on the ways that variable is assumed to be related to other variables of personality within the compass of psychoanalytic theory. For example, once a measure of habitual castration anxiety were sufficiently validated through tests of hypotheses derived from the conceptualization of that variable *per se*, it might be increasingly applied in studies concerning the mediation of that anxiety by various mechanisms of ego defense against heterosexual motivation. If the relevant measures of those mechanisms had been similarly validated in their own right, disconfirmatory results of such studies could be more reasonably attributed to deficiencies in the particular mediational assumptions involved than would be possible if the data had been obtained by more questionable instruments. Neither Lindzey nor anyone else has ventured to suggest how many successful studies are needed for a measure to warrant sufficient scientific acceptance of its construct validity, thus eliminating it as a likely source of failure in nonconfirmatory tests of hypotheses that seek to link psychoanalytic variables. Nevertheless, assuming the scientifically desirable agreement can emerge spontaneously from a *finite* number of studies, the fact remains that very few well-controlled validational experiments have been conducted with any measure of any Freudian variable.

In this book, experiments of this sort have been encouraged through the emphasis that has been placed on the need for evaluating the properties that Freudian theory has attributed to its component variables. Clearly, the evaluation of these variables deserves precedence in any systematic effort to do deductive research on Freudian theory. For to investigate relationships between Freudian variables before their own conceptualizations have been tested would appear to invite the theoretically indeterminant negative findings that Lindzey has so rightly deplored.

Combining longitudinal and experimental
methods in assessing the etiological assumptions
implicit in Freudian concepts

Every predictive test of the effects of a Freudian variable of personality implies a chain of deduction that links it to previous and unobserved patterns of interaction between the child's organismic maturation and his socializing experiences. Insofar as Freudian theory contains no explicit conceptualization of those interactions, one can only assume that the variable in question emerged at some time prior to its study under thus far unimagined circumstances. However, the theory may be quite specific in its conceptualization of the past determinants for a particular variable. For example, Freud (1938b, 1949a, 1949i) offers a fairly definite account of the type of toilet-training likely to have been experienced by adults who may be classified as anally retentive in character.

Naturally, no experimental tests of a Freudian concept's present effects can be taken as an evaluation of the theoretical account of its past interpersonal determinants. For example, Bishop's (1967) findings on the differential reactions to monetary privation of individuals differing in the imputed trait of anal hoarding cannot be offered as evidence in support of Freud's ideas concerning the *etiology* of that trait. At best, such positive results can give encouragement for the direct investigation of that postulated etiology.

For ethical reasons, experimental manipulation of the interpersonal factors presumed to shape the individual's basic personality in childhood is entirely precluded. Such factors can be systematically investigated only through longitudinal studies employing correlational methods of observation.

Thus, the formulation of Freudian hypotheses for experimental purposes will usually involve the use of Freudian concepts as independent vairables. While it may sometimes be possible to conceive of mild and transient experimental manipulations aimed at inducing some direct change in a Freudian variable of personality (Katz, Sarnoff, & McClintock, 1956), a humane science of psychology will have to rely primarily upon correlational methods for investigating Freud's explanations of the etiological determinants of Freudian concepts.

Such longitudinal studies can be systematically combined with experimental ones, repeatedly testing out the empirical implications of the concept as closely as possible in time to its imputed, and operationally identified, emergence in the child's development. Insofar as such repeated tests are affirmative, with individual differences in the effects of the independent variable reflecting measured differences in its own emergent and predicted strength, the experimental results can provide at least a highly circumstantial, albeit not a direct, basis for making inferences about the validity of the theoretical account of the concept's ontogenetic determinants.

On the other hand, insofar as the theory does not systematically conceptualize the etiological determinants of a variable, it is not possible to build specific predictions about them into the longitudinal aspect of such dual studies. In such circumstances, the longitudinal study would of necessity be truly exploratory, with the researcher doing his best to develop his own intimations about, for example, what pattern of interpersonal contact between parents and child should be observed for leads to the factors determining the formation of the variable of interest to him.

*Relating Freudian concepts to volitional
phenomena*

As a physician, Freud firmly believed that success in psychotherapy hinged vitally on a patient's willingness to change himself. Indeed, Freud described the ideal patient as someone who *desires* improvement and is *willing* to spend the time required by the psychoanalytic method of psychotherapy (Freud, 1949c).

But as a psychological theorist, Freud proposed no concepts to deal with the behavioral and experiential effects of willful decisions; nor indeed, with the cognitive schemas involved in the resolution and consequences of such decisions. On the contrary, Freudian theory tends to envision man as basically motivated by forces and controlled by mechanisms that operate unconsciously. Freud never reconciled his general theory of the unconscious determinants of behavior with his therapeutic appeal to freely accepted responsibility, which clearly assumes the capacity of human beings to influence their fate through deliberately activated processes of choice.

Fortunately, human volition, long a central concern of philosophers and novelists, is at last being widely accepted by behavioral scientists as a phenomenon worthy of serious investigation. It is thus becoming increasingly observed that consciously exercised choice (Zimbardo, 1969) and consciously entertained hope (Stotland, 1969) may crucially affect not only an individual's physiological functioning but also the very maintenance of his life (Ferrari, 1962).

On the other hand, recent conceptualizations of volitional phenomena have given scant attention to the unconscious factors that may mediate the content, expression, and effects of freely made choices and commitments (cf. Festinger 1957, Brehm & Cohen, 1962; Kiesler, 1968). Yet Freudian concepts do appear capable of specifying the kinds of individual differences in personality that may provide such unconscious mediation (cf. Bishop, 1967; Gordon, 1966, 1967).

It seems worthwhile, therefore, to relate systematically the deductive powers of Freudian concepts to those emanating from cognitive theories that have been explicitly addressed to the psychological means and consequences of making decisions under various situational and social conditions. In keeping with this suggestion, the author has elsewhere presented concrete examples of the ways in which a mutually useful empirical relationship between Freudian concepts and Festinger's theory of cognitive dissonance may be implemented. The conclusion drawn by that paper also sounds a fittingly ecumenical note on which to end a book devoted to the furtherance of a rapprochement between Freudian theory and scientific psychology:

> Clearly, the psychoanalytic theorist can no longer feel smug about ignoring the psychology of volition. What most laymen believe and what Freud himself felt obliged to invoke, research on dissonance has dramatically demonstrated: conscious decisions, made on the basis of consciously perceived alternatives and highly aware cognitions, can profoundly affect behavior. But to focus entirely on the conscious determinants of behavior is to seek to correct the errors of psychoanalytic theory by committing equally blatant ones. It seems most reasonable, instead, to assume that man's behavior is wholly determined by neither voluntary nor involuntary factors; that the picture of man driven totally and uncontrollably by unconscious urges is just as grotesque a distortion of human complexity as is the image of man functioning entirely on the basis of consciously formulated decisions. Thus, genuine hope for a portrait of man that resembles the actuality of his behavior would appear to reside in a strategy of research, such as is exemplified in the previously mentioned experiment of Bishop (1967), whose objective is to bring together both conscious and unconscious determinants of behavior. By studying the interactions between these determinants, we may begin to sort out how much each contributes to a particular behavioral phenomenon. And such studies may gradually induce psychologists to think in fresh theoretical terms, breaking down the invisible conceptual walls that now separate "depth" psychology from the psychology of cognition (Sarnoff, 1968).

References

Abercrombie, M. L. J. *The anatomy of judgment.* London: Hutchinson, 1960.

Abraham, K. *Selected papers on psychoanalysis.* London: Hogarth, 1927.

Adler, A. *The practice and theory of individual psychology.* New York: Harcourt, 1927.

Adorno, T. W., Frenkel-Brunswik, E., Levinson, D. J., & Sanford, R. N. *The authoritarian personality.* New York: Harper, 1950.

Allport, F. H. The J-curve hypothesis of conforming behavior. *Journal of Social Psychology,* 1934, *5,* 141-183.

Asch, S. E. The doctrine of suggestion, prestige and imitation in social psychology. *Psychological Review,* 1948, *55,* 250-276.

Barber, T. X., & Silver, M. J. Fact, fiction, and the experimenter bias effect. *Psychological Bulletin,* 1968, *70,* 1-29. (Monogr. Suppl., Part 2.)

Bendig, A. W. The development of a short form of the manifest anxiety scale. *Journal of Consulting Psychology,* 1956, *20,* 384.

Bergin, A. E. Some implications of psychotherapy research for therapeutic practice. *Journal of Abnormal Psychology,* 1966, *71,* 235-246.

Bishop, F. V. Anality, privation, and dissonance (Doctoral dissertation, New York University, 1965). *Dissertation Abstracts,* 1966, *27,* (2-B), 596. (Abstract).

Bishop, F. V. The anal character: A rebel in the dissonance family. *Journal of Personality and Social Psychology,* 1967, *6,* 23-36.

Blum, G. S. A study of the psychoanalytic theory of psychosexual development. *Genetic Psychology Monographs,* 1949, *39,* 3-99.

Blum, G. S. A guide for research use of the Blacky pictures. *Journal of Projective Techniques,* 1962, *26,* 3-29.

Bonchek, V. Commitment, communicator credibility and attitude change. (Doctoral dissertation, New York University, 1966). *Dissertation Abstracts,* 1967, *27,* (11-A), 3929-3920. (Abstract)

Brehm, J. W., & Cohen, A. R. *Explorations in cognitive dissonance.* New York: Wiley, 1962.

Bridgman, P. W. *The logic of modern physics.* New York: Macmillan, 1928.

Bromberg, P. M. The effects of fear and two modes of anxiety reduction on social affiliation and phobic ideation. (Doctoral dissertation, New York University, 1967.) *Dissertation Abstracts,* 1968, *28,* (11-B), 4753-4754. (Abstract)

Brunswik, E. *Systematic and representative design of psychological experiments.* Berkeley: University of California Press, 1947.

Campbell, D. T., & Stanley, J. C. *Experimental and quasi-experimental designs for research.* Chicago: Rand McNally, 1963.

Cohen, J. Some statistical issues in psychological research. In B. B. Wolman (Ed.), *Handbook of clinical psychology.* New York: McGraw-Hill, 1965. Pp. 95-121.

Cohen, J. Multiple regression as a general data-analytic system. *Psychological Bulletin,* 1968, *70,* 426-443.

Comfort, A. *The anxiety makers.* London: Panther, 1967. (a)

Comfort, A. *The nature of human nature.* New York: Avon, 1968. (b)

Conrad, E. H. Psychogenic obesity: The effects of social rejection upon hunger, food craving, food consumption, and the drive reduction value of eating for obese vs. normal individuals. (Doctoral dissertation, New York University, 1968.)

Cronbach, L. J. The two disciplines of scientific psychology. In M. T. Mednick & S. A. Mednick (Eds.), *Research in personality.* New York: Holt, Rinehart, & Winston, 1957. Pp. 3-21.

Cronbach, L. J., & Meehl, P. E. Construct validity in psychological tests. *Psychological Bulletin,* 1955, *52,* 281-302.

Dunlap, K. Psychoanalysis and the unconscious. *American Journal of Psychiatry,* 1945, *102,* 330-336.

Edwards, A. L. *The social desirability variable in personality assessment and research.* New York: Dryden Press, 1957.

Ezriel, H. The scientific testing of psychoanalytic findings and theory. *British Journal of Medical Psychology,* 1951, *24,* 30-34.

Ezriel, H. Experimentation within the psychoanalytic session. In L. Paul (Ed.), *Psychoanalytic clinical interpretation.* New York: Free Press, 1963. Pp. 112-142.

Fenichel, O. *The psychoanalytic theory of neurosis.* New York: Norton, 1945.

Ferenczi, S. *Selected papers.* New York: Basic Books, 1955.

Ferrari, N. A. Institutionalization and attitude change in an aged population: A field study in cognitive dissonance. (Doctoral dissertation, School of Applied Social Sciences, Western Reserve University, 1962.)

Festinger, L. Laboratory experiments. In L. Festinger & D. Katz (Eds.), *Research methods in the behavioral sciences*. New York: Dryden Press, 1953. Pp. 136-172.

Festinger, L. *A theory of cognitive dissonance*. Evanston, Ill.: Row, Peterson, 1957.

Festinger, L., & Carlsmith, J. M. Cognitive consequences of forced compliance. *Journal of Abnormal and Social Psychology*, 1959, 58, 203-210.

Frenkel-Brunswik, E. The meaning of psychoanalytic concepts and the confirmation of psychoanalytic theories. *Scientific Monthly*, 1954, 79, 293-300.

Freud, A. *The ego and the mechanisms of defense*. New York: International Universities Press, 1946.

Freud, S. Three contributions to the theory of sex. In *The basic writings of Sigmund Freud*. New York: Modern Library, 1938. Pp. 553-806. (a)

Freud, S. Totem and taboo. In *The basic writings of Sigmund Freud*. New York: Modern Library, 1938. Pp. 807-930. (b)

Freud, S. Character and anal eroticism. In *Collected papers*. Vol. 2. London: Hogarth, 1949. Pp. 45-50. (a)

Freud, S. Fragment of an analysis of a case of hysteria. In *Collected papers*. Vol. 3. London: Hogarth, 1949. Pp. 13-148. (b)

Freud, S. Further recommendations in the technique of psycho-analysis. On beginning the treatment. The question of first communications. The dynamics of cure. In *Collected papers*. Vol. 2. London: Hogarth, 1949. Pp. 342-365. (c)

Freud, S. *The future of an illusion*. London: Hogarth, 1949. (d)

Freud, S. On the history of the psycho-analytic movement. In *Collected papers*. Vol. 1. London: Hogarth, 1949. Pp. 287-359. (e)

Freud, S. *Inhibitions, symptoms and anxiety*. London: Hogarth, 1949. (f)

Freud, S. *New introductory lectures on psychoanalysis*. London: Hogarth, 1949. (g)

Freud, S. Psychoanalytic notes upon an autobiographical account of a case of paranoia (dementia paranoides). In *Collected papers*, Vol. 3. London: Hogarth, 1949. Pp. 390-472. (h)

Freud, S. On the transformation of instincts with special reference to anal eroticism. In *Collected papers*. Vol. 2. London: Hogarth, 1949. Pp. 164-171. (i)

Freud, S. *An autobiographical study*. London: Hogarth, 1950. (a)

Freud, S. *Beyond the pleasure principle*. London: Hogarth, 1950. (b)

Freud, S. *An outline of psychoanalysis*. London: Hogarth, 1955.

Freud, S. *A general introduction to psychoanalysis*. New York: Perma-books, 1958.

Gerard, H. B., & Rabbie, J. M. Fear and social comparison. *Journal of Abnormal and Social Psychology*, 1961, *62*, 586-592.

Goldman-Eisler, F. Breastfeeding and character formation, In C. Kluck-hohn, H. A. Murray, & D. M. Scheider (Eds.), *Personality in nature, society and culture*. New York: Knopf, 1956. Pp. 146-184.

Goldstein, S. *A projective study of psychoanalytic mechanisms*. (Doctoral dissertation, University of Michigan, 1952.) Ann Arbor, Mich.: University Microfilms, 1952. No. 3501.

Gordon, C. M. Some effects of information, situation, and personality on decision making in a clinical setting. *Journal of Consulting Psychology*, 1966, *30*, 219-224.

Gordon, C. M. Some effects of clinician and patient personality on decision making in a clinical setting. *Journal of Consulting Psychology*, 1967, *31*, 477-480.

Greenberg, M. S. Role playing: An alternative to deception? *Journal of Personality and Social Psychology*, 1967, *7*, 152-157.

Grygier, T. G. *The Dynamic Personaliy Inventory*. London: National Council for Educational Research, 1961.

Hartmann, H. *Ego psychology and the problem of adaptation*. New York: International University Press, 1946.

Himmelweit, H. T., Oppenheim, A. N.; & Vince, P. *Television and the child*. London: Oxford University Press, 1958.

Holmes, D. Amount of experience in experiments as a determinant of performance in later experiments. *Journal of Personality and Social Psychology*, 1967, *7*, 403-408.

Hook, S. (Ed.) *Psychoanalysis, scientific method, and philosophy*. New York: New York University Press, 1959.

Hutchinson, E. D. The period of frustration in creative endeavor. In P. Mullahy (Ed.), *A study of interpersonal relations*. New York: Hermitage, 1949. Pp. 404-420.

Insko, C. A. *Theories of attitude change*. New York: Appleton-Century-Crofts, 1967.

Jones, E. *The life and work of Sigmund Freud*. New York: Anchor Books, 1963.

Jones, E. E., & Gerard, H. B. *Foundations of social psychology*. New York: Wiley, 1967.

Jung, C. G. *Contributions to analytic psychology*. New York: Harcourt, 1928.

Katz, D., McClintock, C., & Sarnoff, I. The measurement of ego defense as related to attitude change. *Journal of Personality*, 1957, *25*, 465-474.

Katz, D., Sarnoff, I., & McClintock, C. Ego defense and attitude change. *Human Relations* 1965, *9*, 27-45.

Kelman, H. C. The human use of human subjects. The problem of deception in social psychological experiments. *Psychological Bulletin*, 1967, *67*, 1-11.

Kiesler, C. A. Commitment. In R. P. Abelson, et al. (Eds.), *Theories of cognitive consistency: A sourcebook*. Chicago: Rand McNally, 1968. Pp. 448-455.

Klein, G. S. The investigative uses of psychoanalysis. Unpublished manuscript, Research Center for Mental Health, New York University, 1967.

Klopfer, B., Ainsworth, M.D., Klopfer, W. G., & Holt, R. R. *Developments in Rorschach technique*. Yonkers-on-Hudson: World, 1954.

Krout, M. H., & Tabin, J. K. Measuring personality in developmental terms: The Personal Preference Scale. *Genetic Psychology Monographs*, 1954. *50*, 289-335.

Laing, R. D. *The politics of experience*. New York: Ballantine, 1968.

Lewin, K. *Resolving social conflicts*. New York: Harper, 1948.

Lewin, K. Behavior and development as a function of the total situation. In L. Carmichael (Ed.), *Manual of child psychology*. New York: Wiley, 1954. Pp. 918-970.

Likert, R. A technique for the measurement of attitudes. *Archives of Psychology*, 1932, No. 140.

Lindner, R. M. *The fifty minute hour*. New York: Rinehart, 1955.

Lindzey, G. Some remarks concerning incest taboo and psychoanalytic theory. *American Psychologist*, 1967, *22*, 1051-1059.

Lindzey, G. Psychoanalytic theory: Paths of change. *International Journal of Psychoanalysis*, 1968, *49*, 656-661.

Lish, J. The influence of oral dependency, failure, and social exposure upon self-esteem and depression. (Doctoral dissertation, New York University, 1969.)

Malinowski, B. *Sex and repression in savage society*. New York: Harcourt, Brace, 1927.

Malinowski, B. *The sexual life of savages in Northwestern Melanesia*. New York: Eugenics, 1929.

Milgrim, S. Issues in the study of obedience: A reply to Baumrind. *American Psychologist*, 1964, *19*, 848-852.

Murray, H. A. *The Thematic Apperception Test*. Cambridge, Mass.: Harvard University Press, 1943.

Needleman, J. Systematic explanation and the science of psychoanalysis.

In J. Needleman (Trans.), *Being-in-the-world: Selected papers of Ludwig Binswanger.* New York: Harper & Row, 1968. Pp. 32-58.

Orne, M. T. On the social psychology of the psychological experiment: With particular reference to demand characteristics and their implications. *American Psychologist,* 1962, *17,* 776-783.

Pettit, T. F. Anality and time. *Journal of Consulting and Clinical Psychology,* 1969, *33,* 170-174.

Piotrowski, Z. A. *Perceptanalysis.* New York: Macmillan, 1957.

Rapaport, D. The structure of psychoanalytic theory: A systematizing attempt. *Psychological Issues,* 1960, *2,* (2, Whole No. 6.)

Redfield, R. The folk society. *American Journal of Sociology,* 1947, *52,* 293-308.

Reich W. *Character-analysis.* (3rd ed.) New York: Orgone Institute Press, 1949.

Roethlisberger, F. J. & Dixon, W. J. *Management and the worker.* Cambridge, Mass.: Harvard University Press, 1947.

Rogers, C. R. Toward a science of the person. In T. W. Wann (Ed.), *Behaviorism and phenomenology.* Chicago: University of Chicago Press, 1964. Pp. 109-132.

Rorschach, H. *Psychodiagnostics.* Berne: Verlag Hans Huber, 1942.

Rosenthal, R. *Experimenter effects in behavioral research.* New York: Appleton-Century-Crofts, 1966.

Rosenthal, R. Experimenter expectancy and the reassuring nature of the null hypothesis decision procedure. *Psychological Bulletin,* 1968, *70,* 30-47. (Monogr. Suppl., Part 2.)

Ross, R. Separation fear and the fear of death. (Doctoral dissertation, New York University, 1966.) *Dissertation Abstracts,* 1967, *27,* (8-B), 2878-2879. (Abstract)

Russell, B. *The scientific outlook.* London: Allen & Unwin, 1954.

Russell, R. W. Psychopharmacology. *Annual Review of Psychology,* 1964, *15,* 87-114.

Sarason, S. B., Davidson, K. S., Lighthall, F.F., Waite R. R., & Ruebush, B. K. *Anxiety in elementary school children.* New York: Wiley, 1960.

Sarnoff I. *Identification with the aggressor: Some personality correlates of anti-Semitism among Jews.* (Doctoral dissertation, University of Michigan, 1951.) Ann Arbor, Mich.: University Microfilms, 1951. No. 2647.

Sarnoff, I. Psychoanalytic theory and social attitudes. *Public Opinion Quarterly,* 1960, *20,* 251-279. (a)

Sarnoff, I. Reaction formation and cynicism. *Journal of Personality,* 1960, *28,* 129-143. (b)

Sarnoff, I. *Personality dynamics and development*. New York: Wiley, 1962.

Sarnoff, I. The experimental evaluation of psychoanalytic hypotheses. *Transactions of the New York Academy of Sciences*, 1965, *28*, 272-289. (a)

Sarnoff, I. Signs of the times: cynicism and hypocrisy. Paper presented at the Cooper Union Forum, New York, November 1965. (b)

Sarnoff, I. *Society with tears*. New York: Citadel Press, 1966.

Sarnoff, I. Psychoanalytic theory and cognitive dissonance. In R. P. Abelson et al. (Eds.), *Theories of cognitive consistency: A sourcebook*. Chicago: Rand McNally, 1967. Pp. 192-200.

Sarnoff, I. The university in a humane society. In I. Katz & H. Silver (Eds.), *The university and social welfare*. Jerusalem: Magnes Press, 1969. Pp. 93-108.

Sarnoff, I., & Corwin, S. M. Castration anxiety and the fear of death. *Journal of Personality*, 1959, *27*, 374-385.

Sarnoff, I., Lighthall, F. F., Waite, R. R., Davidson, K. S., & Sarason, S. B. A cross-cultural study of anxiety among American and English school children. *Journal of Educational Psychology*, 1958, *49*, 129-136.

Sarnoff, I., & Zimbardo, P. G. Anxiety, fear and social affiliation. *Journal of Abnormal and Social Psychology*, 1961, *62*, 356-363.

Saroyan, W. *Hello out there*. In B. Cerf (Ed.), *Thirty famous one act plays*. New York: Garden City, 1943. Pp. 549-561.

Sartre, J. P. *Existentialism*. New York: Philosophical Library, 1947.

Schachter, S. *The psychology of affiliation*. Stanford: Stanford University Press, 1959.

Schafer, R. *Psychoanalytic interpretation in Rorschach testing*. New York: Grune & Stratton, 1954.

Schlesinger, V. J. Anal personality traits and occupational choice: A study of accountants, chemical engineers, and educational psychologists. (Doctoral dissertation, University of Michigan, 1963.) *Dissertation Abstracts*, 1964, *24*, (12), 5551-5552. (Abstract)

Sears, R. R. *A survey of objective studies of psychoanalytic concepts*. New York: Social Science Research Council, 1943.

Sears, R. R. *Experimental analysis of psychoanalytic phenomena*. In J. McV. Hunt (Ed.), *Personality and the behavior disorders*. Vol. 1. New York: Ronald, 1944. Pp. 306-332.

Silverman, L. H. An experimental approach to the study of dynamic propositions in psychoanalysis: The relationship between the aggressive drive and ego repression — initial studies. *Journal of the American Psychoanalytic Association*, 1967, *15*, 376-403.

Skinner, B. F. Critique of psychoanalytic concepts and theories. *Scientific Monthly*, 1954, 79, 300-305.

Skinner, B. F., & Ferster, C. B. *Schedules of reinforcement.* New York: Appleton-Century-Crofts, 1957.

Stotland, E. *The psychology of hope.* San Francisco: Jossey-Bass, 1969.

Strachey, J. (Ed.) *The standard edition of the complete psychological works of Sigmund Freud.* London: Hogarth, 1953-1966.

Stringer, P. Masculinity-femininity as a possible factor underlying the personality responses of male and female art students. *British Journal of Social and Clinical Psychology*, 1967, 6, 186-194.

Walster, E., Berscheid, E., Abrahams, D., & Aronson, V. Effectiveness of debriefing following deception experiments. *Journal of Personality and Social Psychology*, 1967, 6, 371-380.

Wertheimer, M. *Productive thinking.* New York: Harper, 1945.

Wisdom, J. *Philosophy and psycho-analysis.* New York: Philosophical Library, 1963.

Wolowitz, H. Food preferences as an index of orality. *Journal of Abnormal and Social Psychology*, 1964, 69, 650-654.

Zimbardo, P. G. Relations between projective and direct measures of fear arousal. *Journal of Abnormal and Social Psychology*, 1964, 68, 196-199.

Zimbardo, P. G. A normative analysis of the Dynamic Personality Inventory (computer generated). Unpublished materials on file, Stanford University, Department of Psychology, 1969.

Zimbardo, P. G., & Formica, R. Emotional comparison and self-esteem as determinants of affiliation. *Journal of Personality*, 1963, 31, 141-162.

Zimbardo, P. G. *The cognitive control of motivation.* Glenview, Ill.: Scott, Foresman, 1969.

Index